Digital Timesca

Digital Timescapes

Technology, Temporality and Society

Rob Kitchin

polity

First published in 2023 by Polity Press

Polity Press
65 Bridge Street
Cambridge CB2 1UR, UK

Polity Press
111 River Street
Hoboken, NJ 07030, USA

ISBN-13: 978-1-5095-5640-3
ISBN-13: 978-1-5095-5641-0 (pb)

A catalogue record for this book is available from the British Library.

Library of Congress Control Number: 2022940568

Typeset in 10.5 on 12pt Sabon
by Fakenham Prepress Solutions, Fakenham, Norfolk NR21 8NL
Printed and bound in Great Britain by CPI Group (UK) Ltd, Croydon

The publisher has used its best endeavours to ensure that the URLs for external websites referred to in this book are correct and active at the time of going to press. However, the publisher has no responsibility for the websites and can make no guarantee that a site will remain live or that the content is or will remain appropriate.

Every effort has been made to trace all copyright holders, but if any have been overlooked the publisher will be pleased to include any necessary credits in any subsequent reprint or edition.

For further information on Polity, visit our website:
politybooks.com

CONTENTS

TABLES

PREFACE

In early 2016, I sat down with my colleagues Claudio Coletta and Liam Heaphy to devise a coding schema for a set of forty-three interviews undertaken with smart city stakeholders in Dublin. The interviews were conducted as part of the Programmable City project funded by the European Research Council. The project was designed to explore how smart city technologies were transforming the production of space and everyday spatialities. In the first interview we jointly coded, however, conducted with a local authority manager, it was references to time and temporality which caught our attention, particularly this description of the traffic control centre:

> Well, I suppose in common with most large cities we have had a traffic control centre for a *number of years*. So our first traffic control centre was built *around 1987 or even 1986* and it has gone through several different *iterations* and expansions and so on. The *latest version* of it was considerably changed in 2013. The traffic management centre itself is a *24 hour, 7 day a week* operation; it is staffed by our own control room operators. At *peak times* it has people from AA Roadwatch, which is the motoring organization here. We have facilities for the police and the public transport service to be here as well, so *at the moment* during the run up to the *Christmas busy time* they are in there *every day*. So we have somebody from the police and somebody from the public transport operators. We also have our own dedicated radio station, which broadcasts *six hours a day, 7:00 to 10:00 and 4:00 to 7:00*. And the idea of that is it provides very detailed traffic information to people in very much a *real-time* fashion using all the cameras and the technology that we have in the traffic control centre. [My emphasis]

Here, several registers of time are mentioned: duration, clock time, cyclic times, the past, the present, real-time and social time. As I

vii

coded the entire interview set, time emerged as a common refrain. Smart city technologies were clearly having a diverse impact on the temporal relations and rhythms of cities, and how the past, present and future are mobilized in the production of smart urbanism. After twenty years of researching the relationship between digital technology, society and space, I was finally discovering that time had been largely absent or implicit in my analysis, and that it was a significant omission. This sparked a personal turn towards temporality, leading to a handful of papers and a book, *Slow Computing*, and the writing of this book.

Digital Timescapes provides a synoptic analysis of the ways in which digital technologies, in a wide range of manifestations (as devices, systems, platforms and infrastructures), are reconfiguring everyday temporalities. The book contributes to a growing literature on the intersection of digital technologies and temporality in four primary ways. First, it is argued that the embedding and growing influence of digital technologies across all aspects of everyday life indicate that we have transitioned to a period where the production and experience of time is qualitatively different from in the pre-digital era. Digitally mediated temporalities have become the key means of structuring temporal relations across many aspects of social and economic life, and of claiming and asserting temporal power. A new temporal doxa, in which new temporal relations have been legitimized, normalized and internalized by individuals and organizations, has been established. Nonetheless, pre-digital temporal forms, relations and regimes endure: clock, sacred and eschatological time, and natural and social cycles and rhythms, continue to shape social and economic relations, and this will remain the case. Second, attention is paid to a much wider range of temporalities and technologies than in other accounts in order to illustrate how all forms of temporalities are being inflected and reconfigured, to a greater or lesser degree, by a multitude of digital technologies. This is achieved by providing an analysis of how digital technologies have transformed the temporalities of six sets of everyday practices and processes: history and memory, politics and policy, governance and governmentality, mobility and logistics, planning and development, and work and labour. Third, the analysis situates the development and use of digital technologies, and the temporalities they produce, within the wider political economy and operations of capital and power, paying particular attention to temporal power and the production of temporal inequalities and temporal arbitrage across different sets of practices, social groups and locales. Fourth, there is active focus on how to challenge and reorder temporal power, developing an ethics of temporal care and temporal justice.

In constructing the argument, my intention has not been to advance a new grand theory of time. Rather, the conceptual contribution of *Digital Timescapes* is two-fold. First, it draws together, builds on and extends the extensive conceptual work undertaken over the past thirty years across a range of disciplines – Science and Technology Studies, Sociology, Geography, Media Studies, Political Science, Philosophy, Anthropology, History, Memory Studies, and Library and Archive Studies – to make sense of digital temporalities. Second, it develops a number of new temporal concepts, including space-time machines, a progressive sense of time, code/spacetime, ethics of temporal care, temporal doxa, temporal realism and slow computing, to aid this work. Throughout, the focus is very much centred on the temporal, but space also remains a consistent aspect of the analysis. Considering one without the other is problematic since temporal and spatial relations are often interdependent. My hope is that the synoptic analysis presented aids our understanding of the inter-relationship between digital technologies, temporality and society, and stimulates further empirical and conceptual work on this key aspect of everyday life.

ACKNOWLEDGEMENTS

The research for this book was conducted as part of the Programmable City project, funded by a European Research Council Advanced Investigator award (ERC-2012-AdG-323636-SOFTCITY) and a Science Foundation Ireland project, Building City Dashboards (15/IA/3090). The book was written during a year-long sabbatical for the academic year 2020–1, supported in part through Maynooth University's Research Investment Fund. I am very grateful to the funders for supporting the research and writing. Several colleagues have helped to shape my thinking on time and temporality and their relationship with technologies and society – in particular, Claudio Coletta, Ayona Datta, Michiel de Lange, Martin Dodge, Alistair Fraser, Liam Heaphy, Aileen O'Carroll and Sam Stehle. The attendees at the 'Slow Computing' workshop at Maynooth University, and the 'On Time' workshop at the University of Siegen, provided useful discussion. I am very grateful to Mark Boyle, Alistair Fraser and Phil Hubbard, and the anonymous reviewers, for reading an initial draft and providing useful, constructive feedback. Many thanks also to Mary Savigar, Stephanie Homer, Neil de Cort, Adrienn Jelinek and Leigh Mueller for shepherding the book through review and publication. The book draws in places on a handful of published pieces (listed in the References), with the material extensively revised and updated.

— Part I —

THE NATURE OF TIME AND TEMPORALITIES

— 1 —

TIME, TEMPORALITY AND TIMESCAPES

The key contention of *Digital Timescapes* is that digital technologies, in a range of guises (as devices, systems, platforms and infrastructures), have profoundly transformed the temporalities of social and economic life, as well as our contemporary conception of time. How time is understood and experienced is different from thirty years ago and the tail end of the dominance of clock time. We now expect to be able to: instantly source a vast array of information and services at any time, from anywhere and on the move; interleave and time-shift activities into 'dead time', such as performing networked labour while waiting at a bus-stop; binge watch a television series made and broadcast in a different jurisdiction on our own schedule and at a playback speed of our choosing; communicate and interact in synchronous and asynchronous ways with a diverse network of social contacts spread across the globe; browse and compare goods, buy them with the click of a button and have them delivered within hours; alter meet-ups and travel plans on the fly in relation to unfolding circumstances; access news occurring anywhere on the planet as it happens; and perform work in more temporally flexible ways. These tasks were largely impossible until recently. Now they are all taken for granted and routine for a large proportion of the population, particularly in the Global North. Just as there was a shift from a task orientation to time to a clock orientation during modernity, over the last three decades there has been a shift to a network orientation to time. Prior to examining this contention in depth in subsequent chapters, it is important to set out the conceptual understanding of time adopted and explicated throughout the book. This is necessary in order to frame and situate the subsequent analysis, as the nature of time cannot be taken as given. This chapter, then, details a

3

contingent, relational, heterogeneous understanding of time; introduces the notion of timescapes; and outlines four cautionary issues to keep in mind when assessing the relationship between technologies, temporalities and everyday life.

The social production of temporality

Philosophers and other scholars have long mused on the nature of time, with a number of conceptual positions elaborated (see Adam, 1990; Burges and Elias, 2016). For some, time is abstract, absolute and essential in nature, best understood through physical laws as inviolate and linear, the irreversible passage from the past to the future that unfolds independently of human existence. Such a view understands time as universal and objective, a phenomenon that can be measured quantitatively and expressed as clock time, and is evident in the cycles of seasons and life and death (Kern, 1983). For others, time is not simply given – a fundamental dimension within which we exist – but is actively produced. Time is contingent, relational and heterogeneous (Adam, 1990). It is perceived, experienced and social. This notion of time is often referred to as temporality, which Hoy (2009: xiii) defines as 'time insofar as it manifests itself in human existence'. Temporality denotes the diverse set of temporal relations, processes and forms that are enacted and experienced through individual and collective action. Temporalities are embodied, emplaced, materialized and experiential (Grant et al., 2015); they are time performed through individual agency, entangled with the temporalities of others, and structured through institutional arrangements and mediating technologies and systems (Sharma, 2014). Temporalities are experienced as a complex entangling of past, present and future, rather than as time's arrow.

That temporality is plural and heterogeneous is well established within the social sciences literature (Adam, 2004). Rather than time being abstract, universal and homogeneous, it is understood as being produced, articulated and experienced in multiple ways. Temporal relations are diverse, non-linear and multifaceted, with people navigating and producing many temporalities simultaneously (West-Pavlov, 2013). For example, Burges and Elias (2016) identify three forms of temporality: time as history (how time is periodized and the relationship between past, present and future); time as calculation (how time is measured and used to structure activity); and time as culture (how time is mediated, embodied, placed and experienced).

4

Each orientates time with respect to a particular framing. Similarly, Leong et al. (2009) identify a tripartite conceptualization of temporality that mirrors Lefebvre's (1991) three forms of spatiality: conceived time (the formal structures and technologies, such as timetables and clocks, that represent and organize time), perceived time (how time is understood and experienced), and lived time (the everyday social practices that enact temporalities) (Humphreys, 2020). These three forms of time collide and work together to produce complex temporalities that vary with context. Peter Osborne (2013: 17) thus writes that the present is not simply experienced 'in' time, but consists of a coming together 'of' times – what he terms 'a disjunctive unity of present times' (cited in Burges and Elias, 2016). These present times unfold dynamically, fluctuating in pace, tempo, rhythm, duration and continuity, 'some long run, some short term, some frequent, some rare, some collective, some personal, some large-scale, some hardly noticed' (Crang, 2001: 190).

The multiplicity of time is made clear when one maps out the diverse set of temporal rhythms, cycles, relations and modalities in which we are enmeshed daily (see table 1.1). We are accustomed to dealing with temporalities 'organized around the individual, family, community, fiscal unit, or legislative entity' and denoted in 'biological (menstrual cycle, lifetime), chronometric (second, hour), calendrical (day, decade), historical (election cycles, technological development), or economic (business cycles)' terms (Houser, 2016: 145). We make and save time, utilize and waste it, use it as reward (holidays) and punishment (serving time) (Hassan, 2009). People enact, and are ensnared within, many intersecting temporal relations that shape the perception and experience of time, and influence how social and economic systems work. Practices and processes unfold at varying paces and tempos; they are diversely coordinated and sequenced; and they produce numerous efficiency and productivity effects. Likewise, everyday life unfolds within and through polymorphic and concatenated temporal rhythms and cycles that produce a sense of continuity, stability or disjuncture. Lefebvre (2004) identifies two main types of temporal rhythms. Linear repetitions are 'imposed structures' enacted through social practices, such as clock time and timetables, whereas cyclical repetitions are 'lived time' originating in 'nature: days, nights, seasons' (Lefebvre, 2004: 8). Individuals commonly encounter and co-produce several rhythms simultaneously. In some cases, rhythms can be eurhythmic, being harmonious and stable though not necessarily in-sync, or isorhythmic, being equal and synchronized, or arrhythmic, being out-of-sync and disruptive (Conlon, 2010).

5

Table 1.1 Multiple forms of temporality

Temporal rhythms/ cycles and measured time	*Natural* Earth seasons; diurnal cycles; body clocks; turning of tides; environmental processes	*Social and economic* National holidays; celebrations; festivals; holy days; working hours; time rules; rush hour; family mealtimes; business cycles; policy cycles; boom-and-bust cycles	*Technical* Product lifecycle; updating; planned obsolescence; phasing; dereliction and ruin; machine time	*Clock/measured time* Second; minute; day; week; month; year; decade; century; millennia; 24/7; standardized time
Temporal relations	*Pace and tempo* Speed; acceleration; refrain; rate; repetition; duration; immediacy; ahead/behind the curve; deceleration; stasis/inertia; hesitation; time flies/drags	*Scheduling* Coordination; sequence; phasing; prioritization; continuity; frequency; routine and habit; just-in-time; on-the-fly; peak time; timetables; deadlines; temporal density and fragmentation	*Efficiency* Productivity; punctuality; simultaneity; rapid response; fast-tracking; leap-frogging; latency; delay; synchronization; multitasking; time shifting; optimization; flexibility; temporal arbitrage	*Time-space compression* Time-space convergence and distanciation; global present; network time; instantaneous time; timeless time
Temporal modalities	*Past present* History; memory; memorialization; heritage; preservation; evolution/ change; trend; legacy; path dependency; forgetting; hindcasting	*Present present* Event; prehension; real-time; of-the-moment; serendipity; always-on; prototyping; liminality; mediated time; nowcasting	*Present future* Pre-emption; trends; short/ mid/long term; projection; speculation; promissory; prediction; simulation; prophecy; premediation; forecasting	*Future present* Aspiration; anticipation; preparedness; foresight; scenarios; long-term; backcasting

Source: created by the author; re-organized and extended from Kitchin (2019a).

Moreover, while the past, present and future act as a chronology against which temporality can be registered – before, now and after – in lived practice they are reciprocally entangled, 'folded into each other in qualitatively different ways' (Koselleck, 2004: 242), rather than being distinct, independent, sequenced categories. The present is an extension built on both the past and an anticipated future. Remembering an event, such as climbing a mountain as a child, entwines past and present, and anticipating its repetition enmeshes the future (Brockmeier, 2002). Similarly, when redeveloping a historic marketplace, replacing it with a shopping mall and apartments, the nostalgia and memories of the past, previous failed proposals, present conditions and activities, and future ambitions become interwoven in public debates and decision-making (Moore-Cherry and Bonnin, 2020). In governance practices, the past and future are produced in the present through algorithmic systems – for example, migration movements across the Mediterranean are simultaneously monitored and tracked in real-time, archived in databases to create a past record, and modelled for future-orientated risk (Tazzioli, 2018). The homepage of an online newspaper has a mixed sense of liveness, blending real-time news with rapidly dating archived stories and the premediation of potential future scenarios, which could all relate to the same unfolding event (Ekström, 2016). In routing and location-based apps, archived data concerning past events guide the present by anticipating and pre-empting potential futures (Thatcher, 2013). This collapsing and enmeshing of past-present-future is common in emergency management, designed to manage immediate risk and pre-empt new events (see chapter 5). This entanglement is captured in Adam and Groves' (2007) use of 'past present', 'present present', 'present future' (the future projected forward from the present) and 'future present' (an anticipated future backcast and imagined in the present), which fuse the terms together, with the present the common denominator 'because experientially, the past, present and future do not have an existence outside of the present' (Dodgshon, 2008: 7).

The heterogeneous nature of time, and the entanglement of past, present and future, are evident in the use of diverse temporalities in fiction, television and film, where time is used to structure narratives and also as plot devices (e.g., flashbacks, replays and recaps; slow motion and fast forwarding; time jumps, time loops and time travel; premonitions). Particular genres are often characterized by their temporal logics, such as the narrative time of soap operas, the real-time of reality shows, and the fragmented and inventive time of science fiction (Keightley, 2012). Similarly, as Kuhn (2010: 299) notes, memories in written texts are 'typically a montage of vignettes, anecdotes, fragments, "snapshots" and flashes', so that 'time rarely comes across as continuous or sequential'. Likewise, video games have temporal continuities and discontinuities: 'game time can be paused, re-loaded, restarted, recorded, connected to others on-line in different time zones' (Reading, 2012: 145).

We are used, then, to encountering 'many forms of time super-imposed one upon the other' (Koselleck, 2004: 2), composing what Burges and Elias (2016: 4) term 'coetaneous temporalities', and Tazzioli (2018: 272) 'coeval temporalities'. We regularly find ourselves enmeshed in several temporalities simultaneously, which may be stretched out across scales and space (Hassan, 2003). For example, a person heading to a 10 a.m. meeting and using their mobile phone to talk to a colleague on the other side of the planet while waiting at a pedestrian crossing for the network-controlled traffic lights to change is negotiating global time and local time, clock time and network time, as well as social and natural time. She is experiencing the pronounced time-space distanciation of a long-distance call (see chapter 2), as well as the localized time-space choreographies of navigating an intersection that is mediated by the algorhythms of an intelligent transport system (see chapter 6). Yet the pace, tempo and rhythms of action unfolding in a real-time present are reliant on the stability, fixity and stasis of telecommunications and transport infrastructures, which evolve gradually or in periodic leaps (Starosielski, 2021). On a daily basis, then, we negotiate complex temporal landscapes with varying temporal relations and modalities. These temporal landscapes often constitute 'chronotopes', wherein the mutual inter-dependencies of time and space produce a signature unfolding of place (Crang, 2007: 70).

Chronotopes vary between locales depending on cultures and traditions, historical and contemporary political economies, institu-tionalized temporal regimes, and globalized inter-connections and interdependencies. For example, Spain has a tradition of siestas and, along with France and Italy, has more leisurely mealtimes, resulting in differing daily rhythms from Northern European countries (Lefebvre, 2004). The institutionalized work pattern of '996' (9 a.m. – 9 p.m., six days a week) in many companies in contemporary China, and its effects on family and leisure time and local food economies (creating a mass demand for meal delivery), is quite different from that of Europe (Shin et al., 2020). As Barak (2013) has detailed for colonial Egypt, and Datta (2018) for present-day India, sacred, modern and (post)colonial temporalities coexist, inflecting each other to produce a plural, hybrid temporal landscape that differs from metropolitan Europe or North America, while simultaneously being partially organized to align with metropolitan time. For example, a significant part of the Bangalore economy functions during the night to align with Western customers and clients (Nadeem, 2009). At a local level, temporalities vary across and within neighbourhoods (e.g., city centre, suburbs, slums) and households (e.g., single, family, empty nesters). In other words, places do not possess a singular temporality, but are composed of multiple colliding, unfolding temporalities that stretch from the local to the global (Crang, 2007). It is little wonder, then, that so many forms of time are identified within time-centred studies: cosmological time, sacred time, mythological time, profane time, clock time, real-time, machine time, network time, mobile time, postcolonial time, patriarchal time, mediated time, geological time, spectral time, quality time, public time, historical time, along with many others.

The production of time

Given that the nature and experience of temporalities are multiple, dynamic and heterogeneous, it follows that they are produced rather than given (May and Thrift, 2001). Time is not an empty, abstract dimension through which we pass. Rather, we create temporalities within social context through a variety of processes and systems, many of which are technologically mediated by devices (such as clocks and timetables), and institutionalized within social structures (such as households, work, governance, religion). Time, as we perceive, generate and experience it, is eventful. Temporalities unfold in contingent, relational, contextual ways, 'coloured and contoured, given shape, diversity, variation and substance through their unique circumstance of creation' (Hassan, 2009: 50). Temporal regimes are (re)produced through social practices that have a temporality (e.g., pace, tempo, rhythm, sequence) and generate temporality (Shove et al., 2009).

An eventful notion of time

In an eventful, processual notion of time, temporalities are always in a process of becoming or unfolding. The countless happenings and encounters in which people take part generate, and are conditioned by, multiple, colliding, intersecting temporalities (Crang, 2005;

Sewell, 2005). The unfolding of temporalities is not predetermined, but is subject to emergence and critical junctures (Grzymala-Busse, 2011). In many cases, unfolding temporalities reproduce predominant temporal patterns and orders, or follow the trajectory of a path dependency (Sewell, 2005). Their constituent practices can be routine and (un)conscious habits that maintain the daily rhythms and sequences of everyday life – waking to an alarm, breakfast time, commuting during rush hour, working 9-to-5, evening mealtime, primetime television, going to bed. Moreover, many are enjoined, following an expected sequence – in a religious ceremony, the leaders and congregation are enjoined to perform rituals in a set pattern that have normalized timings and rhythms; enacting labour involves the enjoining of tasks in a performative order that ensures a job is fulfilled (Schatzki, 2009). Indeed, despite the emergent nature of temporality, it is not in permanent, divergent flux, having durable regularities that create hegemonic, normative time.

Nonetheless, these routines may subtly transform the temporal order through gradual, imperceptible shifts in practices (Anderson, 2015). In other words, the refrain of temporal rhythms is constantly articulated anew through citational repetition, but these mutate through imperfections and interventions (Edensor, 2010). While a system might strive to maintain a eurhythmic state, it is always unfolding in a slightly altered form, or it might be 'punctured, disrupted or curtailed by moments and periods of arrhythmia' and dissolve into noise (Edensor and Holloway, 2008: 485). Planned interventions, such as new policy and regulation, or unexpected or unpredictable incidents, such as emergencies, rupture the temporal order, with critical junctures creating new trajectories (Sewell, 2005). Moreover, happenings are nested, with sub-events taking place within larger events that may have differing durations, speeds, tempo, timings, sequencing and effects (Grzymala-Busse, 2011). For example, the temporal regime of communism in Eastern Europe was transformed in the early 1990s by a range of localized transitions taking place within wider national and regional transformations to a democratic, post-socialist, market-based regime (Goodin, 1998). Some of these transition events were rapid, shock ruptures; others unfolded more gradually. Likewise, work practices may be nested within activities that have differing temporal horizons – an immediate task, a larger job order, an emerging crisis, a yearly target, a medium-term strategy, a long-term economic cycle (Sewell, 2005).

While there is a certain degree of agency in the performance and unfolding of temporalities, they are inflected and structured in a

10

number of ways: contextually, socially and institutionally. The unfolding of events through temporal practices and the reproduction of temporal regimes are contingent on the context in which they take place (Adam, 1990). Exogenous factors, which are external to the systems in which practices are enacted, along with endogenous factors, are at work (Shove et al., 2009). Differing cultures, historical precedents, political-economic situations and local conditions create divergent conventions and expectations (Sewell, 2005). Pressures due to varying circumstances, such as a rush to meet a deadline, create differing conditions and experiences from a leisurely performance. The availability of certain technologies shapes how practices are performed, and their efficiency. Delays might be created by a lack of required technical or embodied knowledge to accomplish a task. Consequently, the weaving together of the temporal texture of daily life never reproduces the exact same pattern, and is always open to tears and breaks (Shove et al., 2009).

While individuals can shape the production of temporalities, they are generally a collective manufacture. We share tasks and environments. We negotiate, coordinate and synchronize schedules, and work to shared deadlines (Southerton, 2006). We align pace and tempo, and collectively produce rhythms. In her analysis of the temporal landscape of an intersection in Shibuya, Tokyo, Sharma (2014) details how multiple interdependent and relational temporalities are tangled together. The time-spaces of those shopping, working, playing and passing through the crossing are inter-twined, if only in fleeting, direct and indirect, ways. The masses of people converging and navigating the intersection are temporally ordered, in part through the design of the space and its regulation through traffic lights, but also through social conventions and patterns of commuting, consumption and servicing (Sharma, 2014). Living in the same household similarly involves producing shared temporalities around activities such as mealtimes, domestic work, childcare and leisure. Our personal temporalities, then, are just one part of a complex hybrid temporal landscape, and we are always in the process of maintaining or transitioning shared temporalities (West-Pavlov, 2013).

(Re)producing temporal power

This collective manufacture of temporalities 'is composed of a chron-ography of power', with individuals having differing abilities and

11

opportunities to influence the unfolding temporal order (Sharma, 2014: 9). Drawing on Doreen Massey's (1993) concept of power-geometry to highlight the unevenness in the production of space, Sharma (2014) forwards the notion of power-chronology to capture the differentiated production and experience of temporal power. She notes that there is a marked imbalance in the relative power-chronography and time sovereignty (ability to control temporal relations) of parents and children, and bosses and workers, in deciding on schedules, pace and tempo, and setting time rules and targets (such as timetables and deadlines) (Sharma, 2014). Women are highly familiar with the operations of power-chronology and the temporal orders of patriarchal time: of domestic and familial time in constant tension with public and capitalist time; of the double shift for working mothers and the sacrifice of leisure time; and of the dangers of night-time (Milojevic, 2008). The working class and people of colour are used to: externally imposed time orders, temporal surveillance and penalties, temporal arbitrage and precarity; working unpopular hours and long commutes; of being behind the curve and late to the newest innovations; of the feeling that time is not theirs to control (Sharma, 2014; Anderson et al., 2020). Likewise, within colonized states, the indigenous population were/are socialized and disciplined into the temporal regime of the colonizer, with the legacy of this regime continuing in a postcolonial era (Datta, 2018). In other words, the control of temporalities is a means through which social divisions relating to class, gender, race, ethnicity, age and other markers of social difference are maintained (see chapter 9).

The differences in power-chronology between groups has remarkable durability, persisting as hegemonic time because their logics are deeply embedded into social relations through institutionalized time rules and policies, social norms and expectations, and the workings and logics of political economies. In many cases, forms of temporal arbitrage operate, where the temporalities of one set of people are organized around those of others (Sharma, 2014). For example, many workers in the Global South align their working hours and body clocks with the schedules of customers in the Global North (Nadeem, 2009; see chapter 8). The daily temporal regime of taxi drivers flexes around the time schedules, pressures and demands of their customers (Sharma, 2014). Similarly, food delivery workers continuously rush to meet customer and company expectations for on-time delivery, in some cases losing pay for lateness (Chen and Sun, 2020). Here, deadlines are simultaneously an objective and a means of supervising and disciplining labour (Barak, 2013). In other words, temporality is a structuring relation of power, used to reproduce and exploit further uneven and unequal social relations and produce a sense of time shaped by and enacted through forms of temporal discipline and control (May and Thrift, 2001; Sharma, 2017).

Temporal power is formally institutionalized in the temporal organization, expectations and rules of state bodies, companies, and civic organizations, framed by and reproducing a wider political economy. Indeed, the control of temporality has been important in the imposition and workings of modernity, colonialism, capitalism and communism. Consequently, portions of daily life are ordered around formalized timetables: work and school hours, opening times, break periods, transport schedules and public holidays. Interactions with the state and law are ordered via appointments and deadlines. State bodies track key dates – such as births, deaths and marriages – and judge eligibility for services based on age and length of service. They can introduce policies and regulations concerning working times, operating hours, periods in elected office or serving on state boards, and curfews in times of emergency (Radoccia, 2013). Companies aim to create efficiencies and productivity through time rules and management practices relating to work pace, rates, coordination, synchronization, scheduling, deadlines and delivery times. In these cases, power can be direct and strategic, creating highly structured temporal relations, or operate more indirectly as a form of 'soft conditioning' designed to coerce or manipulate compliance with temporal regimes (Markham, 2020).

Temporal power is also embedded into technologies and technical systems, expressed through what Mackenzie (2006) terms 'secondary agency'. Wajcman (2018, 2019), for example, demonstrates how ongoing developments in scheduling and time management apps codify the values and lifestyles of their Silicon Valley creators, and reflect their desire to produce intelligent digital assistants that optimize productivity and minimize dead time (see chapter 8). Operational systems such as traffic control have formalized rules regarding timing, phasing, offsetting, cycle lengths, prioritization and road speeds, depending on traffic conditions, direction and types of users (cars, trucks, buses, cyclists, pedestrians) (Coletta and Kitchin, 2017; see chapter 6). Archives are not a neutral, technical means of storing records and artefacts, but rather are social-technical systems created by actors with particular aims, who make choices about what are archived and the terms under which they can be accessed and used, and, in turn, what can be asserted about the past (Bowker, 2005; see chapter 3). In other words, time-mediated technologies are themselves social constructs, invented and institutionalized as instrumental means to articulate and leverage time (Kern, 1983). Timetables and time rules are negotiated, and change; for example, standardized clock time took years to be adopted globally, memory apps evolve through multiple iterations, and so on (Jacobsen and Beer, 2021).

The institutionalization of time and encoding into technical systems normalizes and reproduces temporal power and relations and their differential effects (Sharma, 2014). At the same time, temporal power is also open to resistance, subversion and transgression and moves to claim and assert time sovereignty – that is, having control over one's own time. At an individual level, people employ their own time tactics to challenge temporal relations and time rules (e.g., delaying, working slowly, ignoring schedules or deadlines, being late). Collectively, they can campaign for time policies or regulations (e.g., fixed working hours, holiday allocation, time-off for maternity/parental leave, the right to disconnect) and undertake their own initiatives, such as community-created counter-archives (Cifor et al., 2018; see chapter 10).

Experiential, embodied, subjective time

A major contribution of temporal theorists in the early twentieth century – such as Husserl, Bergson and Heidegger – was to advance an experiential and subjective view of time (Kern, 1983; Hoy, 2009). They argued that it was important to conceptualize and treat time as lived and subjective, rather than abstract and objective, because this is how time thoroughly infuses our sense of self and the production of social relations. We (re)produce temporalities: we perceive, experience and perform time; we possess a sophisticated sense of time consciousness, and our subjectivity is formed through the structures and structuring of temporalities, rather than within them (Nowotny, 1994). We connect temporal events through consciousness and memory (Madanipour, 2017). Time, then, is not something external to and imposed on us, but is also internalized. Time is something we embody in our rhythms of sleeping, waking and eating; the pace, tempo and synchronization of work and play; our social performances and gestures, and our recollections and re-enactments of memories (Nowotny, 1994). It inflects our emotions and view of the world.

As temporal subjects, we have both 'an orientation to time', and are 'disciplined by time' (Lash and Urry, 1994: 226). We are used to

14

processing, living within, and co-producing multiple temporalities, and being entangled within temporal power. For the most part, we encounter these temporal logics and relations with barely a thought: they are everyday hegemonic temporalities we navigate regularly, and experience and perform unconsciously through habits and routines (Hassan, 2009). Indeed, our relations with time are largely normalized and we are well able to handle cognitively their various intertwining and discontinuities. From birth, we are socialized into the logics and patterns of temporalities such as sleep and mealtimes, the school timetable and the working week. We learn how to deal with time pressures and stresses, and to employ time tactics to produce alternative temporalities. We appreciate, at the subjective level, that how we perceive and experience temporalities varies with context, and across individuals and groups. Time 'moves at multiple speeds, relative to lived situations, perceptual perspectives and affective immersions in environments' (Grant et al., 2015: 7). The same event can seem slow or fast, or eurhythmic or arrhythmic, depending on the role and experience of the individuals attending. In an exam, time for the bored invigilator seems to pass slowly, whereas it zips by for the stressed student; one person stuck in traffic might revel in the break from work, whereas another is anxious at the prospect of being late.

The perception and experience of temporal power are uneven in distribution and consequence, with cultural identities formed, in part, through socialization in, and repeated encounters with, oppressive temporal regimes. Lived time is gendered, classed and racialized, with the orientation to and consciousness of time, and experience and perception of temporalities, varying in quite distinct ways depending on social status. It is embodied in temporalized practices, such as rushing to meet deadlines or meet targets, juggling the scheduling of work, home and childcare, and waiting in queues and killing time due to under- or un-employment. The workings of power-chronology, then, produce markedly differing lived temporalities and time consciousness across individuals and social groups. In reshaping the timescapes of domains and sites, digital technologies remediate the unfolding of lived and subjective time, and their relation to our sense of self, and our emotional and physical well-being (Hassan, 2009; Wajcman, 2015). Understanding the relationship between time, technologies and social and economic relations thus requires more than identifying and detailing the processes through which time is produced. It also necessitates charting how these processes and their resultant temporalities are perceived and experienced, and their implications for individuals and communities.

Producing the past and future

As has already been intimated, the production of the past and future are also contingent, relational and multiple, rather than closed, given and fateful (Sewell, 2005; Beckert, 2016). Rather than the past – history, memory, heritage – being immutable, factual, objective records and accounts of what occurred, the past is understood to be a mutable, contested terrain (see chapter 3). History is cast as 'the study of changes of things that change' (Buthe, 2002) and its writing is socially constructed, produced and interpreted by its interlocutors based on records and memories that are themselves social constructions and partial (Sewell, 2005). History is a cultural mediation of the past, socially organized through interpretation and narrativization, and shaped by epistemology, moral and ideological positions, and the concerns of the present (Huyssen, 2003). States exercise their temporal power to organize the past and its telling through their curation of national archives and control of access to records, as well as their role in public memorialization and commemoration. The notion of memory captures some of the ambiguity, relationality and mutability of the past, given it is a remembered or re-presented past that is shaped by the context and circumstances of the event and its recollection, as well as who is remembering. Individuals can remember the same event in quite different ways, and its collective memory is filtered and rescripted through media and state discourses. History, memory and heritage are highly contested in places ravaged by colonialism and war, and in some cases are formally disputed through truth and reconciliation initiatives, such as in post-apartheid South Africa.

The future, too, is contingent and produced, rather than closed and fateful (Beckert, 2016). Legacies of the past and the trajectories of path dependencies undoubtedly create a certain degree of momentum and direction towards the future. Nonetheless, while the future is not random or disconnected from trajectories and prevailing structures, it is not simply a continuation of the present informed by the past. Legacies and trajectories can be interrupted and redirected, and chance and unpredictable events can occur. Indeed, there are many imaginaries and practices through which we seek to envisage and mould the future in ways that maintain, redirect or forge new paths: prognosis, pre-emption, projection, prediction, forecasting, backcasting, speculation, promissories, prophecy, scenarios, simulations, foresight studies, plans and blueprints, and premediation.

For example, states seek to colonize the future through forecasts, foresight studies and development plans in order to create a future in their making (Urry, 2016). Companies aim to realize their ambitions through marketing, investments and speculation. The media condition the public's expectations of temporal orders and possible futures through premediation, discussing potential scenarios and outcomes and their likelihood and consequences (Keightley, 2012).

Futuring practices and imaginaries scope out possible (those that might be realized given available or sought-after knowledge), plausible (those that seem achievable given a present situation), probable (those that are likely given the present trajectory) and preferred (those that are desirable) futures (Amara, 1981, in Poli, 2015). They precondition our imaginaries of and aspirations for the future, and inform actions designed to realize them, such as deciding on life-path choices, making investments, producing innovations, formulating policy, implementing mitigation and prevention strategies, and enacting governance regimes such as predictive policing and emergency management. These actions do double work. On the one hand, they shape how the present is managed in order to realize particular futures – just as the present prefigures the future, the 'future acts as a determining condition of the present' (Uprichard, 2012: 110). On the other, they produce 'latent futures' (Adam and Groves, 2007) – futures in the making that are 'on the way' but have yet to become realized and visible (Poli, 2015). Realization of these latent futures is by no means guaranteed, in part because there is intense competition between individuals and social groups to create preferred futures.

From this contingent, relational perspective, the production of time is not, then, teleological in nature; that is, progressing in a fateful, purposeful, single direction from the past to the present and into the future, following a grand design or transhistorical processes that serve some higher end, purpose or goal (such as eschatological, sacred accounts of time, in which we are heading for the ultimate destiny of humankind, such as the Second Coming or Apocalypse; or Enlightenment notions of progress towards modernity; or capitalism's march towards free markets or to revolution; Sewell, 2005). Temporalities can be organized to serve an ideological purpose, but there is nothing inevitable about how they are produced – the general arc of our past, present and future is not predetermined, and nor is the unfolding of specific events. In other words, there can be radical ruptures in what appear to be stable temporal regimes and how temporal relations are created, organized and institutionalized in society. For example, the Industrial Revolution, capitalism, colonialism and modernity ruptured medieval temporalities centred on religion, seasonal and solar cycles, and task-based work (Kern, 1983). The central premise of subsequent chapters is that a similar set of temporal ruptures have taken place in the digital era.

Time and space

So far, time and temporality have been discussed with little reference to space and spatialities. As Massey (2005) notes, aspatial notions of time are commonplace; space is not acknowledged, or simply provides the backdrop for temporalized processes. Likewise, the production of space is often conceptualized with little attention to its entwining with temporality. Since the philosophical ruminations of Ancient Greece, the nature of time and space and their interrelation has been debated extensively (Crang, 2005). Throughout the Enlightenment, time and space were cast within the natural and social sciences as separate and irreducible to one another, 'polarized components of a conceptual dualism' (West-Pavlov, 2013: 7). From an abstract perspective, space is considered a three-dimensional container in which we exist, and time is the irreversible passage from the past to the future (Kern, 1983). From a lived, experiential perspective, space is related to being, stasis and the dimension in which life exists, and time is related to becoming, progress and the trajectory through life (May and Thrift, 2001). Time reveals 'relations of succession or change', whereas space concerns 'relations of structure or organisation' (Dodgshon, 1999: 610). Giving analytical precedence to one dimension or the other prioritizes an understanding of society in terms of how it has developed through time, or how it is organized and operates across space (Massey, 2005). Dodgshon (2008) refers to this analytic separation as spaceless time (in which temporalities are examined with no reference to space other than as backdrop) and timeless space (in which space is charted with no reference to temporality, other than as occurring at a point in time). For May and Thrift (2001), the prioritization of time produces an aspatial historicism, whereas a prioritization of space leads to an atemporal spatial imperialism.

In contrast, the relationship between time and space can be conceptualized in at least three other ways that recognize that everyday life always occurs in both time and space: separate but related (time *and* space); separate but interdependent (time-space or space-time); or

18

dyadic, in which they are thoroughly fused (timespace or spacetime) (Dodgshon, 2008). Time and space being intimately connected, but not necessarily interdependent, is evident in time-geography. Developed by the geographer Torsten Hägerstrand (1967), time-geography initially treated space and time as an abstract, absolute four-dimensional container in which activity takes place. Given that the temporal and spatial dimensions are fixed, independent scales, time and space have no influence over each other; they merely provide an inert backdrop. In later iterations, time-geography casts space and time relationally, acting interdependently in shaping social action (Schwanen, 2007; Sui, 2012).

As interdependent dimensions, time and space are understood as being irreducible, yet they directly shape each other. Massey (2005: 55, 56), for example, argues 'neither time nor space is reducible to the other; they are distinct. They are, however, co-implicated.... [There is a] mutual necessity of space and time. It is on both of them, necessarily together, that rests the liveliness of the world.' Likewise, Parkes and Thrift (1975) contend that space is timed, and time is spaced. That is, the production of space is shaped by the temporalities of the processes involved (e.g., the use of timetables to order the operations of transport infrastructure; the use of futuring in developing urban plans), and the production of time is influenced by spatialities (e.g., the spatial structure of a city guiding scheduling, sequencing and timings of events and timetables). In time-space compression, time and space work interdependently, with a reduction in the time taken to traverse and communicate across space speeding up the flows of information and goods, making the world seem smaller and more interconnected (see chapter 2). Sui (2012) notes that the interdependence of space and time can take a number of forms given their multiplicity, including chronos and choros (clock time and geometric space), kairos and topos (social time and lived place), and chronos/topos, and kairos/choros.

For some, time and space are seen as being two sides of the same coin: since everything happens at some time in some place, they are intimately conjoined and inseparable. In other words, it is impossible to separate time and space into interdependent components (time-space) or consider them as separate phenomenon that instigate discrete processes (time and space) (May and Thrift, 2001). Instead, time and space are a fused dyad; 'a single mode of dimensionality': time-space (May and Thrift, 2001; Malpas, 2015: 26). For Malpas, the happening of place is inherently a time-space, what he terms 'topos'; a temporal/spatial unity cast through mutual dependence.

19

Our lived experience unfolds through topos. In the natural sciences, Einstein's theory of relativity has similarly led to the fused notion of spacetime, a hybrid, dynamic composite (West-Pavlov, 2013). My own view is that time and space are highly interdependent dimensions (time-space), which can, but do not necessarily, operate dyadically to produce time-space formations.

Time-space pervades the analysis presented throughout the book. However, rather than provide equal weight and focus to both elements, the focus of attention is directed more towards temporality in the conjunction of time-space. This is to foreground time and enable an in-depth examination of the ways in which digital technologies produce a multiplicity of temporalities and reconfigure our experience and sense of time, without losing sight of the interplay with spatialities. Indeed, spatialities are intimately and explicitly bound into the processes and practices examined. While some might feel the particular focus on the temporal creates an imbalance in charting the tempo-spatialities of everyday life in the digital era, it is intended to help to rebalance the relative lack of attention paid to time in accounts of digital geographies and sociologies, which to date has overly prioritized the spatial (Datta, 2018, 2020; Kitchin, 2019a). The means by which the time-space analysis is conceptually mobilized is through Barbara Adam's notion of timescapes.

Timescapes

Adam (1998, 2004) describes a timescape as a cluster of associated temporal features and relations that collectively work to (re)produce a temporal regime and landscape. Whereas other scapes, such as landscapes, cityscapes and seascapes, prioritize 'the spatial features of past and present activities and interactions' (Adam, 1998: 10), timescapes emphasize their temporal features while being mindful of their associated spatialities. Indeed, Adam (2004: 143) contends that the notion of 'scape' is important because it 'indicates, first, that time is inseparable from space and matter, and second, that context matters'. By prioritizing time, the timescape perspective enables the operations, salience, multiplicity and unfolding of temporal relations and lived time to be intricately charted.

Adam (2004, 2008) identifies a number of temporal features that compose a timescape (see table 1.2). These features are inter-related and together shape the production and constellations of time, though they are not necessarily of equal importance to

20

Table 1.2 The elements of a timescape

Timeframes (in what time frame?)	Bounded, beginning and end, seconds, days, years, lifetimes, generations, eras, epochs
Temporality (how?)	Process, internal to a system, ageing, growing, irreversibility, impermanence
Tempo (at what speed?)	Pace, velocity, intensity of activity, rate of change
Timing (how synchronized/ coordinated?)	Synchronization, coordination, kairos (right/ wrong time)
Time point (when?)	Moment, past, now, instant, juncture, future
Time patterns (how organized?)	Rhythmicity, periodicity, cyclicality, repetition, change
Time sequence (in what order?)	Series, phasing, cause and effect, simultaneity
Time extensions (temporal length and future horizon?)	Duration, continuity, instant to eternity
Time past, present and future (modality?)	Horizons, memory, anticipation, past present, present present, present future, future present

Source: created by the author; based on Adam (2004, 2008).

unfolding temporalities and the reproduction of temporal regimes (Adam, 2004). Variances across the features produce a multiplicity in temporal relations and timescapes of differing character, and mapping them out reveals their constructed and provisional nature. It also highlights that timescapes are palimpsest in nature, containing the legacy and layers of multiple historical temporal regimes (Stine and Vollmar, 2021). Hence, the temporalities of clock time (e.g., defined working hours) persist alongside network time (e.g., organized around the synchronous and asynchronous logics of digitally networked technologies) in workplaces (see chapter 8). Control of the features of timescapes enables temporal power, and relative stability in their arrangements creates temporal continuities within sites such as the home and work. Multiple timescapes, with differing temporal features and logics, coexist, sometimes working in concert to shape the wider temporal landscape, or vying for dominance. As we live our everyday lives, we traverse through and co-produce these timescapes: we are able to recognize their composition, characteristics and expected practices, and their interrelations, frictions and discontinuities, and use time tactics to subvert and resist their temporal order (Hassan, 2009).

To illustrate the utility of the timescapes perspective, Adam (1998) maps out the timescape of industrial time with respect to environmental economics, politics and issues. Pre-digital industrial time, Adam proposes, is primarily composed of machine (clock time), economic (time as a resource) and laboratory (measure of abstract motion) time. Together, these compose a timescape in which time frames are a measured quantity; temporality is fixed, regulated and controlled; timing is rationalized; tempo is maximized and optimized; the time point is extended; time patterns are even and eurythmic; time sequences are controlled; time extensions are investments, opportunity costs and goals; and the time future is prospected, produced, predicted and pre-empted (Adam, 2004). Hassan (2009) details the timescape of an airport, which has a complex amalgam of clock and network time, with a timetable of flights, the sequencing of passengers through a complex system of practices and checks, and the use of real-time automated systems (e.g., for passenger profiling and baggage routing). These produce a diverse set of temporal relations and rhythms (waiting, rushing, dead time) with respect to different zones and activities (check-in, security, departure lounge, immigration control, baggage pick-up, arrivals hall). Numerous other studies chart specific timescapes: for example, Dyson (2009) maps the timescape of European economic governance; Ladner (2009) examines the interrelations, differences and gendering of the timescapes of postindustrial workplaces and homes; Liu (2021) charts the timescapes of domestic living; and Kitchin (2019a) details the timescape of smart cities.

The remainder of the book details the extent to which digital technologies have reconfigured temporal relations, transformed timescapes, and produced a new time consciousness. The next chapter examines the interrelation of technology and temporality from a historical and contemporary perspective, identifying core issues and relations. Part II then charts the timescapes of six sets of processes and practices in the digital era. While by no means exhaustive, the chosen foci are key components of everyday life and social and economic activity. Examining them enables a number of temporalities and timescapes – how these vary across people and place, and the effects of a diverse range of technologies on their (re)production – to be detailed. The final part of the book examines the more troubling aspects of how digital technologies are reshaping temporalities, the ways in which uneven and unequal temporal power might be challenged and reconfigured in emancipatory and empowering ways, and future research agendas.

In developing the argument, I try to be mindful that it is quite easy for four problematic issues to arise in assessing the relationship between technologies, temporality, and everyday activities. The first is the extent to which temporalities are a factor in, or an artefact of, the ways in which digital technologies and processes interact. For example, is speed a by-product or temporal description of how digital technologies are shaping urban development, or is the demand for speed and a quick turnaround in profit a causal mechanism driving fast urbanism (Chien and Woodworth, 2018; see chapter 7)? 'Just because rhythms can be identified' in relation to certain actions, 'it does not necessarily follow that it is time which determines that patterning of activity' or explains the organization of practices; rather, the rhythms might be the artefact of another process (Southerton, 2020: 154). It can be quite tricky to 'determine unambiguously the analytical status of ... time', to 'distinguish clearly between independent, dependent and, possibly, intervening variables', to treat forms of temporality as discrete variables, and to situate temporalities and untangle whether they are proxies for other factors, or are the outcomes or active agents in urban processes (Goetz and Meyer-Sahling, 2009: 181; Grzymala-Busse, 2011).

The second issue is the danger of slipping into a technologically deterministic analysis in which digital technologies are seen to determine, in cause-and-effect ways, various temporalities and other social relations. As noted, time is fundamentally socio-technical in nature – thoroughly contingent, relational and contextual in its unfolding. Technologies might offer temporal affordances that play a significant role in the production of time, but they do not universally determine temporality. Indeed, digital technologies are themselves shaped by temporal processes, and are in and of time, rather than impinging on time from outside (Erickson and Mazmanian, 2017). Moreover, the mechanisms, processes and practices enacted by or in conjunction with digital technologies are distinct from the temporalities (e.g., duration, tempo, pace and timing) of those actions, though they are interrelated in terms of producing an outcome (Grzymala-Busse, 2011). By placing the focus of analysis on the temporal effects of digital technologies, many studies that claim to adopt a socio-technical perspective allow a latent form of determinism to slide back into the analysis (Keightley and Pickering 2014). Such latency needs to be guarded against.

The third issue is maintaining an even-handed and credible assessment, seeking to avoid overstating the extent to which digital technologies have transformed temporalities, and the salience of digitally mediated time. Digital technologies have undoubtedly reconfigured the production of time, yet the temporal relations and regimes of the pre-digital era persist and remain important. Clock time and fixed timetables, for example, remain key means of structuring social relations such as meal and break times, school and work hours, retail opening hours and business meetings, and television and sports schedules. Sacred and eschatological time remain important for religious believers in terms of service, prayer and festival times, and they continue to impinge on wider society through associated public holidays and time rules (such as Sunday shop-opening hours). These times have not been usurped and fully replaced by network time, but rather they coexist and inflect each other, along with other forms of time (e.g., postcolonial, mediated, gendered, etc.). Digital technologies have instigated significant changes in temporalities, but these need to be framed and contextualized in relation to temporal continuities (Erickson and Mazmanian, 2017). As Keightley and Pickering (2014: 591) note, we need to 'understand change against continuity, and continuity against change, with both gaining or retaining their significance through their mutual interaction'.

The fourth issue concerns the situatedness and framing of the analysis in two senses: my own positionality, and the literature from which I am drawing ideas and empirical examples. Undoubtedly, my own experiences and observations relating to time are shaped by my own socialization and social status. I am a white, middle-aged, abled-bodied, childless man who has a relatively high degree of temporal autonomy in my work and home life. I am presently more likely to instigate and expect temporal arbitrage than to perform it, and to reproduce temporal inequalities than experience them. I have lived my entire life in Ireland and the UK and been socialized into their temporal regimes and orders. My temporal perceptions, experiences and expectations, my time consciousness, are grounded in this positionality, and that no doubt colours my view of the workings of temporal relations. Ireland might be a postcolonial country, but in a quite different way from former colonial countries in the Global South, and it is very much a European nation. Moreover, I am limited to the English language, and my education, and the literature I have engaged with, are overwhelmingly Anglo-American centric. As many other scholars have detailed, quite different conceptualizations and orientations to time exist across cultures and places (Appadurai, 2013; Barak 2013). I have tried to be sensitive to these differences, but the analysis is nonetheless Eurocentric in its framing, argument and the majority of illustrative examples.

— 2 —

DIGITAL TECHNOLOGIES AND TEMPORALITIES

The intimate relationship between technologies, temporality and everyday life is long established. Technologies structure the pace, tempo and rhythms of activities. Time-centred technologies, such as clocks and calendars, enable the measurement, planning, scheduling and synchronization of events. Labour-saving technologies speed up work processes and create efficiencies in the undertaking of tasks (though the time saved is usually filled with additional work). Transport and communications technologies reduce the time taken for goods and information to move between places, and reconfigure the organization of logistics and the spatial arrangement of the economy. Media and archiving technologies provide a means of recording and storing information, producing historical accounts, and accessing and sharing personal and collective memories. This chapter examines the relationship between technologies, temporality and everyday life from two perspectives. In the first section, a brief historical account is charted. Rather than mapping out key developments and transitions across civilization, the discussion concentrates on the era of modernity and the role of clock and standardized time in industrialization, the time-space compression created by new communications and transport technologies and infrastructure, and how these temporal transitions were key to the workings of capitalism and colonialism. The second part of the chapter considers the difference the digital makes to how technologies inflect the temporality of everyday practices and social and economic relations. A case is made that a temporal transition has occurred over the past thirty years as forms of network time have become common and normalized.

Technologies, temporality and modernity

Modernity is considered both a historical period encompassing the seventeenth century through to the mid twentieth century and a collection of sociocultural norms associated with capitalism, secularization, liberalization, colonialism and globalization (Berman, 1982). Following the late-medieval era, the period includes a wide range of cultural, political, social and economic phenomena and processes – Enlightenment ideals, scientific advances, industrialization, democracy, mass media, urbanization and new forms of governmentality and government, undergirded by a sense of progress towards liberty and quality of life (Giddens, 1990). The transition into the modern era was accompanied by a shift in temporality linked to the growth of reliable, affordable clocks, with clock time vying with sacred time and task-orientated time to shape social organization, eventually becoming the dominant temporal order.

While the transition to clock time has its roots in the medieval period (Thrift, 1990), it is no coincidence that mechanical clocks, and their associated temporal practices of timekeeping and time management, became key social technologies at the same historic moment as industrialization and the rise of capitalism (Thompson, 1967). Clocks abstracted time from natural (e.g., seasonal cycles) and sacred time, replacing them with consistent, measurable and trackable temporal units (e.g., 60-second minute, 60-minute hour, 24-hour day) (Burges and Elias, 2016). This enabled time to become an abstract exchange value, with workers paid for their time rather than by task or the use value of their goods or services. Time became a context-independent (one hour is an hour, regardless of situation) 'value by which products, tasks and services [could] be evaluated and exchanged' with respect to monetary value (Adam, 2004: 38). A worker's time became a commodity that was assigned an economic value, with units of time exchanged for remuneration that could be spent on other commodities. In parallel, for employers, the amount of time that needed to be purchased to produce goods and services became a calculable measure for production costs (Southerton, 2020). Time, in other words, became synonymous with money, and, in turn, treated as a resource that could be harnessed, traded and exploited.

As an abstract exchange value, time became an integral component of production, with the optimization of time to perform a task producing efficiencies and increasing productivity (Adam, 2004). From this perspective, saving time equates to making profit (Wajcman,

27

2008). Increasing the rate of production reduces the cost of a product and increases its competitiveness and potential to capture market share. In order to stay competitive and profitable, commodified labour as abstract exchange value had to be intensified (Adam, 2004). Speed and efficiency thus became essential for business – a key means through which to maximize profit (Tomlinson, 2007). Clock time made economic operations and organization predictable and manageable by facilitating the coordination of scheduling, and synchronization in activities (Hassan, 2009). Time-centred technologies and time management strategies became essential tools to intensify, reorganize or rationalize labour, optimize resources and logistics, and compress product creation and distribution (see chapter 8). Consequently, workers increasingly competed against the clock to meet productivity targets (West-Pavlov, 2013).

The adoption of clock time within work and public services had significant impacts on social and spatial organization of society, creating clear distinctions between home and work, and public and private spaces (Thompson, 1967). These time-space divisions were separated along gendered lines, with women performing time-geographies organized around domestic labour and childcare, and men around work and public activities (Milojevic, 2008). In addition, new public infrastructure related to energy, lighting, water and sewage decoupled social rhythms from natural cycles (Elsner et al., 2019). The synchrony of social life – the temporal ordering of schooling, work and social activities – established a sense of engroupment, (re)producing and reinforcing social identities and a shared sense of belonging (Freeman, 2016). Indeed, the embedding of clock time into the social fabric, and the ordering and regulation of everyday life, created a new type of time consciousness and temporal subjectivity that thoroughly permeated temporal-spatial attitudes and behaviour, in relation to both the self and others (e.g., concerning punctuality, lateness, slowness, etc.) (Thrift, 1990). This deeply ingrained time consciousness in turn became a central aspect of governmentality through the self-disciplining of behaviour with respect to the expectations of the prevalent temporal regime (see chapter 6).

In addition to labour production, speed, synchronicity and efficiency were similarly applied to: market processes, in terms of accessing finance, the logistics of sourcing materials and distributing goods, and being the first to get new products to the market; and to consumption, in terms of the lifespan of new products and their continual replacement with innovations, creating fashion and fads (Tomlinson, 2007). In other words, the 'turnover time' of business

– 'the total time necessary for the production of the commodity, its launching onto the market and distribution, and finally, the return of the profits to cover the original outlay invested' – was significantly reduced (West-Pavlov, 2013: 131). In parallel, the 'half-life' of commodities – the length of time before a product becomes obsolete, replaced by the latest model or fashion – shrank, providing new market opportunities (Harvey, 1989). Schumpeter (1942) famously described this as the creative destruction imperative of capital: through innovation and competition, current products are rendered obsolete, ceaselessly replaced with new ones. Even relatively long-term temporal and spatial fixes for capital, such as real estate, cycle through phases of disinvestment, dereliction, regeneration or replacement as capital seeks fresh opportunities (Harvey, 1989; see chapter 7). The reduction of turnover time was aided by three significant temporalized processes: time-space compression, the standardization of time globally, and the colonization of the future.

Enormous time-space compression took place during modernity – that is, a significant shrinkage in the time taken to traverse and connect across space, making the world seem smaller and interconnected (Harvey, 1989). Time-space compression consists of two related processes. Time-space convergence is the reduction in time taken to travel or communicate between locations (Leyshon, 1995). Steam-powered shipping and railways radically increased the speed of movement, while also enabling larger volumes of people and goods to be moved at cheaper rates. Travel time across the Atlantic shrank from between two to four months to less than two weeks with the introduction of steam ships; travel from New York to Chicago shrank from three weeks by stagecoach to two days by train (Leyshon, 1995). Likewise, the invention of the telegraph drastically reduced the time taken to transfer information between distant places. In 1870, letters posted from London took up to forty days to arrive in Calcutta; a relayed telegraph message, just three days (Leyshon, 1995). Subsequent technological innovations – trams, cars, buses, planes, telephone, radio, cinema and television – and their associated infrastructure increased time-space convergence, while also extending its effect to more places and people at more affordable rates. The second process, time-space distanciation is an increasing synchronicity between places so that they become interdependent through rapid communication and travel (Giddens, 1984). Time-space distanciation enabled states to direct their diplomats and converse with other states in a timely fashion, and colonial governments to react quickly to political and military issues in their dominions. It also

29

facilitated the expansion and organization of corporate operations across the globe. Distanciation enabled: workers and tasks in one location to be overseen by managers in another; the exploitation of differences in labour, resource, and overhead costs to create global production networks; an expansion into new markets guided from the centre; and quick and cheap distribution to markets globally (Dicken, 2007). Space-time convergence and distanciation have meant that the friction of distance has been progressively annulled through speed – or, to put it another way, space has been overcome by time.

Time-space compression was a key facilitator of colonialism, which generated its own complex temporal affordances. The coordination and synchronization of time locally and with the metropole was a key aspect of colonial modernity (Appadurai, 2013). Barak's (2013) account of the introduction of new transportation and communications infrastructure in Egypt (e.g., Suez canal, train, trams, telegraph, telephone, radio) from the mid nineteenth to early twentieth century, and the imposition of British time technologies, temporal expectations and its Gregorian calendar, demonstrates the ways in which clock time, timekeeping and timetables (of transport, public institutions, work) sought to reorder and civilize the seemingly disordered, slow, natural and sacred 'Egyptian time', and make Egypt a key node in the global temporal order of the British Empire (with nearly all transport, post and telegraph messages to the East passing through the territory). At the same time, not every aspect of British temporality was imposed, or it was imposed unequally – for example, while British workers on Egyptian railways were full-time employees paid monthly salaries based on clock time, most Egyptian workers were employed as day labourers paid per task (Barak, 2013). Moreover, 'Egyptian time' was retroactively invented, with roots in Islamic traditions and rural folklore, and claimed as a resistive counter-tempo to the expediency, promptness and synchronization of colonial time (Barak, 2013). Barak's (2013: 2) analysis thus highlights how modernization in Egypt was accelerated under colonialism, while 'always remaining one step behind'.

The adoption of standardized, universal time independent of location further extended the separation of economic activity from local temporalities (Kern, 1983). There were 300 local times in the United States in 1860, and many more in France until the end of the nineteenth century (Kern, 1983). This disparity of times, alongside the effects of time-space compression, created issues of synchronization of services such as railway and postal systems.

Greenwich Mean Time (GMT) was adopted as a universal clock time to supersede local times in the UK in 1847 as a way to synchronize railway timetables. In 1870, there were 80 different railway times in the United States; these – and, by association, local times – were standardized to a universal time in 1883, which divided the country into time zones (Kern, 1983). In 1884, the political process to create a global standardized time centred on the Greenwich meridian was initiated, being formally adopted in 1898. Global standardized time greatly enhanced the coordination of transportation and communications and facilitated the organization and operations of logistics, trade, politics and warfare (Giddens, 1990).

Throughout modernity, the colonization of the future became a key imaginary of progress and a resource for seeding and sustaining capital. In pre-modern societies, the future was generally viewed as the direction of temporal travel and part of a circular repetition of events (such as seasons). In contrast, capitalism viewed the 'future as open containing opportunities to be seized and risks to be calculated' (Beckert, 2016: 22). In essence, the future was mobilized as resource for the present. Credit is a means to lend tomorrow's money based on expected income and profits to present-day investors and consumers, with interest paid as a fee for the service and to cover any potential losses, and the future is the location where generated profits will be spent (Sewell, 2005; West-Pavlov, 2013). Credit, then, is drawn from a hypothetical future in which investors utilize projected future profit to pay off debt incurred on present investments. In other words, credit allowed 'firms to engage in economic activities that could not otherwise be undertaken, using resources they have yet to earn' (Beckert, 2016: 4). Competition to capture future markets and derive profit drives innovation and the creation of products to be experienced in the future. Firms and employees are thus encouraged to be future-aware, to develop new forms of work (efficiency and productivity gains), new products and new skills that ensure credit can be successfully paid off and there are opportunities to re-invest returns (Beckert, 2016). Those who cannot generate a surplus profit lose access to credit and go out of business. Capitalism thus 'depends on the future', though 'that future is its weak spot not only because investments may not bring a return, but also because there may not be an opportunity to re-invest those returns' (West-Pavlov, 2013: 134).

Just as the future became a resource, so too did the past, though the motivation was figured more around civilization, knowledge, bureaucracy and collective identity than capital (Huyssen, 2003).

Within modernity, particularly in the late nineteenth century, there was an explosion in the number of institutions centred on history and memory (e.g., museums, archives, libraries, galleries, public records offices and historical societies) (Huyssen, 2003). This was accompanied by development of formalized archiving systems and associated technologies concerning storage, display and circulation of materials. In addition, there was a growth in memorialization and public monuments, commemoration, and the start of movements focused on preservation, conservation and heritage (Lynch, 1972). The time consciousness of the general population was not just, then, being orientated around the clock and the future needs of capital, but also with respect to the past, creating a different form of temporally mediated social identity.

For Stephen Kern (1983), a crucial period for temporal and spatial relations during modernity was 1880 to 1918. During these years, time was standardized; clock time and time management were strongly institutionalized; new communication, media, transport and utility technologies (e.g. telephone, radio, cinema, motorized vehicles, air travel, electrification) were introduced; and the telegraph, railways and use of industrial machinery expanded rapidly. Together, these technologies radically reshaped everyday temporalities and time consciousness, producing a new temporal doxa that remained in place throughout the twentieth century. A temporal doxa can be said to exist when a temporal regime is hegemonic in society: its logic, configuration and operation having been normalized and accepted as necessary and legitimate. A central assertion developed throughout the rest of the book is that a similar transition has taken place since the early 1990s, reaching a tipping point in the late 2010s, wherein the digital has become vital to the production of temporalities in the Global North, reshaping the temporalities of everyday life, and producing new time competencies and consciousness that are thoroughly normalized and internalized by people and institutions. The digital age has ruptured the temporal logics of modernity, with the network time of digital devices, systems, platforms and infrastructures reconfiguring the timescapes of society.

Digital technologies and temporality

Since the 1950s and the birth of digital computing, everyday life has become ever more entwined with the digital. Initially, given their cost, digital computers were used in military, scientific and limited industrial applications. By the late 1950s, they had started to be enrolled into government and civic uses to monitor and control utility and other infrastructures, and for modelling social, economic and environmental scenarios. In the late 1960s, the promise of digital developments dovetailed with cybernetic thinking, leading to attempts to model, plan and run social and economic systems using computation (Forrester, 1969). During the 1970s, mainframe computers started to be adopted within government and industry for processing records and extracting insights from them, and the nascent Internet started to expand, with its use spreading beyond the military and academia by the end of the decade. In the 1980s and 1990s, personal computers began to become widespread in central and local government, along with specialist software, used for administration, the delivery of services, and to manage assets. Digital technologies and information systems started to be adopted across commerce and industry as a means of improving the flexibility and efficiency of processes and of enhancing productivity. Computers became increasingly networked in the 1990s and 2000s with the rapid growth of the Internet, accompanied by large investments in e-government (the delivery of services, and interfacing with the public via digital channels) and e-governance (managing citizens and their activities using digital tools) (Castells, 1996). This also extended to the networking of infrastructure, such as the wide-scale adoption of traffic management systems and surveillance cameras (e.g CCTV) (Lyon, 1994). At the same time, personal computers and gaming machines became common in homes, which were increasingly being connected to the Internet. By the mid-to-late 1990s, commentators across disciplines were detailing how the organization, processes and practices of various sectors of society were being transformed by the digital turn. For example, a substantial literature emerged charting how the digital was transforming the operations and nature of work and business (Castells, 1996; Cairncross, 1997), and government and governance (Poster, 1995; Snellen and van de Donk, 1998). Urban and regional theorists started to detail the nature of an emerging networked urbanism, wherein ICTs became increasingly critical to how cities and the activities within them functioned (Castells, 1996). The Internet and networked infrastructure were found to be having profound effects on urban–regional restructuring by enabling pronounced time-space compression and the temporal-spatial reorganization of businesses and institutions.

In the 2000s, computation became ever more mobile with the rise of smartphones and other portable digital devices, and computation started to become pervasive, ubiquitous and instantaneous (that is, embedded into everything, available everywhere, and responsive in real-time) with growing scales of economy in digital products, networking and storage, and the rollout of the Internet of things. By the late 2000s, personal and mobile computing, networked devices, access to cloud services, platforms and infrastructures permeated home, work, consumption, travel and play. Commerce and work had become thoroughly digitally mediated, with the routine employment of networked digital technologies and an increasing use of big data and automation across all aspects of business (see chapter 8). Whole new digital industries had emerged related to software production, internet commerce, cyber-manufacturing, and the digital mediation of services and goods, quickly growing to become significant sectors of the economy. The concept of 'smart cities' – cities that combine forms of entrepreneurial and networked urbanism – started to gain traction and investment (Townsend, 2013). Reconnecting with cybernetic thinking and aligning with the political economy of neoliberalism, smart urbanism envisages a thoroughly digital city in which city services, infrastructures and populations are managed in real-time using networked technologies (Kitchin, 2014a). Aspects of rural life also became digitally mediated, with small and medium enterprises embracing digital technologies to remain competitive and access new markets, and agriculture and food production adopting them to facilitate and automate work and create trust through farm-to-fork traceability of products (Dodge, 2019; Fraser, 2019). These trends continued in the 2010s as more and more activities were drawn into the digital fold.

Consequently, we now live in an age where networked digital devices, infrastructures, systems and platforms are thoroughly interwoven into how society operates and is managed, governed and planned, how economies function and are interconnected globally, and how people perform everyday life. People routinely interact with and co-produce the digital – sometimes in a direct manner, other times indirectly or with little awareness. For example, table 2.1 details a selection of digital technologies and systems shaping social and economic practices and processes that are examined in more detail in part II of the book. These technologies act as space-time machines, significantly disrupting and reconfiguring temporality, as well as spatiality, to produce a new set of time-space relations and engender a new time consciousness. While these space-time machines have specific temporal effects with respect to sites and domains, they also modulate timescapes more generally, with respect to rhythms and cycles; pace and tempo; time-space compression; scheduling; efficiency; the past, present and future – and are central to the production of network time and real-time.

Moreover, they produce what might be termed code/spacetime. That is, a dyadic entwining of the digital, space and time in which space-time relations are dependent on digital technologies in order to be produced in particular ways (Kitchin, 2019a). This is a temporal extension of the concept of code/space, wherein code is essential in the production of expected spatiality (Kitchin and Dodge, 2011). For example, in a modern supermarket, if the checkout tills crash, then the space is produced as a warehouse rather than a store, as there is no longer a manual means to sell goods. In order for the space to operate as a supermarket, code and space are mutually constituted, hence code/space being expressed as a dyad. Code/space, however, ignores the temporality of events and practices, hence its reformulation as code/spacetime. For example, an intelligent transport system controls the flow of traffic through junctions (sites) by altering the phasing and sequencing (timing) of traffic lights. If the code fails, in the sense of the system crashing, then the traffic lights either fail to work or operate on default settings, meaning that the chronotope intended is not produced and congestion and gridlock will quickly follow. This dyadic relationship does not exist in all cases, however. The digital might make a difference to how space-time is produced but is not essential, in which case coded space-time (separate but interrelated) is generated (Kitchin 2019a). Key elements in the production of code/spacetime are network time and real-time.

Network time, real-time and the present

Hassan (2003) contends that networked digital technologies produce 'network time' – a temporal modality in which time is reconfigured by digital mediation. The technologies detailed in table 2.1 render time largely instantaneous and global, creating a shared 24/7 society of immediate connection across the planet. Network time, Adam (2007) notes, is 'globally networked rather than globally zoned. It is instantaneous rather than durational or causal. It is simultaneous rather than sequential.' People across the globe can share temporal alignments in play (e.g., online games) and work (e.g., online conferencing), organizing themselves temporally around their networked interactions rather than local clock time. Network time enables stock markets to work in concert across time zones, networks of traffic

Table 2.1 A selection of digital technologies shaping social and economic practices and processes and their related temporalities

Domain	Digital technologies and systems	Related temporalities
History and memory	Digitization, archiving systems, data infrastructures, data management systems, digital humanities software, memory apps, museum apps	The past, memory, history, heritage, memorialization, preservation, hindcasting
Politics and policy	24/7 traditional media, digital communication (email, web forms, texting), social media, collaborative platforms, polling instruments, time management tools, performance and predictive analytics, simulation and modelling, dashboards	Timing, time rules, time tactics, path dependencies, legacies, sequencing, synchronization, fast policy, policy cycles, prototyping, futuring, prediction
Governance and governmentality	Administrative systems, e-government, decision support systems, control rooms, utilities management systems, predictive policing, emergency management systems, sensor networks	Real-time, optimization, efficiency, longitudinal analysis, pre-emption, anticipation, prediction, forecasting
Mobility and logistics	Intelligent transport systems, scheduling apps, location-based social networking, mobility platforms, real-time passenger information, supply chain management systems, rostering systems	Time-space compression, real-time, just-in-time, on-the-fly, synchronization, efficiency, rhythm and refrain, sequencing, forecasting, serendipity, temporal density and fragmentation, nowcasting
Planning and development	Consultative planning apps, geographic information systems, building information management systems, city information modelling, augmented/virtual reality platforms, housing and real-estate platforms, financial systems	Speed, fast urbanism, futuring, projection, foresight, speculation, development cycles, deceleration, obsolescence, postcolonial time, mythological time
Work and labour	Specialist work software and digitally mediated machines, time management tools, enterprise resource planning systems, customer relations management systems, platform/gig apps, work surveillance systems	Productivity, efficiency, time management, time-space distanciation, temporal arbitrage, flexibility, precarity, multitasking

Source: created by the author.

lights to be concurrently controlled, and consumers to purchase goods or to download online content anywhere on the planet with the click of a button. Consequently, for Hassan (2003, 2009), network time is undermining and displacing the salience of clock time (though not negating or cancelling it) and we are transiting to a new normative temporal regime that is defined by speed, connectivity, flexibility, and radical time-space compression.

Similarly, Castells (1996) argued that ICTs produce what he termed 'timeless time', wherein localized clock time is erased, suspended and transformed – 'all expressions are either instantaneous or without predictable sequencing' (Castells, 1998: 350), with networked systems being 'simultaneously present' across time zones. Urry (2000) likewise argued that networked technologies produce 'instantaneous time' – real-time, on-demand, at-a-distance, synchronous connection and response. Hassan (2007) notes, however, that network time is also fragmented and not necessarily synchronous. For example, an email is delivered to a receiving server at the speed of light with little latency, though it might be read several hours later, and responded to days after that (or not at all). Network time is also fragmented, since it is produced across multiple platforms that do not necessarily share the same temporal logics or relations. Network time is 'perceived more in terms of abrupt and discontinuous irruptions of varying intensities' than as a continuous, even arrow of time (Virilio, 1997; Purser, 2002: 162). Consequently, as Crang (2007: 84) notes:

[t]here are multiple speeds implied in network time-spaces. Rather than thinking simply of an endless onward rush, we might look at them as a turbulent-torrent. There are back eddies, ripples, fast parts, slow pools, and so forth, and flows may be braided and overlain ... Some people may be slowed, others accelerated. Some times may be densified or fragmented and others extended or attenuated in long waits.

Real-time is a particular form of network time, though the two are often treated as synonymous (Hassan, 2009). Heim (1993: 49) defines real-time as 'simultaneity in the occurrence and registering of an event', with little to no latency in temporal duration. Real-time systems enable instantaneous communication and continuous synchronicity across a network that might span the globe. Real-time enables the close management of the here-and-now, with its power derived from the seeming annihilation of space *and* time to the point where life takes place within a 'perpetual present' (de Lange, 2018). As discussed in chapter 5, a significant part of the appeal of smart city technologies is their seeming ability to enable city systems to be used and managed dynamically in real-time. Data concerning the activity and performance of an infrastructure or system are generated by sensors, actuators, transponders and cameras and fed back to a control room for instant processing and response by a management system, which sends out instructions for how the system should operate, given present conditions. These data can be shared via publicly facing dashboards, APIs (Application Programming Interfaces) and open data repositories, and plugged into mobile apps. Such control rooms and dashboards seek to create instantaneous corrective actions before problems grow and multiply, to manage emergencies and conduct surveillance, and to create more efficient and optimized system operations, as well as providing accountability, transparency and a resource for civic hacking (Kitchin et al., 2015; Luque-Ayala and Marvin 2020).

The ability to perceive and respond to distant events in the world in real-time creates what Virilio (1997) calls 'chronoscopic time'. Writing with respect to the real-time media coverage of global events and the general use of telecommunications, he argued that, rather than unfolding in succession as a conventional narrative of before, during and after, or events being documented after the fact, audiences have become accustomed to the real-time instant in which narrative time implodes (Purser, 2002). Media coverage on a 24/7 basis creates an eternal, unfolding present of spatially and sociopolitically disconnected snapshots, with instant rather than reflective analysis in which the 'event is fused immediately with event reactions' (Luke, 1998: 165). Likewise, real-time control rooms and spatial media produce chronoscopic time in which cities and personal time-geographies are managed in the perpetual present, with continual recalibration in response to emerging events and serendipity (Crang, 2007). In turn, many people have become fixated on knowing and taking part in the perpetual present – checking for new emails and responding, seeking out current news or weather, browsing the newest posts on social media and commenting, checking-in to places on locative media, discovering when the next bus/train is due, and checking personal performance metrics on wearable devices.

The generation of data in real-time also enables an anticipatory extending of the present in which data are used to predict the present and the very near future (micro-seconds to a few days), to guide action in the present in relation to these predictions, or to estimate what occurred in the very recent past (for example, to calculate more timely official statistics; Kitchin, 2015). Such predictions are termed 'nowcasting' (Bańbura et al., 2010), in which the past, present and future are folded into each other, using past records and current conditions to predict the very near future. Nowcasting is the dominant form of weather forecasting to report expected conditions in the next few hours and days. Nowcasting is a long-established practice within the financial sector to pre-empt stock market and currency exchange rates, and is a core feature of intelligent transport systems seeking to anticipate and prevent congestion. More recent uses include predictive policing that seeks to nowcast patterns of crime in order to direct police patrols accordingly (see chapter 5); real-time polling and measurement of television viewer responses to political or news debates (see chapter 4); and apps that provide predictions of bus arrivals, travel time, car parking spaces or bikeshare availability, and so on, in the next few minutes or hours (Stehle and Kitchin, 2020). As Uprichard (2012: 133) notes, the aim is often not simply to know now and predict the immediate future, but 'to know about now before now has happened'. This is leading, she contends, to the present being increasingly embedded into institutional structures, and vice versa, with the result that the 'present itself becomes more and more plastic, to be stretched, manipulated, moulded and ultimately "casted" by those who can access more of it in the supposed "now"'. From this perspective, control rooms cast the present by iteratively pre-figuring it through ongoing responses.

When one examines real-time systems closely, it is apparent that they are never quite real-time in practice; the data generated and processed are sampled, with a small latency between discrete data points (Mackenzie, 1997). Weltevrede et al. (2014) note that social media and news platforms have varying latencies in their back-end processing and delivery of content, producing differing temporalities. In their study of the velocity of twenty-six types of urban big data, Kitchin and McArdle (2016) detailed that the data were temporally differentiated in two ways: with respect to how they were generated, and to how they were analysed, acted upon and shared. In the first case, data were categorized as either 'real-time constant' (always on and operating) to denote data that are endlessly generated (e.g., a weather sensor that continuously records measurements), or 'real-time sporadic' to denote data that are generated only at the point of use (e.g., clickstream data that is continually measured but only whilst a user is clicking through websites). In both cases, there is latency in data recording, with data being sampled every few milliseconds, or every ten seconds, or every five minutes, or whatever temporal rate the system had been programmed to perform. In the second case, data processing, analytical functions and publishing occur in some systems as the data are generated, with only slight latency (e.g., as a tweet is tweeted, it is recorded in Twitter's data architecture and, microseconds later, it is published into user timelines); in other systems, the data are sampled in real-time, but their transmission, processing or publication is delayed (e.g., mobile LiDAR scanning by a vehicle captures scans of streetscapes every second, but these are stored on a hard disk and transferred to a data centre at the end of each day).

The temporal rate of data measurement and sharing is in part chosen and in part imposed. Parikka (2018) divides real-time systems into three categories: those with a strict upper limit on the time within which a response must be performed; quasi real-time systems where a lack of speed or delay might cause annoyance rather than damage; and systems where the response time is not critical. Systems are configured in relation to these requirements, with decisions made regarding prioritization in sorting, routing, queuing and waiting for network and software events (such as the passage of packets across multiple networks) (Parikka, 2018), and balancing data resolution and noise (data quality) against system configuration and performance (e.g., life of batteries, costs of data transmission/ storage). The system components and architecture also affect temporality. All digital processing involves latencies related to memory buffering, CPU (Central Processing Unit) scheduling, process rates and interrupts, and complexity and size of a task. Indeed, technologies consolidate many temporalities. For example, 'a modern car going at 60 miles per hour is likely to have wheels rotating at around 800 revolutions per minute, an engine firing at 2,000 revolutions per minute, and a microprocessor calculating at 2 GHz, or 120 billion cycles per minute' (Stine and Volmar, 2021: 15). Within a networked digital device, several temporalities are simultaneously at play – for example, 'seek time, run time, read time, access time, available time, real time, polynomial time, time division, time slicing, time sharing, time complexity, write time, processor time, hold time, execution time, compilation time, and cycle time' (Mackenzie, 2006: 2). In complex systems, composed of many devices and networks (e.g., sensors, computers, routers, servers, etc.), these temporalities multiply.

Mackenzie (1997) thus contends that real-time is a fabricated temporal condition, and Weltevrede et al. (2014: 127) conclude that there are varying forms of 'realtimeness'. As such, there is a multiplicity of the present (Coleman, 2018). For example, 'Twitter creates a real-time, live connected present, while Netflix produces ... a suspended or expanded present; ... the present is not a static or homogenous temporality but rather it is (capable of being) stretched and condensed, expanded and contracted, sped up and slowed down, in various ways' (Coleman, 2018: 3). Real-time is differently compressed and paced (Coleman, 2020) and the present is active, flexible and malleable (Coleman, 2018, 2020). Moreover, realtimeness is provisional, always potentially subject to disruption through faults such as network outages and software crashes, more malicious interventions such as hacking, and scheduled maintenance (Hope, 2006; Stine and Volmar, 2021). Weltevrede et al. (2014: 140, 141) thus conclude that real-time 'does not unfold as a flat, eternal now or as a global, high-paced stream, but ... unfolds at different speeds in relation to different devices'. This realtimeness produces distinct 'real-time cultures' within platforms and systems.

By radically compressing time and space, network time and real-time have a number of associated temporal effects relating to pace and tempo, scheduling, and rhythms and cycles, as well as spatial effects relating to the geography of the economy and urban development (see chapters 7 and 8). Some of these effects are highly problematic and 'the tyranny of real-time' (Virilio, 1997: 19) is discussed in chapter 9. It should be noted that, while network time and real-time are key temporalities of the digital era, they are complemented by other temporal modalities, such as mediated and mobile time (see chapter 6), and they are not the only modalities through which speed and acceleration are being operationalized (e.g., fast policy and fast urbanism only partially operate in real-time; see chapters 5 and 7).

Pace, tempo, rhythms and synchronicity

A key assertion of scholars studying the relationship between digital technologies and temporality is that network time, in its varying manifestations, is having a significant impact on everyday temporal relations in several ways. In particular, speed and acceleration are identified as key temporal effects in the digital era (Rosa, 2003; Tomlinson, 2007). Rosa (2015) details three forms of acceleration. Technological acceleration is the speeding up of technical processes. This feeds into and propels an 'acceleration in the pace of life', in which there is a decrease in the time needed to undertake processes and actions, and an 'acceleration of social change' in which social relations (e.g. attitudes, values, practices, habits), structures (e.g. communities, workplaces) and institutions (e.g. public services) increasingly lack stability and are open to transformation. These forms of acceleration are driven by and serve the desires of capitalism by further speeding up the turnover time of capital accumulation, while simultaneously extending its spatial extent (see chapters 6, 7 and 8).

Acceleration does not necessarily lead, however, to an increase in free time, as any additional time produced can be colonized by other activities. The always-on nature of networked technologies and the availability of mobile access mean that people are becoming always–everywhere available (Green, 2002). A consequence of perpetual connectivity is the 'time shifting of activities to formerly unavailable time slots' (Crang, 2007: 71). Time outside of work can be colonized by work-related activities, and so-called 'dead time' or 'wasted time' endured during various forms of commute can be transformed into 'productive time' (such as phoning, texting, emailing, searching information and sending files) (Wajcman, 2008). Moreover, the time-shifting property of networked technologies expands the possibilities for time-deepening activities, such as multi-tasking and interleaving, so that several tasks can be performed simultaneously or overlap, rather than be performed sequentially (Crang, 2007). Consequently, digital technologies often produce ever-more-extended and complex networks of tasks to attend to.

In addition, the temporal organization of activities is becoming more flexible and de-coupled from clock time (see chapter 6). Instant and mobile communication, plus the sharing of location information, are altering coordination in space by enabling 'perpetual contact' and on-the-fly scheduling of meetings (Katz and Aakhus, 2002), and serendipitous encounters with nearby friends (Sutko and de Souza e Silva, 2010), as well as new forms of activism such as swarming and flash mobs (Willis, 2016). The scheduling and planning of activities and events thus shifts from planned actions at specific times and places to continual recalibration and reaction for any time, any place (Crang, 2007). Spatial media have also enabled access to information about the real-time conditions of transportation networks, facilitating dynamic route planning, and spatial search and location-based services provide information on nearby businesses permitting contextual choice- and decision-making rather than advanced search and planning. Consequently, set mealtimes, clocking-in/out, timetables, pre-arranged meetings and so on, built around the measure of a clock, have been traded for greater temporal flexibility.

Acceleration, time shifting, fragmentation, interleaving and a decoupling from clock time have associated consequences for the concatenated temporal rhythms and beats of everyday life. Acceleration speeds up the rate of temporal repetition, temporal density creates overlaps and disturbs synchronicity, and temporal fragmentation creates ruptures. Constellations of rhythms that were harmonized can be 'punctured, disrupted or curtailed by moments and periods of arrhythmia' (Edensor and Holloway, 2008: 485). While some technologies might create disruption, others are deployed to augment and regulate the multiple rhythms of social and economic systems – to limit arrhythmia and produce eurhythmic systems that maintain a refrain. Many smart city technologies, for example, are designed to perform new forms of algorithmic governance with the intention of producing consistent rhythmic patterns. In effect, these systems' algorithms act as 'algorhythms' producing 'measurable time effects and rhythms' (Miyazaki, 2012: 5), with the space-time unfolding of place algorhythmically mediated to produce a consistent, desired refrain (Coletta and Kitchin, 2017; see chapter 6).

At a personal level, changes to pace, tempo, rhythms and other temporalities mean that, while digital technologies are often promoted on the basis that they create time and aid the management of temporal relations, everyday life is generally experienced as more flexible, fragmented, frenetic and lived-in-the-moment (Crang, 2007; Hassan and Purser, 2007). Indeed, a common conclusion is that digital technologies, far from freeing up time, have created temporal density, squeezes and pressures (see chapter 9). Temporal density occurs when a person experiences several temporalities simultaneously, caused by overlapping rhythms, the fragmentation of time, a multiplication of tasks, and social pressures to respond or comply (Southerton and Tomlinson, 2005; Wajcman, 2015). Networked computing produces ever more extended and complex sets of tasks to attend to, accompanied by a temporal regime that compels people into a persistent engagement (Hassan, 2009). Quickly transitioning situations on multiple fronts: new innovations that swiftly become obsolete; rapid shifts in culture, fashion and politics; saturation in 24/7 news cycles and social media exchanges; accelerated and intensified work practices and processes; ever-tightening deadlines; pressures to alter schedules on the fly to capitalize on opportunities and avoid wasted time, and to respond to family, friends and employers in a timely fashion – all give rise to a sense of being pressed for time at the same time as losing some level of temporal autonomy (Rosa, 2015; Wajcman, 2015). This can lead to time scarcity and feelings of being rushed or harried and that there are not enough hours in a day to do all the things needed (Hassan, 2007).

These time pressures are uneven and do not affect all people in the same ways (see chapter 9). Power-chronology ensures that some people are more strongly ensnared in temporal density and fragmentation, experience time pressures and time poverty, and have less temporal autonomy (Sharma, 2014). For example, some individuals work a 'normal' working week of 9-to-5, Monday to Friday, and have a degree of autonomy in how they temporally structure their work; others will be working shifts and unsocial hours or have irregular work patterns at the behest of others (Sharma, 2014). Men and women both experience the effects of acceleration, but can do so to different extents (Milojevic, 2008; Wajcman, 2015). Women's time is often more fragmented than men's, consisting of more events each day, and more events of shorter duration (Southerton, 2020). They are more likely to be managing workplace demands along with more domestic and caring work, with pressures being exacerbated for single mothers and those in dual-income households (Wajcman, 2015).

Past and future

Just as modernity led to changes in the temporalities and use of the past and future, and their entanglement with the present, the wide-scale use of digital technologies is similarly shifting how the past and future are conceived, produced and utilized. Smart city technologies, for example, seek to leverage information about the past and data generated in real-time to manage more efficiently the present, and to anticipate and shape the future. Similarly, analyses of past performance, trends and trajectories related to urban development help to shape investor decisions and the form and nature of future environments (see chapter 7). Digital technologies thus use the past and future as resources, working across temporal modalities to produce new time-spaces.

As discussed in detail in chapter 3, digital technologies are having significant effects with respect to how we interface with and create history, and how memory is mediated. The mass digitization of historical artefacts (letters, records, surveys, art, photographs, sound recordings, films, cultural objects) and the making of community and counter-archives are producing new sets of digital data concerning the past. Technologies such as LiDAR (light detection and ranging) scanning and ground-penetrating radar and virtual reality also provide new means for uncovering, reconstructing and visualizing past landscape features and human activity (Bruzelius, 2017; Koramaz, 2018). New data infrastructures enable these data to be accessed from afar, harmonized, combined, analysed, and re-used for low marginal cost. In addition, the digital mediation and datafication of everyday life is producing vast quantities of big data of the present – that is, continually produced, highly granular data (usually at an indexical scale; e.g. related to a person, object, transaction) which are exhaustive to a system (e.g. every indexical entity) (Kitchin, 2014b). While some of these data are exhaust and are deleted after immediate use, vast quantities are being archived for future re-use and value-extraction.

Data resources for uncovering and charting the past enable new ways to make sense of and narrate history, and potentially democratize who can do so (Garde-Hansen et al., 2009; Hoskins, 2018a; see chapter 3). Community archives provide a wider evidence base of ordinary and marginalized lives, rather than the narrow view of institutional archives controlled by elites. Big data and new data analytics provide an unprecedented level of information and insights for future historians, though much of these data are owned and controlled by states and companies. As Kinsley (2015: 169) notes, big data holdings provide a high degree of temporal power to their holders concerning 'level of control over what is remembered, how it is remembered and what influence this can have on contemporary socio-spatial experience'. The digital thus potentially produces a richer understanding of the past, and provides a resource for plotting the path to the present and for forecasting the future. It can also create a means for history to be selectively narrated for political purposes in the present, enrolled into fake news, disinformation, propaganda and ideological conflict, and used to (re)shape individual and collective memory.

Digital technologies and their computational processes have become an important means of mediating the present future and casting the future present. The present future is the future from the standpoint of the present; it is the future to be created, which unfolds from past and present trends (Adam and Groves, 2007). In contrast, the future present deploys the future in the present, using possible or anticipated outcomes to rethink current practices, which in turn reshapes the future created (e.g., identifying a desirable future then backcasting to devise policies and interventions to lead from the present to that future) (Poli, 2015). Algorithmic futuring, using analytics and models, has become a key means to forecast and make the future (see chapter 5). Complex models can quickly be calculated for various scenarios and over varying time horizons. The models produced predict what the future might hold, but also create a disposition toward realizing or pre-empting and transforming that future (Beckert, 2016). Similarly, technologies such as City Information Modelling (CIM) can render 3D virtual models of future urban development plans, giving a sense of the urban fabric if buildings are constructed and their potential impact on the existing environment (e.g., shadows, viewsheds, drainage and flooding) and urban activities (e.g. traffic and retail footfall) (Thompson et al., 2016). The models can be quickly adapted to remove, alter or replace buildings or to reconfigure the plan (see chapter 7).

Such future predictions and prognoses recursively impact how the present is managed in order to try to realize particular futures – in other words, just as the present pre-figures the future, the future impacts on present actions (Uprichard, 2012). For example, the smart city movement actively seeks to shape future urbanism and create an extended timeprint in its vision through the practices of experimental urbanism. Here, innovators prototype and trial new technologies in real-world settings in order to test, learn about and promote possible and desirable urban futures. Smart city testbeds and living labs thus work to produce 'latent futures', which can be scaled up to the rest of the city and translated to other cities (Adam and Groves, 2007; Evans et al., 2016). Testbeds involve a continual churn of innovation, with Halpern and Günel (2017) noting that constant prototyping is a form of temporal management that aims to anticipate and respond to present and impending future threats, but in a manner that consistently defers a definitive answer. On the one hand, the 'repetitive incompletion' of experimental urbanism works to enact 'preemptive hope' – creating a sense that an uncertain social, economic and environmental future is being proactively tackled (Halpern and Günel, 2017: 2). On the other hand, it creates a transition pathway to a particular vision of a smart city. Smart city advocates also seek to invoke the future present through foresight and backcasting initiatives (Dixon and Tewdwr-Jones, 2021). As White (2016) details, smart city advocates have developed a set of styles, practices and logics that map out and draw extensively on future scenarios both to rationalize technological intervention in the present and to pre-empt and plan new urban trajectories. In the smart city case, White argues that three crises act as a motivator for imagining alternative futures: population growth and redistribution, global climate change, and fiscal austerity. By evoking alternative future imaginaries and contrasting them to a present future that fails to take a path of smart city investment, advocates seek to prepare the ground for a new form of urbanism that will respond effectively to existing and coming crises.

Conclusion

This chapter has provided a general discussion of the relationship between digital technologies, temporalities and everyday life, arguing that digital technologies (in the form of devices, systems, platforms and infrastructures) act as space-time machines. Through their logics and operations, they actively transform temporal and spatial relations, as both an intended and inherent consequence of their production and use. Just as temporality was reconfigured during modernity with new technologies, industrialization and the rise of capitalism and modern government, temporal relations are being remade in the digital era in diverse ways. In particular, the temporality of everyday activities and social and economic relations are being increasingly disconnected from clock time and, instead, driven by network time. Indeed, we have now reached a point where network time has become embedded and taken for granted: digitally mediated temporalities have become the dominant means of temporally structuring social and economic relations, and asserting temporal power. Critically, these new temporalities and associated temporal practices and competencies have become comprehensively normalized – 'melted into the interstices of practical consciousness [to] become just another part of the ordinary, taken-for-granted world of lived existence' (Thrift 1990: 106). A new time consciousness has developed in which network time, and its new temporal practices, orderings and regimes, have been thoroughly internalized. A new means of perceiving, orientating, organizing and acting temporally has emerged in which the temporalities of network time are no longer exceptional, but expected, routine and habitual. In turn, how we understand the past, present and future and their interrelationship has been reshaped.

In other words, the embedding of digital technologies across all aspects of everyday life has led to the development of new temporal experiences, sensibilities and competencies that have become second nature for a large proportion of the population. Consequently, compared to thirty years ago, individuals and organizations have a quite different conception of time, and have altered their orientation and actions to create and exploit new temporal relations, or to accommodate new forms of temporal arbitrage and inequalities.

Yet, as the following chapters illustrate, network time consciousness has diffused unevenly and has contextual and geographical specificity dependent on the roll-out and adoption of digital technologies, the extent to which they mediate everyday activities, and the degree to which they have been embraced or resisted. While a new time consciousness has emerged, it is important to recognize that it is not unified, unitary and non-contextual in nature (Thrift, 1988). Moreover, previous temporal regimes persist. As Adam (2004) notes, just as clock time did not eradicate sacred and eschatological time or natural cycles and rhythms, network time is not fully replacing clock time. Rather, 'instantaneity, simultaneity, networked connections, ephemerality, volatility, [and] uncertainty' are running alongside and being superimposed on the 'linearity, spatiality, invariability, clarity and precision' of clock time to create new 'temporal multiplicity and complexity' (Adam 2004: 65).

— Part II —

DIGITAL TIMESCAPES

— 3 —

HISTORY AND MEMORY

The production of history and the generation and recollection of memories has long been technically mediated using a plethora of analogue media (e.g., documents, photographs, sound recordings) and storage, cataloguing and search mechanisms (e.g., archiving systems). This chapter explores the transformative effects of digital technologies with respect to history and memory through four sections. The first examines the intensification of datafication (a step change in the volume and granularity of data being generated and stored for future re-use) through the use of digital media and mnemotechnologies (tools that enable memory to be stored and communicated). The second details the rapidly expanding creation and maintenance of data infrastructures, and the migration of traditional archives into digital form. What digital technologies and digital archives mean for personal and collective memory is detailed in the third section, examining how digital devices and archives act as memory machines in ways that differ from analogue forms of prosthetic memory. The fourth section details what mass datafication, data infrastructures and digital archives, and new suites of digital tools and analytics, mean for historical analysis and how the past is understood, narrated and used as a resource in the present. This includes a discussion of the epistemology of historical research and new modes of presenting history, such as interactive museum displays, historical GIS (Geographical Information System), and heritage walks mediated by augmented reality. What the analysis makes clear is that our relationship with and understanding of the past is being reconfigured through digital mediation.

Datafication and mnemotechnologies

Over the past couple of decades, there has been an extensive effort to digitize analogue materials, scanning millions of documents, newspapers, books, photographs, artworks and material objects, and to archive these into digital databases, along with associated metadata. These made-digital data are being complemented by born-digital data about the past, generated by a range of new technologies and their associated software and analytical techniques. For example, LiDAR scanning, aerial/drone photography, and remote sensing are being used to examine past landscape features (Koramaz, 2018). Precise 3D models of former buildings, sites and objects can be constructed using 3D laser scanning and photogrammetric modelling employing digital cameras, and ground-penetrating radar can be used to detect buried features (Bruzelius, 2017). Consequently, there has been an explosion in digital data about the past.

These person-directed forms of data generation are being accompanied by automated data generation and archiving in which systems automatically record data relating to their use. All of the technologies in table 2.1 generate what are termed big data – that is, data that are generated continuously in real-time, are exhaustive to a system, and are fine-grained and indexical (usually at the level of an individual person, object, transaction, location) (Kitchin 2014b). For example, a social media platform such as Twitter captures all posts by all posters, plus all the associated media (images, gifs, videos, sound files) and metadata, not a sample of posts or posters. Similarly, many devices constitute 'logjects' – that is, objects that record their own use (Dodge and Kitchin, 2009). For example, a smartphone is a logject that records and stores data from its various sensors (including accelerometer/motion, three-axis gyroscope, compass, GPS, barometer/altitude, proximity to screen surface, ambient light, moisture, temperature, touch ID, face ID, camera, microphone, Wi-Fi and radio) (Dodge and Kitchin, 2009; Costello, 2020). Various apps on the phone can make use of these data to provide information, services and entertainment, as well as to generate a large amount of additional data through the interactions with the app (e.g. inputted data, searches, posts, tagging, commenting, game play, check-ins, purchases, likes, bookmarks, etc.).

The state and companies are massive generators of big data. For example, through the introduction of e-government, interactions with government departments and state agencies are increasingly digitally mediated. Likewise, operational systems for managing state services and infrastructure rely on digital technologies. Companies are now thoroughly digitally mediated, using a variety of technologies and systems to plan and manage their operations. Enterprise resource planning, supply chain management and customer relationship management (see chapter 6) are big data systems that enable real-time and historical views of performance and allow the dynamic coordination of activities and workers across dispersed sites and complex arrangements. In many cases, big data are volunteered for the purpose of self-monitoring – for example, using a fitness tracking app. Such self-recorded data might include a person's performance (e.g. miles walked/run/cycled, hours slept and types of sleep), consumption (e.g. food/calorie intake), physical states (e.g. blood pressure, pulse) and emotional states (e.g. mood, arousal) (Lupton, 2016). In recording such data, 'we are invited to view ourselves as longitudinal databases constantly accruing new content' (Schull, 2016: 9). These data, along with résumés, family photographs and videos, personal and family stories, and personal thoughts, used to be considered sensitive and private, and were shared only with a handful of selected people. Now, they are freely and publicly shared. Since self-recorded data are generated in order to archive them, the future-past shapes action in the present – that is, behaviour in the present is guided by the expectation of what the future self will want to re-visit as memories (Reading, 2009). In addition, we store large personal data caches. For example, I have tens of thousands of emails, thousands of digital photos and videos, hundreds of pieces of writing, and research data from dozens of projects stored on a laptop, external hard drives, and in the cloud.

Mass datafication constitutes a seismic shift in the temporality of data generation, and the granularity and coverage of datasets. Rather than data being sampled temporally (e.g. every quarter, year, five years) and across populations (e.g. every hundredth person), digital devices and systems automate data generation and the storage of those data. Consequently, digital technologies are producing a massive amount of fine-grained, time-stamped or time-series data, relating to a wide variety of phenomena. Rather than being transitory, with data deleted after immediate use, these data are being stored for future re-use in data infrastructures and digital archives that take a number of forms and serve many constituencies. Importantly, many systems and devices, along with data infrastructures and archives, also act as mnemotechnologies (Stiegler, 2009, 2011) – that is, they store, organize, add value to (by generating new information about them and applying analytics) and present memories. This is in contrast to what Stiegler terms mnemotechnics, such as a paper diary or photo that simply records or signifies a memory. Mnemotechnologies systematically organize memories so that they can be revisited and relived. They act as 'cognitive artefacts ... used to aid not just memory, but all kinds of cognitive tasks and processes such as navigating, calculating, making inferences, and problem-solving' (Heersmink and Carter, 2017: 418). The smartphone is a mnemotechnology since its apps act as repositories for data and provide a number of means to access and view those data (e.g., searching, browsing, timelines, graphs, maps, summary statistics, dashboards), and/or they recall and present the data as memories (Prey and Smit, 2019; Jacobsen and Beer, 2021). As such, the smartphone is a 'wearable archive of the everyday' (Reading, 2009: 90). Moreover, since the device is networked, the data can be easily shared with third parties, either through the app covertly sending data to its producer (and their selected partners), or the user openly sharing the data as an inherent aspect of interacting with the service. The digital era has massively expanded the scope, reach and resolution of mnemotechnologies. It has also pushed aspects of memory production onto individuals (as opposed to an institution such as a broadcaster) through their direct use of technologies. In turn, these memories become searchable and opened up to queries and analytics by their generator and their holder. In some cases, these memories are presented to individuals without their request (such as Facebook automatically presenting a 'memory' into a timeline from five years previously) (Jacobsen and Beer, 2021). Here, the past is inserted into the present, producing an affective response that might shape how the future unfolds. As such, mnemotechnologies have profound consequences for personal and collective memory, for history, and for how the past is used in the present.

Digital archives and data infrastructures

Archives are formal collections of data and information that are actively structured, curated and documented, with plans regarding preservation and access (Lauriault et al., 2007). They have existed throughout recorded history as sites where key documents are stored. In general, what was archived was important manuscripts and information derived from data, such as summary documents, graphs, maps, articles and books (rather than the data themselves) (Kitchin,

2014b). The state, in particular, has been a key actor in creating and maintaining national archives, and archives associated with public bodies. Those in positions of wealth and power also maintained archives relating to their estates and commercial interests. Likewise, some companies initiated long-term archiving endeavours, though many kept records for a certain period before destroying them when their legal or commercial retention was deemed unnecessary. Similarly, universities created libraries and repositories to store key published work and scientific data, but typically did not retain all the data holdings of staff once they retired.

Indeed, the vast bulk of data and information generated throughout history has been lost or destroyed. The materials retained and preserved were archived because they were deemed historically important records, or they might have future re-use value. In part, a degree of 'prospective retrospection' – anticipating what will be needed in the future – has been applied in deciding what to archive; in part, decisions represent particular interests and values (Roberts, 2015). Typically, the volume and focus of records kept have been skewed towards elite interests, with most people and enterprises either footnotes or erased from history, with marginalized groups in particular largely absent or misrepresented (Caswell et al., 2017). Gaining access to traditional analogue archives is often not straightforward, with individuals needing to gain permission from gatekeepers and to spend time in their location. Using the archive and finding information requires specialist knowledge regarding its organization, and a lot of effort to sift and search through the material.

Since the 1980s, and particularly post-millennium, archives have been transformed by the application of digital technologies. As noted, millions of existing archival sources, along with their associated metadata, have been digitized and enrolled into networked archival architectures consisting of an assemblage of databases, software, interfaces, operating systems, hardware and networked infrastructure (this assemblage is often termed a data infrastructure; Kitchin, 2014b). Digitization, and building and maintaining archival architecture, is a relatively expensive endeavour, and involves a number of technical and institutional challenges (see Borgman, 2007). It is considered a worthwhile endeavour as it opens up potentially valuable information to a wider audience (who can access the resource via the Internet), enables the sources to be easily and quickly searched and browsed, facilitates re-use and repurposing, and permits new analytical tools to be used to make sense of the material (Beagrie et al., 2010). In addition, it is easier to link together and scale archival collections into larger federated repositories, enabling connections to be made across records and databases and further insights to be garnered. In other words, digitalization transforms traditional archives into networked mnemotechnologies that use computation to organize, add value to, extract insight from and present information.

Data infrastructures are designed to handle and store digital data, including born-digital data consumed and generated in data-driven systems. They are not just essential for the digital version of traditional archives, but have become widespread across state bodies, scientific initiatives and companies, for managing data resources and conducting business. Data infrastructures do not necessarily have any long-term archival ambition, though they nearly all serve that purpose; rather, they enable present operations to take place (the data might be deleted at a future date). No online business would be able to function without a robust data infrastructure; nor would the state be able to run e-government services. Data infrastructures are not simply data stores, but are actively planned, curated and managed, staffed by specialist personnel, and governed with respect to legal and industry standards (regarding ethics, privacy, data standards, security). As new techniques and technologies are developed, data infrastructures evolve. For example, the development of relational databases in the 1970s enabled structured data to be stored and queried in sophisticated ways, and the rollout of NoSQL databases in the 2000s enabled the same for massive, unstructured data (paving the way for Web 2.0, including social media). New data analytics – such as visualization, statistics, modelling, data mining, pattern recognition – have led to a significant change in how sense is made from the data and insights extracted (Kitchin, 2014b).

Data infrastructure developments have transformed the archiving of data and the archival landscape, along with initiatives such as open data, open government, civic media, and the development of data capitalism. Significantly, the creation of big data, and exhaustive, networked data-driven systems, has, on the one hand, democratized access to many archives that were formerly limited to relative small numbers of users, and, on the other, made it possible for 'ordinary lives' to be documented in detail (Arthur, 2009). Along with an overhaul of state-run archives, there has been a growth in community archives, as well as a massive expansion in commercial data infrastructures. Community archives complement or provide a counter-point to the authority of state archives. They seek a more locally grounded selection and curation of what materials hold enduring value, aiming to shape collective memories of shared pasts and reveal history from the bottom up (Caswell et al., 2017; Cifor et al., 2018). These archives might relate to a specific place (such as a neighbourhood) or identity group (such as people of colour or disabled people), or both. Many are specifically political projects, undertaken as counter-archiving endeavours in response to the official narratives of the state, designed to unsettle and challenge mainstream histories, with the archivists self-identifying as activists and advocates interested in issues of justice, public engagement, and the politics and praxes of archives and the history they produce (Cifor et al., 2018; see chapter 10). In some cases, the archives document a political movement – for example, the archives created by the Occupy Movement, which also sought to practise a decentred approach to archiving that underpinned how the movement operated (Erde, 2014). Community archives can also challenge how archives function through shifting the role of archivist from gatekeeper and curator to trainer and facilitator of co-creation and co-management with community members (Erde, 2014; Burgum, 2020).

Commercial data infrastructures are largely black-boxed enterprises. Some might have a public face to part of the data – for example, it is possible for users to search Twitter for tweets and tweeters, though each search reveals just a slither of the entire repository of data, which is only available in a limited sample through an API. Or the data are selectively fed back to users at a personal level – for example, enabling access to one's own data, but not those of others – or through memory services such as 'On this Day'. Most data infrastructures, though, are considered prized assets, with no – or very constrained – access. Data brokers, for example, hold enormous data banks about individuals (e.g., in 2019, Acxiom was thought to hold data on '2.5 billion addressable consumers' in 'more than 62 countries' across more than '10,000 attributes'; Melendez and Pasternack, 2019), but, even for a fee, they rarely share core data, providing instead derived data or associated data analytics or services. Part of the reason commercial data infrastructures are so enormous is because, rather than selectively curating data, the approach has been to record and store everything possible, given that it might have potential future use (Zikopoulos et al., 2012). Consequently, massive amounts of fine-grained, longitudinal data are being produced, collated and controlled by companies, much of which has salience for memory and is of value for future historical analysis, but at present remains limited to narrow commercial use.

Digital memory

Memory is the means by which the past manifests in the present (Hoy, 2009). Memories are remembered pasts – the recollection of and engagement with past events, experiences, thoughts, viewpoints and emotions that are triggered by encountering people (e.g., old friends), places (e.g., former residences), objects (e.g., photos, scrapbooks) and practices (e.g., conversations, holding hands, playing sports, parades). Memories can be disclosive, revealing how the present relates to the past, and how the past can guide the present and the future (Hoy, 2009). Some memories are utilitarian, such as fitness data recorded to be viewed later, whereas others are more denotive and meaningful, such as a photograph of an important event (Özkul and Humphreys, 2015). Memories can be mistaken, latent, forgotten and contested. They can be personal or collective, vernacular or official (Haskins, 2007). They can be enacted, participatory and public, such as a group visiting a memorial and performing a ritual – and they can be affective, inciting an emotional response (Garde-Hansen et al., 2009). They are produced and experienced by everyone, relying on personal and shared knowledge, rather than a select, elite group drawing upon archival sources, as is often the case with the production of history (Garde-Hansen et al., 2009). Memories are essential for maintaining identities and producing meaningful narratives about life trajectories (Barassi, 2020). Collective memory emerges from shared experiences and their mediation through storytelling and various forms of media (e.g., broadcast media, social media), shaped by and reinforcing inherited cultural memory in the form of 'language, rituals, myths, songs, monuments, institutions' (Blom, 2017: 14).

Digital technologies are transformational for memory, giving rise to digital memories that are qualitatively different from those captured and conveyed by analogue media. At a basic level, digital technologies enable far more information to be recorded and stored, and thus more potential personal and collective memories to be surfaced. As noted above, digital devices and data infrastructures act as prosthetic memory, storing massive amounts of data beyond what might be produced and retained by the human mind (Hoskins, 2011). Due to their digital quality, these data are rewritable, and more fluid and less durable than analogue counterparts (Hand, 2016). Some of this information forms direct memories, and some, such as a set of data analytics, is associative. Here, there is a danger of conflating memory with storage, the difference being that memory relates to the qualities of the information recorded and how it is experienced when encountered (Parikka, 2013).

Crucially, the networked nature of digital media enables emergent memories characterized by 'immediacy, mobility, flexibility and inter-activity', as well as connectivity, sharing and circulation (Hoskins, 2014: 55). Digital technologies act as mnemotechnologies that have significantly different qualities from analogue aide-memoires; databases, algorithms, analytics, interfaces shape what and how memories are configured and narrated, and are 'often explicitly mnemonic, encouraging users to "look back" on their ... memories' (Garde-Hansen et al., 2009; Lambert et al., 2016: 157). Digital mediation opens up 'new ways of finding, sorting, sifting, using, seeing, losing and abusing the past' (Hoskins, 2018a: 1). Here, memory is not simply triggered by digital technologies, but happens through them (van Dijck, 2009). Such digital mediation – and decisions about what is remembered, how it is remembered, how it is re-presented, and what is left silent – is often performed in automatic, autonomous, automated ways (Prey and Smit, 2019). How memories are presented and narrated is thus crafted by algorithms: filtered, merged, rearranged, rendered, dropped into timelines and prompts to share (Hand, 2016; Lambert et al., 2016). As Jacobsen and Beer (2021) note, social media platforms can act as memory devices, actively sorting and surfacing the past on behalf of users. Quite unlike a diary or photo album, a platform's algorithms decide which former posts or profile information are meaningful and worthy of revisiting and potentially re-sharing, or suppressing. For example, based on reactions (e.g. emojis) and keywords associated with resur-faced memories, platforms such as Facebook attempt to identify automatically what kinds of memories to promote or suppress (Jacobsen and Beer, 2021). These processes can take place without any understanding of context; algorithms work with data without remembering, forgetting or affect, relying on human intelligence and the meaning-making abilities of people to add sense to the material surfaced (Esposito, 2017). This digital mediation has consequences for both personal and collective memory.

As Jacobsen and Beer (2021) note, 'being targeted by memories on social media is not a passive experience. It initiates an interactive and iterative process of interpretation and reinterpretation of an "imagi-native reconstruction" of the past and our relationship to that past'. The digital storage of personal data and information, and the appli-cation of diverse tools to manage, surface and interact with them, provide a powerful means of critically reflecting on, understanding and re-composing oneself and our relationships, including one's sense of place and belonging within a place (Özkul and Humphreys, 2015). They enable us to consider who we are, where we come from, how we used to be, and who we want to become, and construct life narratives of an imagined past, present and future self. In this sense, they do not just remind people of the past, but participate in the production of the past (Jacobsen and Beer, 2021). This engagement can be active and deliberate, enacted purposefully by an individual searching an archive, or it might be received and reactionary, such as engaging with a memory placed automatically into a timeline. In both cases, the performance of memory takes place in dynamic and interactive ways with and through their digital mediation (Kuhn, 2010). These memories can be shared via messaging and platforms and connected to the memories of others, with consequences for personal memory through engagement and feedback. For example, while the circulation of a printed photo album can be controlled by its owner, photos uploaded to social media or stored on platforms such as Flickr can circulate well beyond personal control and invite comments and critique (Hand, 2016).

Digital mediation affects collective memory through the sharing, circulation and remediation of personal and institutionally narrated (by organizations, states, companies) memories. The circulation of such memories enables the formation of second-hand memories (not rooted in first-hand experiences) constructed from peer-to-peer sharing and the fast and unscripted commentary of many voices (who can edit, tag, like, link, forward and chat about memories) (Garde-Hansen et al., 2009; Hoskins, 2018b). Such second-hand memories, and what Hirsch (2008) refers to as post-memory (memories transmitted so deeply to individuals that they constitute their own memories), used to be predominantly created through testimony and telling stories to friends and family, or the reporting of broadcast media (e.g., television news, documentaries, newspapers, factual books and biography). They were consumed memories rather than co-generated by audiences (Garde-Hansen at al., 2009). Through online networks, all kinds of information and stories from ordinary people – rather than official or powerful vested-interest sources – are distributed to strangers to become part of the conversation and enactment of collective memory. While sources might be scattered across platforms, they are easily searched, linked and shared (Hoskins, 2018b). Moreover, the digitalization and networking of archives means that material that was limited in access, housed in a single location or controlled by a gatekeeper can be sourced on demand by entire populations, opening it up to interpretation and remediation by all (Haskins, 2007). Collating together official sources with biographical and personally generated information – such as drawing together surveillance footage and bystander witness testimony / video recordings in the 9/11 terrorist attack in New York, or the 7/7 attack in London – produces a bricolage collective memory composed of multiple views and perspectives on the same event (Garde-Hansen et al., 2009).

This access, sharing and participatory engagement produces diverse affective responses, from empathy at a distance to deepening hate and conflicts between individuals and groups. As Hoskins (2009: 28) notes, 'the digital era opens up conflicting and simultaneous horizons (or even "fronts" on the past) that are rapidly being assembled, torn up and reassembled in more self-conscious and reflexive ways by individuals, groups, nations, politicians, news organisations, terrorists'. The performance of memory becomes fractured and contested, with memories opposed by counter-memories (Kuhn, 2010). Indeed, the scale, connectivity and speed at which memories can surface, circulate and be debated online disrupts what might have been relatively stable collective memories (Kansteiner, 2018). This signals for Kansteiner (2018) that there is no collective view, public sphere or mass imaginaries to speak of in the post-broadcast world, but rather there are mutable, emergent ensembles that lack stability, assembling and disassembling around particular issues. Hoskins (2018a) characterizes this change as a shift from the collective to the multitude.

Due to their propensity to circulation, memories in the digital era often evade intended curation and forgetting (see chapter 9). Moreover, they have the potential to be mediatized ghosts since they are easily copied and can circulate outside the control of individuals or the platforms on which they were created, so are difficult to erase or delete (as discovered by anyone who has deleted a tweet to then see a screengrab of it circulate afterwards) (Garde-Hansen et al., 2009). Memories can also surface through hacking and malicious use, such as revenge porn, and be discovered or presented wholly out of context (Hand, 2016). Here, distinctions between public and private, personal and collective, and active and passive memories blur (Hand, 2016). Such contestation and blurring raise political questions about the intersection and interplay of memory with cultural and national identity, citizenship and belonging, democracy, truth, conspiracy theories and fake news (Huyssen, 2003; Hoskins, 2018a).

In making sense of the relationship between digital technologies and memory, it is important to recognize that digital memory is a commercial endeavour and is highly industrialized (Reading and Notley, 2018). Digital devices, apps, platforms, analytics and cloud services are produced and maintained by many actors, most of whom are profit-driven. Consequently, far more entities, bound into complex arrangements, are involved in memory work than in previous eras, and their endeavours are underpinned by capitalist interests (Reading and Notley, 2018). These actors are seeking to take advantage of the economic value (exchange and utility) of memories, where the associated data are commodities to be monetized and exploited, employed to profile and target their users (Terranova, 2017). As such, digital memory is a key aspect of data capitalism (Sadowski, 2019), and is enrolled in what has been termed data colonialism (Thatcher et al., 2016). Data colonialism refers to a process of capital accumulation through data dispossession, where users of a platform provide their labour and their data/memories for no payment, as a feature of a product or service, to those who control the means of production (Thatcher et al., 2016; Sadowski, 2019). These data are then employed to target users for further value extraction, either directly through the app/service, or indirectly through downstream data uses (e.g. through the work of data brokers) (Andrejevic, 2009). Many of these companies are ill prepared to police the multitude and memory conflicts, which also runs counter to their business model of garnering more information, encouraging exchange and pushing advertising.

Digital history and heritage

History is how the past is narrated. Heritage is those pasts that are preserved and presented for public consumption. Digital technologies are having a number of significant effects on history and heritage with respect to who can narrate the past, how the past is constructed and understood, which pasts are preserved, and how the past is communicated and engaged.

Through their digital rendering, the nature of archives and archival work has been transformed. Collections can be interlinked and cross-referenced against other archival sources, and can be searched and browsed in new more efficient and effective ways. Their databases are malleable and can be reconfigured in ways that do not conform to the organizational structures of traditional archives, enabling new data ontologies that create further avenues of exploration and analysis (Berry, 2017). Data are opened up to a variety of interactive management and curation tools, and the application of data analytics that offer new ways to make sense of and interpret the archived material. These new data analytics offer an epistemological challenge to the practices of conventional history (Kitchin, 2014b).

The piecing together and telling of history have traditionally been undertaken by professional historians. Like broadcast media, the production of history is largely a one-to-many approach that is authoritative and institutionalized in nature (Garde-Hansen et al., 2009). Historians generally use official documentary sources housed in archives that require in-person attendance to access. These archives hold state and corporate records and materials relating to the elite interests of society (such as letters, diaries, ledgers, deeds), with generally little detail beyond specific facts (e.g., household or workplace demographics) concerning the wider population. In contrast, digital archives and data infrastructures open up historical resources for use by anyone who has access to the Internet. Community archives provide a wider view of society and greater, more contextual information about ordinary people and places, with more recent big data infrastructures set to provide fine-grained, extensive archives of the recent past. Hoskins (2018b: 89) thus suggests that the digital mediation of archival sources changes the parameters of the 'who, what, when and why of remembering'. Digital archives and data infrastructures democratize who can produce history and widen the scope of history to include the lives of ordinary people and those marginalized and excluded in society, and facilitate the narration of unpopular, forgotten or counter-histories that challenge official grand history (Cifor et al., 2018; Pogačar, 2018). There are concerns, however, that this democratization also 'softens history' (Hoskins, 2018a), producing elective histories and historical conflations (Pogačar, 2018), with official narratives of the past countered by a cacophony of personal opinion. In the words of David Lowenthal (2012: 3, cited in Hoskins, 2018b): 'No longer what elites and experts tell us it was, the past becomes what Everyman chooses to accept as true.'

Typically, the production of history is conducted through a close reading and narration of the past. As Sewell (2005) notes, how this close reading has been practised has been divided between a humanities approach and a social sciences approach. Both are interested in identifying the critical junctures and sequencing of how the past unfolded. However, the humanities approach tends to focus on context, 'contingency and temporal fatefulness' of particular events, and the roles of key actors and processes (Sewell, 2005). It usually examines sources through a discursive lens to construct a historical narrative. The social sciences approach is more focused on identifying trends and patterns and their causes that are generalizable beyond particular cases (Sewell, 2005). Alongside constructing narratives, it can employ techniques such as process tracing and stochastic modelling, which attempt to identify causal mechanisms that explain historical outcomes, and tools such as historical GIS (Buthe, 2002; Rast, 2012). Humanities scholars tend to leave their theory implicit, social scientists are more explicit, using their historical analysis to construct and test theory (Calhoun, 1998; Pollitt, 2008).

Digital tools and data analytics provide tools to aid close reading, such as: qualitative analysis packages that facilitate data management and the coding, classification and linking of documents; historical GISs that produce time-series mapping of patterns of change, and historic building information modelling (in which historical information can be embedded within 3D scans and photogrammetric models); and virtual reality models that enable the digital recreation and examination of buildings, settlements and landscapes (Gregory and Geddes, 2014; Koramaz, 2018). They also enable a wider, more distant reading performed through and with algorithms and other kinds of analytics. The computational approach to history is a key part of what has been termed the digital humanities (Gardiner and Musto, 2015). The digital humanities use digital tools and techniques, such as descriptive statistics, graphing, mapping, virtual reconstruction of places, content and sentiment analysis, to provide a distant reading of multiple sources to identify relations and patterns that are unlikely to be spotted through a close reading of a handful of sources (Moretti, 2005; Manovich, 2020). For those analysing history from a social sciences perspective, digital archives and data analytics enable a more rigorous analysis of datasets through visual analytics, statistics and modelling in order to identify causal explanations. Past events and their sequencing, key conditions and critical junctures can be modelled and simulated, and predictions made as to how these might project forward into the future (Grzymala-Busse, 2011; Beckert, 2016). This is particularly useful for evaluating and modelling path dependencies, assessing how the past can be learned from, and calculating how a situation might unfold in the future under various conditions (see chapter 5).

The digital humanities and computational approaches to history have not been universally welcomed, with detractors arguing that they foster weak, surface analysis, rather than deep, penetrating insight – that is, they are overly reductionist and crude in their techniques, sacrificing complexity, specificity, context, depth and critique for scale, breadth, automation and general patterns (Kitchin, 2014b). Moreover, some are critical of work conducted at a distance using only digitized materials and digital search, as opposed to being embedded in physical archives and browsing and sifting through the records and viewing them in context (e.g. finding related records physically stored next to each other that a digital search would not identify) (Hoskins, 2018a). Nonetheless, the digital approaches make use of the power of computation and databases to perform analysis and draw new insights that would have been difficult or impossible using analogue archives and techniques.

Digital media are also transforming how history is narrated and communicated to different audiences and how people engage with the past. This includes the interfaces and tools of websites and history-related apps, interactive museum displays, and 3D spatial media such as augmented and virtual reality. Websites provide interactive and hyper-connected media that enable users to navigate their own path through presented material, to engage with and query information (such as selecting different forms of visualization, turning on/off layers), to access source archival material, and in some cases to contribute actively to the resource (e.g. by uploading demographic details, photographs and scans of key documents to a genealogical site, or eye-witness video to a commemoration site, or providing comments and feedback) (Roberts, 2015). Historical data stories have become a feature of data journalism. For example, the BBC produced a multiple-threaded, audio-visual hyper-narrative concerning the 7/7 terrorist attacks in London, with content aggregated from a spectrum of official and amateur sources plotted on graphic timelines across the four locations that viewers could interactive with and explore (Hoskins, 2011).

Many museums have an accompanying app that allows those visiting to scan QR codes to find out more information (usually audio, text, photographs and video) about displays, or acts as an after-the-visit reflection tool (Kansteiner, 2017). They also have interactive screens or displays (such as immersive video, and map projections onto 3D printed models) in the museum that provide videos, animations, games and quizzes designed to engage visitors and educate them about the past. For the museum, these create an engaging, enriching experience while retaining control over the narrative framing of history and memory (Kansteiner, 2018). For the user, they enrich the learning experience and enliven history (Koramaz, 2018). A number of AR (augmented reality) apps have been produced to enable users to explore heritage sites and former landscapes as they navigate an environment. For example, Speed (2012) details an app that allowed users to overlay historical maps of Edinburgh, ranging from 1773 to 1961, over Google Maps, and invited them to traverse the city to explore how it has been transformed. The Museum of London's 'Streetmuseum' app allows users to point their camera along a street and then overlay an image of the same street from years previously (Speed, 2012). A similar app allows visitors to the site of the Bergen-Belsen concentration camp to walk through what is now a forest and have the former buildings and infrastructure reappear on the screen in what were their locations (Kansteiner, 2017).

Conclusion

Digital technologies have produced a number of significant effects on memory and history. This chapter has examined some of the transformations taking place, including the rise in datafication and the use of mnemotechnologies; the digitalization of archives and the growth in data infrastructures across domains and actors; how digital mediation is reshaping the nature and circulation of, and engagement with, personal and collective memories; and how digital archives and technologies are transforming the epistemology of historical research and the narration of the past. These developments have produced a timescape in which more of the present is captured and stored for potential re-use, more memories can be resurfaced, and past records and artefacts are more accessible and circulate more widely, and can be used and made sense of in diverse ways. As more archives become digitized, the temporal extension of the past is lengthened and widened for the general public, accessible in an instant from anywhere with an internet connection, rather than mediated by professionals searching through physical archives. The past remains a key resource for understanding the present, with new tools opening up novel means to make sense of history and memories, including methods for uncovering the timing, synchronization, time patterns and sequencing of past events. Datafication of the present and the digital archiving of historic records also provide a new means to commodify memories and the past.

The analysis presented in the chapter has been necessarily brief and partial, and there is much more to say about the digitally mediated temporalities of the past. A host of other issues were hardly examined at all – such as decline, ruins, erasure, nostalgia, heritage, conservation, the intersection of memory and history with identity and with capitalism, and how the past impinges on the present and the future. Further, the chapter shied away from a discussion of issues such as presentism, revisionism, forgetting, loss of information / fragility, the costs of memory, data sovereignty and archive colonialism, some of which are examined in chapter 9. Indeed, there is a sizeable literature focusing on the impact of the digital on memory, history and heritage, and a thorough treatment of relevant ideas, theories, empirical observations, and applications would require a book-length thesis. It is clear that the impact of digital approaches to memory and history will only deepen over time as further historical archives are digitized, born-digital data continue to be retained, and new technologies, tools and techniques for managing, making sense of, and communicating and engaging with memories and historical data are produced. These developments will require ongoing critical reflection on the digital mediation of the past and its relationship with the present and the future.

— 4 —

POLITICS AND POLICY

How societies and economies develop and function are shaped by the ideologies and praxes of politics and the formulation and enactment of policies. There is an enormous interdisciplinary literature on politics and policies, but the vast majority of analysis focuses on the politics and policies per se and their operations and effects. While a good portion of the analysis considers their socio-spatial context and geopolitics, their temporalities are often rendered implicit or largely ignored. In contrast, this chapter examines the production and operation of chronopolitics (Sharma, 2017) in a relatively broad sense, considering the role of digital technologies in their production. It is divided into two main parts. The first part explores the relationship between politics and time and how digital systems and platforms – such as 24/7 multiplatform traditional media, social media and time management tools – are reshaping the temporalities of politics. The second part details the temporalities of policy-making, structured using Strassheim's (2016) observations that policy-making takes place in time and using time, and time is reconfigured through enacted policies. In particular, issues of legacy and path dependencies for shaping policy options, and the phenomena of digitally mediated fast policy, monitoring, prototyping and testbedding, are discussed.

Politics

It seems obvious that time is central to the operations of politics, yet there is remarkably little detailed analysis of political temporalities. Political time is plural and multiform, with varying rhythms, cycles, tempos and durations at play. The branches of liberal democratic government, for example, have different embedded temporalities. The judiciary are orientated towards the past, with an emphasis on tradition and precedent; the executive is geared towards the present and responding to unfolding events; and the legislatures are focused on the future, and anticipating and planning new laws and their consequences (Scheuerman, 2004; Hassan, 2009). Similarly, political institutions have their own temporal orders (Schmitter and Santiso, 1998). For example, public bodies, such as planning departments and welfare offices, have their own rhythms, tempos and beats, often involving bureaucratic procedures (Hassan, 2009). These temporalities become routine and fixed in place through institutional practices, though they are open to mutation and to transformation through reform and the introduction of new technologies (such as online e-government services that negate the need to spend time travelling and queuing), and rupture through unfolding events and regime change. Executive branches of government, in contrast, are expected to act quickly and flexibly in response to crises, such as natural disasters, war and economic collapses (Hassan, 2009). For example, emergency services such as the police and fire services are organized to be temporally agile to respond to unfolding events (see chapter 6).

Democratic government is *pro tempore*; it has temporal delimitations on length of terms that create time scarcity and pressures to deliver election promises in a timely manner (Linz, 1998). Political actors have a period of time – an election cycle, a window of political opportunity, an allocated slot in a debate schedule, attendance at various committees, a soundbite media interview – in which to make political progress or defend a position. With a clear beginning and end, the limits on the duration of office – for politicians and political appointees in institutions, such as courts, central banks, boards of public bodies – have a profound effect on how political work is temporally organized over a term (Goetz and Meyer-Sahling, 2009). Political actors are thus constantly asking themselves: When is the best time to act? How much time will be needed? How fast should we proceed? In what order should things happen? What is the best tempo to ensure progress (Nowotny, 1994)? The answers to these questions are prescriptive claims concerning the right temporal frames for action, which are often countered by those opposing the proposed interventions ('it is too early or late'; 'too long or short'; 'too slow or fast'; 'in the wrong sequence') (Schedler and Santiso, 1998: 12). Consequently, temporal rhetoric is a common refrain in the pronouncements of politicians: 'It is time for a change, the time is not ripe yet, first things first, better late than never, one thing at a time, times have changed, we have to keep up with the times, things will sort themselves out, and so forth' (Schedler and Santiso, 1998: 12).

Regardless of the rhetoric of temporal choices, political work has to be fitted into a dense temporal grid – schedules of formalized, timetabled meetings (parliamentary sessions, committees, boards, constituency hours) and informal meetings (breakfast, lunch, dinner engagements; media interviews; quick conversations between sessions). The temporal grid of formal meetings creates regularity, predictability and the intra- and inter-institutional synchronization of actors and activities, and is structured by the ordering force of time rules (Goetz and Meyer-Sahling, 2009). Time rules determine the basic parameters of practices and processes, such as their lifespan, timing, time budgets and timetables (Schedler and Santiso, 1998; Dyson, 2009). They establish norms about the timing and timeliness of procedures and actions, fixing when events do and do not take place, and the lapses between them. The rules are often designed to force resolution and avoid inertia, but also to foreclose hasty or surprise decisions and ensure periods to reconsider or to conduct negotiations and reach compromises (Linz, 1998). They are crucial then to the political machinations of government and public admin-istration, with temporal grids and recurring patterns of political activity constituting the basic political rhythms of domains and jurisdictions (Goetz and Meyer-Sahling, 2009). Coordination of these time rules and the organization of meetings are complex timetabling conundrums that are increasingly solved and managed using time management and rostering systems (Wajcman, 2019). These systems parse the various rules and temporal obligations into a schedule of events and align the diaries of actors. Moreover, diaries are often shared, allowing aides to monitor and rearrange diary appointments in relation to unfolding events, enabling politicians to have greater control and flexibility in scheduling.

The ability to control the allocation and functioning of time rules is a significant power as it frames the conditions under which politics is practised. The less frequent and shorter the meetings, the less debate and input members can make to influence an issue (Linz, 1998). A host of other time tactics, in which time is employed as a useful resource (as opposed to a constraint), can be used to influence the political landscape. Time tactics include seeking to exploit, game or subvert time rules, seeking to gain time by expanding the expected time frame for outcomes and creating a longer margin of confidence

(Linz, 1998), or to speed up processes to foreclose opposition, or to delay or postpone to obstruct progress (such as with filibusters and moratoriums), or to stagger or parcel out a process (Goetz and Meyer-Sahling, 2009). Many gifted and successful politicians have a well-honed sense of timing, able to judge the right time to act, and in what tempo and sequence, and when to hold fire (Goodin, 1998). A number of time tactics are presently mediated by digital technologies, especially related to news and social media, which are key channels for influencing voter views on political issues and processes. However, controlling information flow, timing and messaging in the social media age, where information can leak, mutate and be quickly countered by alternative and false views, has become more tricky, though public relations teams have adapted to try to corral or take advantage of social media's unruliness.

Complicating this temporal landscape is the multi-scalar nature of political organization and activity, which is fragmented and nested across scales (e.g., neighbourhood, city, regional, national and supranational). Local politicians are acutely aware that the political systems in which they operate are multi-scalar, with the political power to make decisions and determine budgets and policies that affect their constituency often residing outside of their control at higher levels in the political hierarchy (e.g., nation-state, supranational) (McCann, 2003). Moreover, political action and rhetoric take place not just in institutional settings, but also in the public sphere that transcends scales and has its own temporal logics. Digital communication channels (e.g. email, web forms, web news sites, video channels, polling instruments), social media and collaborative platforms challenge the political status quo, shape political narratives and foment political change. Traditional media operate across scales and are updated 24/7, often across multiple interlinked platforms (television, radio, websites, social media channels), with quickly transitioning news cycles that create a succession of political storms that demand quick reaction. Social media are a maelstrom of public opinion on political topics, which foments public reaction and creates demand for quick political action. They can rapidly elevate issues into political crises, as well as form a medium through which political organization and activism can take place (Kaun, 2017; Lauermann and Vogelpohl, 2019; see chapter 10).

As the Internet grew rapidly in the 1990s, it quickly became apparent that its media had political consequences. For some commentators, the Internet opened up pathways to communicate directly with politicians and their aides, and created fora in which citizens could share and debate political ideas and ideals, thus enhancing democracy (Poster, 1995). Others argued that, given the absence of territory and place online, the Internet was undermining traditional place-based political systems by, on the one hand, organizing politics around interests and issues rather than locales, and, on the other, by bypassing established political institutions, channels and gatekeepers (Thu Nguyen and Alexander, 1996). At the same time, websites provided new channels of political communication for politicians and parties to supplement traditional media, municipal governments created their own forums for facilitating place-based public conversations about local issues, and e-government systems were implemented to provide services and communicate directly with citizens (Graham and Marvin, 1996). As such, a number of somewhat contradictory political processes were under way simultaneously. In each case, however, the temporal effect was to enable speedier, distributed communication and political action that negated the need for travel and in-person meeting.

These political trends were further enhanced by the development in the mid-2000s of Web 2.0 and mass participation in social media platforms (Highfield, 2017). News channels and social media have become powerful means for communicating (mis)information, creating a groundswell of support, and mobilizing action beyond the channel, such as street protests. Traditional media sites have been supplemented with a variety of new internet-only news channels that, while often trying to convey a sense of neutrality and objectivity, are generally right- or left-leaning and promote strong ideological views (e.g., Breibart, The Blaze, Buzzfeed, Daily KOS). Social media act as a means of circulating and amplifying the 'news' stories of these channels by prompting sharing, reaction and debate. Relatively local events and stories can quickly gain traction and become viral, circulating widely, stimulating additional linked stories, transferring into traditional media and mainstream political debate (e.g., the Ferguson and George Floyd protests and #MeToo stories) (Bonilla and Rosa, 2015; Bode, 2016; Highfield, 2017). Moreover, through social media, the reach of political information, often encountered incidentally as a by-product of using the platform, is extended to groups who typically shun traditional media, have relatively little political interest and knowledge, and lower abilities to shift, sort and evaluate political messaging (Bode, 2016). The speed of circulation and relatively unpoliced nature of social media make the momentum of stories and their downstream effect difficult to control and counter. It demands rapid engagement and responses by politicians to capitalize on the public mood or to quell public sentiment. The distributed, open nature of social media also makes them an effective means for mobilizing and coordinating fast activism that seeks to synchronize resistance to neoliberal capitalism and autocratic governance by matching their pace of political action through temporary and well-timed campaigns (Lauermann and Vogelpohl, 2019; see chapter 10).

While enabling protest and activism, social media have also been embraced by the political establishment as a communications tool for directly engaging with the public, along with other digital innovations such as the production of big data. For example, social media and big data have transformed political campaigning and lobbying strategies, enabling a greater, more targeted reach that is reactive to issues as they emerge. In the 2008 and 2012 presidential campaigns, Obama's team made extensive use of social media, web channels, and data acquired from data brokers and public sources, alongside data generated by polling and face-to-face canvassing, to record and analyse voter intentions and the political landscape continuously, using the information to guide its messaging and political actions in near real-time (Issenberg, 2012). In the 2016 and 2020 campaigns, Trump's team similarly made extensive use of big data, targeting particular voting groups, spreading extensive misinformation and fomenting political division, with key lines of attack timed to maximize impact and sow distrust (Happer et al., 2019). In these cases, political teams are constructing databases and making sense of political data in a highly time-sensitive manner, running campaigns that employ time tactics that are reactive to unfolding events, rather than trying to maintain consistent, stable messaging (Issenberg 2012).

Importantly, networked media and the use of digital systems, platforms and infrastructures are contributing to four synchronization issues that pose significant challenges for politics, the operations of government, and the time rules designed to harmonize political temporalities. The first is the synchronization of the work of politicians and their teams. Politicians are exposed to many more channels of communication and engagement and are enrolled in 24-hour news cycles and unfolding events and crises, with associated temporal demands to react in a timely fashion. They are expected to be anytime-everywhere available, and increasingly find themselves caught in temporal densification and fragmentation, navigating and synchronizing on-the-fly multiple traditional time regimes and rules (of government, institutional offices and institutions, constituency work) along with daily unfolding issues that need redress. It is no surprise, then, to see many of them glued to their smartphones between engagements. The second is the synchronization of political temporalities between institutions, actors and processes operating across jurisdictions and scales. The terms of service length and election cycles are polyrhythmic and vary across scales and institutions, potentially creating misalignment and disrupting or stagnating political decision-making. By altering the temporalities of political processes, digital technologies further disrupt this synchronization.

The third is the synchronization of political action and policy-making, which are encumbered by time rules and institutional processes, with the rapid unfolding of political crises and public and media demands for quick response. Politicians are increasingly operating in public maelstroms, with little time for deliberation and reflection, and pressure to concentrate on dealing with immediate and short-time issues rather than the longer-term (see chapter 9). The fourth is the synchronization of political time and the economic time of the market and capitalism (Hassan, 2009; Rosa, 2015). This temporal mismatch has long been in place, but the uneven impact of the accelerating force of digital technologies across the public and private sectors has widened the gap between the slower-moving apparatus of political institutions and the speedy processes of business driven by the desire to reduce the turnover time of capital (Hassan, 2009; Fawcett, 2018). It is this asynchronicity that is driving calls for acceleration and greater efficiencies in politics and public services (see chapters 5 and 7) and the generation of fast policy, to which the chapter now turns.

Policy

Policies are the means by which politics is converted into directed action. A policy defines a problem that needs redress, how it should be resolved in general terms, and details the specific steps required to be enacted to ensure success in practice. Temporality pervades the policy process in three main ways: policy-making in time; policy-making by time; temporalities produced through policies (Strassheim, 2016). This section focuses on the first two, with the latter discussed and illustrated within the other chapters in part II.

Policy-making in time

Policy-making takes place in time. Policy formulation, preferences and actions, preconditions and outcomes are structured by legacy arrangements, path dependencies, sequencing and temporal cycles and time rules (Strassheim, 2016). A standard assumption in policy analysis and policy-making is that policies pass through a policy cycle that has a temporal order. That is, they proceed through a diagnosis phase (in which evidence is generated, the problem is identified and initial debates take place), to a technical phase (in which potential interventions are identified, assessed and selected), to implementation and administrative phases (progressing through milestones), to phasing out or replacement with an updated or new policy depending on its perceived success (Newman and Howlett, 2014). Each phase might involve different actors, processes and institutions. At any stage, this cycle might be broken, depending on circumstances and interventions, such as a new event changing the political and domain landscape, or new policies at different political scales superseding it (e.g. a new national policy overriding a local policy), or a new political party coming to power and adopting a different approach. Indeed, formulating policy is a complex, contested process that ceaselessly takes place, with policy cycles rarely unfolding as planned due to disruption, delays, realignments and cancellations. While there might be time rules concerning timelines, milestones and deadlines, and the scheduling of meetings, publications and consultations, policy debates within domains never stop. Stakeholders argue over the effectiveness of existing policies and whether they require tweaking, a major overhaul or replacement.

Policy-making takes place in the context of present conditions, inherited policies and regulations, legacy systems and infrastructures, institutional memory, and existing attitudes and cultural norms among experts, politicians, policy-makers and the public (Pollitt, 2008). As such, 'policymakers are heirs before they are choosers' (Rose, 1990: 263). Moreover, they may be inheriting processes that are progressing along paths that are difficult to redirect or derail, due to the force of trajectory and lock-ins. The future, then, is not an open-ended horizon – rather, the path forward is conditioned by enduring and resilient existing socio-technical arrangements (Tutton, 2017). Path dependency theories contend that some – not all – historical sequences of events extend forward from a critical juncture along a trajectory that produces a self-reinforcing direction (Rast, 2012). While a number of paths are initially possible and probable, once a given path has been established its trajectory gradually becomes self-affirming and 'locked in' (Greener, 2002). Lock-ins are set in motion by contracts, regulatory conditions and technology choices that mean deviating from a trajectory has significant costs

(Greener, 2002; Rast, 2012). Within this view of how policies gain a certain embedded, self-reinforcing path, history is important, as 'contemporary outcomes are directly traceable to contingent events in the distant past' (Rast, 2012: 17; Beckert, 2016).

In practice, variations in sequencing, timing, pace, tempo and duration create variation in paths and outcomes (Grzymala-Busse, 2011). Policies and their responsible institutions and programmes change incrementally over time. Moreover, a trajectory might be severely disrupted and redirected if conditions change sufficiently (e.g., a crisis or a regime change, or the rollout of a new technology), creating a turning point or critical juncture that opens up a new window of opportunity to make/take a different path (Rast, 2012). Moss (2021: 1) thus argues that, while path dependency and transition accounts explain the development of some phenomena, 'neither are well suited to capture the complex dynamics, non-linear developments, alternative pathways and hybrid configurations that become apparent when taking a long-term perspective'. Focusing on the development of urban infrastructure, he argues that a wider set of historical framings and analysis are needed to capture messy and contested ways in which systems unfold in practice. Drawing on assemblage thinking, he details six approaches – tracing out legacies, analogies, non-linear trajectories, palimpsests, hidden/ignored pasts, and past futures – through which to examine the contingent and contextual ways in which phenomena emerge that diverge from ideal narratives such as a path dependency (Moss, 2020, 2021).

Regardless of the framing and mechanisms through which phenomena emerge and track, a historical view emphasizes the importance of policy and regulatory inheritance in shaping the present and future. One means to try to short-circuit the weight of this inheritance is to disregard and discard the past in favour of innovation and fresh thinking. Here, the past as a referential base is largely ignored and replaced by momentary meaning and analysis of the present (Dodgshon, 1999), and unanchored consideration of future possibilities (Amoore, 2013). There might still be the use of evidence-based policy-making, but this often has a short historical time horizon and focuses on a narrow range of variables that can be presented in descriptive form (as graphs, maps and tables) or inputted into models and interpreted with limited historical context (in its worst manifestation, the data are assumed to 'speak for themselves'; Kitchin, 2014b). Data analytics, simulation and forecasting models are key means for producing evidence-informed analysis that is largely decontextualized in nature, in that it excludes the conditions that led to the situation that the data reveal and the history of previous policy interventions (Pollitt, 2008). Such evidence-informed and possibility-based analysis can thus 'become a way of absorbing or assuming away critical contextual differences which are crucial to understanding why a particular programme or activity works reasonably well at one place or time but not at another', and pushing through policies that serve particular interests (Pollitt, 2008: 12). In contrast, contextual policy analysis informed by the past has a number of benefits, including the avoidance of predictable failures, enhancing the legitimacy of choices, and reducing the chance of being accused of short-sightedness and naivety (Pollitt, 2008). The question, then, is how best to take account of the past in order to shape the future?

While the past and the present shape the policies being proposed, policy-making is undoubtedly future-orientated. Policies are designed to create particular future visions and outcomes. Policy-makers, then, need to conceive of what a desirable future might be, the pathways to achieving it and the viability of it being realized. In other words, policy-making is an explicit attempt to colonize the future – to determine the future yet to come and put in place mechanisms that will help to realize it. To aid this visioning and colonization, policy-makers utilize a range of methodologies and techniques – including prediction, simulation and optimization models, foresight studies and backcasting – that are now predominantly digitally mediated. Large-scale datafication and the generation of big data (see chapter 3), a massive growth in computational power, and significant advances in data analytics have led to an increasing use of analytical models in policy-making (Kitchin, 2014b). Predictive models seek to forecast what might transpire in the future, given trends and certain conditions. Simulation models aim to replicate how a system works, and then calculate how it might function under alternative scenarios. Rather than forecast the future, optimization models seek to identify an optimal course of action to enact a desired future by improving performance under varying conditions. Foresight studies aim to imagine prospective and preferred futures, and to determine long-term strategic plans and priorities for achieving them, drawing on forecasting, expert opinion, the views of key stakeholders, and public consultation through surveys and town-hall meetings (which are often now internet-based, reaching much larger constituencies) (Dixon and Tewdwr-Jones, 2021). Backcasting imagines some state that we might wish to achieve by a certain date and then works back to the present to try to define the steps or pathway needed to make such a future a reality (Adam and Groves, 2007). All of these approaches are normative and are shaped by cultural and political values and desires concerning potential futures (Strassheim, 2016). The use of GIS, 3D spatial media and various forms of social media for envisioning and debating planning and development futures is discussed in chapter 7.

Once a policy has been drafted, there is no guarantee that it will survive intact its passage through political debate and any required legislative process. Those policies that do become official guiding principles for stakeholders have to be translated into programmes of work and implemented. Increasingly, there has been a move towards tracking longitudinally whether policies and programmes are producing the desired outcomes (see chapter 6). A means to operationalize such performance management is through indicators and dashboards. Indicator projects have proliferated since the early 1990s, driven by the adoption of new managerialism and the desire to run administrations in an evidence-informed manner (Kitchin et al., 2015). Indicators are recurrent quantified measures that can be tracked over time to provide longitudinal information about stasis and change with respect to a particular phenomenon. In other words, they enable diachronic comparison. The progress of a policy is usually monitored using administrative and survey data, but increasingly also includes real-time data where available. Single indicators track the performance of a specific, measurable phenomenon, whereas composite indicators combine several single measures using a system of weights or statistics to create a derived measure (Maclaren, 1996). Contextual indicators provide key insights into a particular issue, diagnostic and target indicators reveal whether a policy intervention is working and meeting expectations, and predictive and conditional indicators are used to forecast and simulate future scenarios and performances (Franceschini et al., 2007). Benchmarking consists of comparing indicators within and across entities to establish how well one entity (e.g. a system, institution, place) is performing vis-à-vis other locales, or against expectations and targets – that is, synchronic comparison. The process is often accompanied by scorecarding, whereby tables of rankings, ratings and changes in relative position are produced to reveal which entities are doing well and which have fallen behind (Kitchin et al., 2015).

Typically, suites of indicators are displayed and monitored using dashboard interfaces, which consist of interactive graphs and maps that enable accessible, detailed information concerning performance and trends (Kitchin et al., 2015). For example, city administrations use indicators and dashboards to monitor the roll-out of policies and programmes and the performance of individual workers, departments, organizations and sectors, and to guide operational practices and decision-making. For example, a number of cities in the United States use a system called Citistat to track and benchmark indicators. In Baltimore, city managers meet once a week to review the performance of departments, set new targets, and discipline under-achievement (Gullino, 2009). Phenomena that used to be monitored annually or sporadically are now being assessed weekly, and, in the case of real-time, indicators can be tracked by the second. While such timeliness seems useful for oversight, it presumes that patterns and trends can be redirected through quick acting policy levers, ignoring the fact that social and economic processes work at a different pace, tempo and rhythm (Kitchin et al., 2015). Indicator monitoring demands responsive change in the here and now, but some policies might take decades for effects to mature and pay dividends. Similarly, a focus on synchronic comparison – for example, league tables – prioritizes whether an organization or place is performing better or worse than others, rather than whether progress is being made over time locally, which is actually the intended outcome, with the desire to improve rankings potentially negatively disrupting policy implementation (Pollitt, 2008).

Policy-making by time

The short-circuiting of history, decontextualizing policy analysis, and selectively using various methodologies and techniques for colonizing the future are examples of using time as a strategic resource in policy-making. Time is a medium and motive of policy actions. Indeed, policy-makers deploy a range of temporal tactics to seize windows of opportunity, to set the tempo, timetabling and deadlines of the policy process, and to track progress and milestones in deployment and react accordingly. Key actors will use temporal tactics to try to create favourable conditions ('the right time') for their agenda and to disrupt the proposals of others, and to delay implementation. In some cases, actors might act with short-term goals in mind for immediate political gain, or they might play a longer game. Another tactic is to combine diachronic and synchronic arguments, contending the present state of play in an area is out-of-sync or behind the curve with respect to another place (Kitchin, 2019a). Being a laggard and falling behind the pack in terms of policy innovation reduces competitiveness and can create a downward spiral of decline. There is thus an appeal for an administration to catch up with new policies, technical innovations and practices implemented elsewhere to ensure that it gains competitiveness. In some cases, the aim is not simply to catch up but to move ahead, shifting from a second or third mover to a first-mover innovator, where policy and associated programmes and technologies might be immature, but the location gains from new ideas, enhanced competitiveness, economic and cultural spillovers, and innovations that can be exported (Florida, 2002). There are risks associated with being a first mover and being ahead of the curve, however, including teething troubles, a failure to realize ambitions, becoming locked-in to first-generation solutions, and being leapfrogged by late-comers who learn from initial forays and have new innovative, cutting-edge solutions (Goodin, 1998). When to innovate and when to follow are thus important considerations in formulating and implementing policy.

Two other temporal tactics employed by stakeholders to drive an agenda and gain competitive advantage by being ahead of the curve, or to keep up with rival places or to leapfrog them, are: prototyping and testbedding; and the use of fast and mobile policy-making. Prototyping and testbedding are processes designed to speed up the development process of new policies or new technologies and infrastructures. Programmes and innovations are iteratively trialled and tested in real-world settings much earlier in the development cycle than normal, and well ahead of being formally launched as new products. In the case of cities, this is sometimes termed 'experimental urbanism' (Evans et al., 2016) or 'living labs' (Dutilleul et al., 2010). The process is facilitated by local government (though it can involve purely privately owned spaces), who provide permission and supports for trialling to occur, usually designating an area as a testbed (Halpern et al., 2013). The approach has become common amongst aspiring smart cities globally, who have designated 'smart districts' for companies to trial new technologies that aim to transform how city spaces are managed and governed. Usually, such schemes form part of an economic growth and urban development strategy that seeks to foster innovation and encourage start-ups, to attract companies to the city by offering real-world trialling, and to place the city ahead of the curve on using technology for solving urban problems.

Fast policy concerns the rapid pace at which policies are formulated, worked through the political system and translated into active, on-the-ground programmes, and the speed at which policies developed and applied in one location diffuse across the globe and are imitated by other cities (Peck, 2002; Peck and Theodore, 2015). In recent decades, government and public bodies have been under pressure to become more proficient in their day-to-day work, and nimble and timely in their response to unfolding events. This includes accelerating all aspects of the policy-making process to intensify and compress the policy cycle. Adding to the sense that speed is of the essence is the constant churn and systemic institutional turbulence created by neoliberal rounds of creative destruction in the public sector (Peck, 2002). Public officials are thus being put under pressure to produce policy solutions quickly, and to implement them rapidly in an ever-changing context. This is often accompanied by an expectation that they will swiftly bear fruit, or be replaced briskly if they underperform. This compression is driven by the desire to emulate the success of others and increase efficiency and competitiveness, but is also a political tactic to fast-track decision-making – deflecting and reducing opposition by narrowing the range of participants in the policy process; foreclosing and foreshortening opportunities for deliberation, consultation and negotiation; and rapidly establishing a path dependency that ensures a preferred outcome (Jessop, 2008). As discussed in chapter 10, this political tactic of speed is being countered by 'fast activism' that seeks to mobilize quickly to push back against or block quickly moving policy agendas.

A common means for achieving compression, and to increase the likelihood of swift results from the policy implemented, is to import tried and tested policy solutions from elsewhere (McCann and Ward, 2011). Supranational agencies such as the European Commission actively facilitate mobile and fast policy through its many programmes that require institutions to actively share knowledge and collaborate on initiatives and funded projects (McCann and Ward, 2011). There is also an enormous industry of expos and conferences designed to circulate 'ideas that work' and create a global epistemic community wedded to certain ways of knowing and doing, and consultancy firms that advise governments and agencies on policy responses, often formulating and promoting 'best practice', 'silver-bullet' solutions rooted in documented case examples (Peck and Theodore, 2015). Websites, blogs and social media aid rapid circulation and promotion of these events and practices, and help to extend and cement social networks. By engaging with these actors and activities, local stakeholders shorten the learning curve for identifying potential policy responses, access ready-made solutions that only require tailoring to local needs, and gain an established discourse and inter-referencing that provide convincing support for the preferred solution (Peck, 2002; Peck and Theodore, 2015).

Present policy-making is thus polycentric and relational, and less likely to be a purely endogenous, domestic enterprise (Peck and Theodore, 2015). However, in travelling, policies and their outcomes never transplant in quite the way intended. Policies are imported into a local context that has a different history of previous programmes and legacies; a different set of political actors, institutional stakeholders and governance arrangements; and different cultures and social relations. Imported policies mutate, being refashioned for the particularities and politics of the new application. In some cases, this might lead to a degradation in their effectiveness; in others, innovations might become a potential new extension to the best-practice model. Rather than following an orderly diffusion path, policies then travel along complex and splintering trajectories, but they do so at a quickening pace (Peck and Theodore, 2015). Such trajectories and the use of fast and mobile policy are discussed with respect to planning and urban development in chapter 7.

In addition to producing policy in time, and using time as a strategic resource, policy-making reconfigures and produces new temporalities through the effects of policies on governmentalities and activities. Policies often define the sequence, timeframes and tempo in which actions are to be delivered, and how benefits or costs are to be applied, which then shape how domains operate temporally (Goetz and Meyer-Sahling, 2009; see chapters 6, 7, 8). Policies designed to increase efficiencies, productivity and competitiveness all seek to transform the temporal orders and sensibilities of particular activities, and in so doing alter their nature and how they are experienced. In some cases, the policies explicitly seek to define new temporalities by dictating the timing, pace and tempo of activities. Examples are time policies that concern the opening hours of business, the operating timeframes of public services and the scheduling of public events, or labour policies that dictate working hours or holiday entitlements (see chapter 10).

Conclusion

This chapter has highlighted the extent to which politics and policy-making are thoroughly temporally mediated activities, how the enactment of different temporalities constitutes forms of political practice, and the effects of digital technologies on the production of political and policy temporalities. It has drawn on a relatively limited pool of literature as, perhaps somewhat surprisingly, comparatively little attention has been paid to the relationship between temporality, politics and policy-making. Instead of charting chronopolitics, analysis is much more likely to focus on the geopolitics of politics and policies, and the production of space and spatiality; it is synchronic, rather than diachronic. In such studies, temporality is largely reduced to the passage of time, or just a single facet is highlighted, such as speed or acceleration, and often in a largely descriptive manner (e.g., politics/policy-making is becoming 'fast', without necessarily unpacking this theoretically or the complexities of how fastness works in practice). How politics and policy-making unfold in time, how temporality is used as a strategic resource, and how temporalities are reshaped by political practices largely remain unexamined. Yet, as detailed, temporalities and their chronopolitics play a significant role in shaping how everyday life is planned, managed, governed and experienced, and the digital is profoundly influencing the timescapes of politics and policy-making.

With respect to politics, the digital is influencing the timing, sequencing and synchronization of political time rules and tactics, with 24/7 news cycles and the rapid circulation of ideas and responses on social media accelerating the speed at which politics and their fallout are conducted. They also tend to shorten the time horizon of political action and leadership, with attention focused on the immediate present, the short term of days and weeks, and the period of news attention and the election cycle. Long-term and generational time horizons are as much to do with how issues play out in the present as they are about the future. Time remains a crucial political resource, and digital media enable a responsive and flexible means of seeking to control and coordinate political action, or to disrupt the status quo and foment resistance and change. Likewise, the timescape of policy has been accelerated but also stretched to create time-space compression in the gathering and diffusion of ideas and practices. Digital media influence the timing, sequencing, pace, tempo and duration of the policy cycle, as well as providing a means of closely monitoring and responding to its unfolding and effects. Simulations, prototyping, futuring and prediction are used to produce a forward-looking vista, a means of colonizing and making a future yet to come that is unencumbered by the legacy of the past, though such an aspiration is undermined by the path dependencies of inherited policies, legacy systems and institutional memory.

— 5 —

GOVERNANCE AND GOVERNMENTALITY

Government – and its many agencies and programmes – is the key institutional means by which society is managed and governed and public services are delivered. Since the 1950s, digital technologies have been used to facilitate and augment governance and management, with their scope and employment expanding with the development of sophisticated hardware and software and the creation of the Internet, becoming ever more embedded and central to the management of populations, services and infrastructures. In turn, the nature of governance has mutated, becoming more technocratic, calculative, real-time and anticipatory (predictive and pre-emptive), driven by discourses of creating efficiencies, productivity, value for money, citizenship, empowerment, security and safety, and alignment with the logics of neoliberalism. This chapter considers these changes, charting how the digital has become ever more central to the operations of governance and the logics of governmentality, paying particular attention to their temporalities. The chapter opens with a discussion of governance, governmentality and temporality. It then details how digital technologies, such as the Internet of things and control rooms, facilitate real-time management and response to present condi-tions. Next, attention is turned to anticipatory forms of governance, considering how they seek to predict, prepare for, prevent, pre-empt and respond to events, illustrated through a discussion of predictive policing and emergency response and management.

Governance, governmentality and temporality

Temporality is central to the logics and operation of governance. As with policy (see chapter 4), governance is embedded in and structured

84

by time, it uses time as a central resource in the conditions and workings of governance, and the nature and production of temporalities are reconfigured by governance regimes. Governance systems build incrementally, mutating as time unfolds, occasionally transforming in relatively radical ways that nonetheless are shaped by the past (e.g. through embedded knowledge and values, legacy systems and infrastructure, sunk costs, unfolding debates). They are inflected by sequencing and exogenous time rules that have a profound effect on their operations. They are time ordered in their formulation, implementation and operation, and pass through a regulatory lifecycle. For example, Newman and Howlett (2014) detail a seven-stage model of a regulatory regime lifecycle that progresses from a period of gestation, in which an emerging problem is identified as needing a governance response, through various forms of institutional regulatory response, to its discontinuation or replacement by a different kind of regime. They postulate that regulatory regimes 'pass through the same stages in the same order, but the duration of the various stages will be controlled by exogenous factors' (Newman and Howlett, 2014). In addition, they note that differences in governance across jurisdictions is not necessarily a result of fundamental variations in the constitution of systems, but might be reflective of the temporal stage of regulatory regimes within each state (i.e., variance across space might be the result of temporal variances in the lifecycle) (Newman and Howlett, 2014).

The control and regulation of temporality are fundamental aspects of power and are a key feature of governance systems (Pollitt, 2008). We live in a society saturated in time rules and expectations, and control of one's own time is often a privilege and can denote a high degree of social status. For example, senior managers have autonomy and control of their diary, but ordinary workers have to follow convention or orders (Sharma, 2014). Age-related criteria often delimit access to places and systems. Opening and closing times, work hours, break periods, holiday entitlements, and expected work rates and outputs within a designated period constitute the temporal order and time rules of work (Gregg, 2018). In accessing services, one can wait in a queue or be issued with a ticket that denotes the order of being attended to, or one can book time-appointed slots (Henckel and Thomaier, 2013). The circumscribing of time is commonly exercised as a penalty by removing personal control of one's own time: for example, detention periods in school, being grounded at home in the evenings and weekends, or the loss of a driving licence for a number of years. A curfew is a means of controlling the times at which people can access public space, and might be a limited state intervention (Lynch, 1972) or more systematically implemented as a familial form of control (Datta, 2020). While residing in prison is a spatial constraint, it is no coincidence that it is called 'serving time'; prisons are highly time-controlled environments from lights on/off, periods outside the cell or to exercise, to visiting hours; they are full of waiting and 'dead time', and living 'out of time' and 'killing time' (Kaun and Stiernstedt, 2020). Visions and plans of the future are designed to cater for particular kinds of valued citizens, with others pushed to the margins. For example, the smart city and associated fast urbanization is a future designed for the middle and upper class (Datta, 2020), and largely excludes the poor from its spatial enclosure other than as service workers whose working times constitute a form of temporal arbitrage, being subservient to those they serve (Sharma, 2014). Evaluation and decision-making by states and companies draw on archives of past data to assess and control how individuals should be treated in the present.

All of these cases reconfigure the temporalities of everyday life in direct and indirect ways. Lives become organized around the time rules and expectations of governance rules, from daily concerns such as when we wake, how we plan our diaries, how we make decisions about what activities we might do, to longer-term concerns such as where we live (e.g., choosing to reside near to schools or work to make commutes more time-efficient). In the case of relatively rigid systems, such as schools or prisons or 9-to-5 workplaces, the imposed temporalities of governance regimes produce a daily and weekly rhythmic pattern and familiar cadence to everyday life (Lefebvre, 2004). In other cases, such as shift-work, gig-work or zero-hour contracts, there might be little pattern in working hours, with an expectation that a worker has to comply with temporal demands and to organize other aspects of their lives with respect to them (see chapter 8). We are so conditioned by these imposed temporal arrangements that they become habitual and routine. We often anticipate and self-regulate our behaviour in relation to them (Rosa, 2015). Such figurings have multiple spill-over effects. For example, direct impacts on one person have knock-on consequences for other family members (e.g., working hours influence the frequency and scheduling of family activities; being in prison affects the time an outside partner has to spend on care-giving, working, visiting). An awful lot of social organization involves coordinating and trying to synchronize our multiple temporalities to align with those demanded by governance regimes. Households have to figure out how to coordinate the timing of school runs with getting to workplaces on time, factoring in traffic conditions or transit timetables, along with coordinating multiple other household-related tasks across the day. The activities of workers, who have their own specific temporal demands and orders to fulfil, have to be aligned within workplaces and in conjunction with the other workers. Time pressures and failures to coordinate and synchronize timings are often the cause of household and workplace conflict and stress (Wajcman, 2015).

How time is mobilized as a strategic governance resource and the effects of governance on everyday temporalities are strongly influenced by the use of technologies in systems of management and control. As noted in chapter 2, the space-time compression of modernity, enabled by developments in communications and transport, enabled profound space-time distanciation and the more timely control of distant populations and dominions. Along with bureaucratic systems of accounting and recording, they transformed how populations were monitored and policed locally and beyond. Information was more rigorously and systematically generated and recorded, and made easier to search and cross-index via the introduction of indexical identifiers (e.g. finger prints, and social security, passport, case file, employee and bank account numbers) and could circulate more easily and widely. Technologies such as traffic-light systems regulated the flow and timing of vehicle movements, clocking-in and chronometer technologies regulated the working hours and breaks of workers, and surveillance and policing technologies enabled monitoring and recording of populations of interest (Lyon, 2007; Barak, 2013).

The introduction of networked digital technologies, and their embedding in every social and economic domain, have had a profound effect on how governance is conceived and enacted in a number of ways. Such technologies have characteristics that qualitatively and quantitatively change how populations, infrastructures and spaces can be monitored and managed, including transforming how time can be used as a strategic resource. Fundamentally, networked digital technologies enact network time (see chapter 2). They can produce, process and act on fine-grained, individually indexical data in real-time with very little latency (Hassan, 2009). They can do so for whole domains and from a distance. Systems such as automatic number plate recognition (ANPR) systems monitor every vehicle passing, not a sample of them (Kitchin, 2014b). Similarly, tap-in/tap-out public transit systems record every entry and exit (see chapter 6). Network time facilitates rapid, data-informed response to unfolding events. Advances in machine learning and artificial intelligence mean that these responses are increasingly made through forms of 'automated management' (Kitchin and Dodge, 2011) in which systems operate in automatic, automated and autonomous means to make decisions related to how systems perform and people can act. Database design and cloud computing have enabled vast quantities of data to be stored for future re-use. The production of indexical data and metadata increases the legibility of those to be governed, enabling more targeted and timely responses, and allows associated data across systems and domains to be conjoined, permitting further relationships to be identified (Dencik et al., 2019) and the coordination of activity and responses, such as during an emergency situation (O'Grady, 2018). New data analytics can extract greater insight and value from these datasets. This includes advances in simulation, optimization and prediction that can be used to plan for and pre-empt future events.

Importantly, digital technologies are becoming ubiquitous and pervasive – mediating ever more daily tasks, with computation and data processing becoming embedded into the social and urban fabric (e.g., into objects, streetscapes, buildings, infrastructures) and available from everywhere (Kitchin and Dodge, 2011). As such, they are in a prime position to augment, modulate and regulate how life takes place, and increasingly perform that role. A smart television, for example, does not simply provide access to television programmes, but seeks to nudge viewer experiences and habits through recommendations – it modulates behaviour. A checkout till in a supermarket does not just facilitate the addition of prices for payment, but is an instrument that monitors and disciplines worker performance (keeping a track of the scan rate and instructing the operator to speed up if too slow), as well as tracking customer purchases (Kitchin and Dodge, 2011). The means of performing work becomes the means of regulation; rather than the worker self-disciplining behaviour due to the possibility of being monitored, their work is constantly tracked and modulated through persistent monitoring. With respect to the customer, the data generated are utilized by the company for customer profiling and nudging future consumer behaviour. The data can also be sold on to third-party data brokers who offer data services in which consumer profiles contribute to consequential decisions concerning access to work, tenancy, mortgages, loans and so on, forming a core element of surveillance capitalism (Zuboff, 2019). Public spaces (e.g. streets and parks) and private–public spaces (e.g. shopping malls, plazas, train stations) are becoming ever more saturated with surveillance technologies (including digital CCTV cameras, ANPR cameras, and sensors that measure various phenomena), as well as technical architectures to monitor and control movement (such as swipe-card doors and barriers) and a host of smart city technologies that are designed to monitor systems and infrastructures and perform urban management (Lyon, 2007; Kitchin and Fraser, 2020). Crucially, then, digital technologies extend the scope and range of governance, and transform the mechanisms through which it is enacted. Governance becomes more technocratic, prescriptive, algorithmic and rule-based, with management taking place through data and formalized procedures, rather than the discretion and judgement of bureaucrats (Rieder and Simon, 2016).

In turn, the nature of governmentality has shifted in character (Kitchin and Dodge, 2011; Vanolo, 2013). Governmentality constitutes the logics, rationalities and techniques that render societies governable and enable governmental institutions and other agencies to enact governance (Foucault, 1991). Governmentality transforms over time, mostly slowly mutating, but occasionally its nature transforms radically. For example, in the move from a feudal to modern society, the mechanisms to monitor society and ensure compliance with societal rules moved from localized, communal monitoring and forms of terror to instil obedience to more centralized, institutionalized bureaucracy and a disciplinary regime designed to instil particular habits, dispositions and expectations, and to corral and punish transgressors (Rose, 1996). A new form of 'bio-power' – the management of populations – was put in place, which worked at two levels: first, a new 'art of government' enacted through an interlocking array of institutions, administrative and technical systems, and laws and regulations; second, the micro-power of social norms and self-management in relation to expected behaviours (Walter and Andersen, 2013). Here, people are endowed with the autonomy to act within restrictions, with bio-power policing the boundaries of social action. Not everyone, however, is viewed as having the capacity to act autonomously, with differences in how people are treated varying along lines of class, gender, race, ethnicity, disability and sexuality.

Digital technologies are producing a shift in governmentality to enhanced disciplinary regimes through pervasive surveillance, and to new forms of social control (Kitchin and Dodge, 2011; Beer, 2019). In the latter case, governmentality moves from a disciplinary regime in which people self-regulate behaviour based on the fear of surveillance and sanction, to a control regime in which people are corralled and compelled to act in certain ways, their behaviour steered or nudged through their embedding in or use of systems (Vanolo, 2013). The example of the checkout operator illustrates this shift from discipline to control. Governmentality is no longer principally about subjectification, in which subjects are encouraged to act in certain ways, but about control, where behaviour is actively guided (Martinez, 2011). Temporality is an explicit component of such biopolitics, with the control of time a means to maintain and exert power. For example, a demanded speed is built into the checkout operator's work, as it is with many other jobs, from keystroke rates of administrative workers to the number of items collected per hour in a warehouse (see chapter 8). Similarly, the use of time management tools by companies indicates temporal expectations regarding the rate of activity and working hours, while also providing greater institutional control over how time is spent. A biopolitical economy of time is thus in operation, with different groups experiencing varying levels of temporal arbitrage in which their time is organized around the priorities of others (Sharma, 2014).

Real-time management

Urban services and infrastructures are increasingly managed and regulated using networked digital systems, producing what is commonly referred to as the smart city (Townsend, 2013). While there are competing notions of what constitutes a smart city, it is generally accepted that a key characteristic is the instrumentation of urban systems and the use of digital technologies to mediate human activity and service delivery in real time (Kitchin, 2014a). Smart city technologies are quite broad in scope, ranging from city operating systems, performance management, coordinated emergency response, intelligent transport infrastructures, bikeshare, smart parking, real-time passenger information, environmental sensor monitoring, smart grids (energy distribution) and smart metering, building management, and locative and spatial media (Kitchin, 2014a). These data-driven, algorithmic systems work to make cities knowable and controllable in new, dynamic, reactive ways. They are often feathered into or layered on top of existing systems and infrastructures, using sensors, actuators, cameras and other means of generating real-time data to monitor conditions, with instructions then being issued to recalibrate performance. For example, as detailed in chapter 6, real-time data from inductive loops, cameras and traffic radar at major junctions throughout a city are gathered together in a traffic control centre where they are used to recalibrate constantly the timing and phasing of traffic lights in order to try to minimize congestion. Such systems perform everyday management, seeking to regulate automatically the multiple rhythms of cities, to limit arrhythmia and produce eurythmic systems that maintain a refrain. They are also used for responding to unfolding emergencies, using the real-time data to try to contain an issue and direct responses that de-escalate the causes and mitigate their effects (O'Grady, 2018; Delaney and Kitchin, 2020).

The two critical elements for the real-time operation of these technical systems are the production of big data and some degree of automation. The level of automation varies by domain and system, with three levels of human participation (Docherty, 2012):

- human-in-the-loop: the system identifies and selects profiles and targets, but human operators perform the key decision-making and actioning (e.g., facial recognition matches being manually assessed before proceeding);
- human-on-the-loop: the system identifies and selects profiles, targets and decisions and automatically acts on them, but under the oversight of a human operator who can actively intervene and override (e.g., intelligent transport systems controlling traffic light phasing, with operators monitoring and intervening when necessary);
- human-out-of-the-loop: the system is fully automated and identifies and selects profiles, targets and decisions and acts on them without human input or interaction (e.g., automatically processing traffic-violations and issuing of fines based on captured data; or crash avoidance in autonomous vehicles).

All three levels of participation produce forms of 'automated management' (Kitchin and Dodge, 2011), wherein algorithms are key agents in decision-making and how systems are regulated. In general, automated management is a method of control that modulates the actions of those using or navigating those systems: the traffic control system might not dictate the path through a road network, but it does control the pace and timing of the traverse with little room for deviation; a driver steers and dictates the pace of a modern car, but thousands of autonomous micro-decisions made by the thirty-plus embedded computational devices nudge behaviour and assert control where necessary.

Control rooms are key sites for coordinating and overseeing the operation of these systems, especially for those involving human-in- and human-on-the-loop levels of automation that require human input. Data are displayed to operators through dashboards, very often in a form that shows performance over time. Operators can cycle through the data feeds, run analytics and models as required, tweak and reset operational parameters, react to issues that the system identifies as problems requiring solutions, override system decisions, liaise with personnel in the field, and coordinate responses with the operators of other services (Coletta and Kitchin, 2017; O'Grady, 2018). In most cases, control rooms relate to a single system, but they can also host a range of systems and stakeholders. In Rio de Janeiro, the real-time data feeds of 32 agencies and 12 private concessions (e.g. transport and energy companies) – relating to traffic and public transit, municipal and utility services, emergency and security services, environmental conditions, weather, and the public via social media – flow into a single control room (Luque-Ayala and Marvin, 2016). The centre is complemented by a virtual operations platform that enables city officials to log in from the field to access and upload real-time information. The Centro de Operacoes Prefeitura do Rio (COR) operates 24/7 and employs 400 staff, and includes a media section that enables journalists to monitor the city in real-time for incidents. Each agency located in COR is autonomous and continues to maintain its own control room, operative systems and response protocols, with COR providing a site of coordination and horizontal integration (Luque-Ayala and Marvin, 2016). COR is a large-scale endeavour to manage the unfolding time-spaces of the city and it diversely mediates – often in real- or near real-time – the temporalities of operations and urban experiences across a set of domains. Through coordination across agencies and systems, the integrative approach aims to ameliorate arrhythmia quickly and maintain eurythmic rhythms and beats. That said, the system has significant blind spots, in particular relating to the extensive favelas that exist in a state of exception to the normalized system infrastructure practices elsewhere in the city (Luque-Ayala and Marvin, 2020).

In New York, the Office of Emergency Management (OEM) is housed in a purpose-built 65,000-square-foot facility in Brooklyn and hosts a Watch Command Center that utilizes a Citywide Incident Management System (CIMS) (Smith, 2006). The building includes a suite of operational and training rooms, including workstations for 130 agencies (from city, state and federal bodies, plus non-profit entities and private-sector partners), video conferencing, secure communications, several large video displays, and back-up power generation, as well as a Joint Information Center for media communications during an emergency (Delaney and Kitchin, 2020). As such, it draws together and shares real-time data from across the city and, in return, directs emergency responses to ongoing crises. Such centralization provides enhanced intelligence and greater coordination across the multiple actors that are involved in such responses. Control rooms can also be mobile, deployed in the field to be nearer the site of action, using wireless and satellite communications to transfer data and commands.

While real-time management of single systems has become common across all cities, in practice, coordinated management and emergency response has not proven straightforward to implement. Issues blocking cooperation and integration across systems are technical and institutional (Delaney and Kitchin, 2020). Technical systems are designed and built using various approaches, technologies, software and standards that can limit interoperability with other systems. They are operated by organizations that have embedded institutional cultures, structures and working practices. When asked to cooperate with other bodies, they often act in protectionist ways to defend their independence and resources. Addressing these issues requires significant investment of resources in technical architectures, and political energy to reconfigure institutional and structural arrangements. Both of these requirements have been slow to materialize in many jurisdictions. Consequently, response systems are used independently with coordination between agencies being reliant on existing, often inefficient, institutional structures, or are piecemeal and ad hoc, as Delaney (2019) has demonstrated with respect to the response to the Boston Marathon bombing and the Irish agency response to extreme weather events.

Anticipatory governance

Governance has long had some anticipatory qualities, seeking to pre-empt and predict possible events and to be prepared for, prevent and mitigate their potential effects (Anderson, 2010; Stockdale, 2015). The future is brought into the present, shaping how the present unfolds in order to realize an aspirational future. Digital technologies have had a significant impact on such anticipatory governance by: widening the pool and timeliness of data used to make calculations and judgements; enabling more sophisticated models, predictions, forecasts, scenarios and simulations of future outcomes and the likely effects of different responses; and providing a means through which to coordinate and direct responses in an effective manner – including real-time, automated actions – and to construct contingency plans. Anticipatory systems are increasingly being employed by states across a range of domains to make predictions about future potential events and to intervene pre-emptively to limit, prevent or prepare for any unwanted outcomes, thus exerting some level of control of the future by taking action in the present (Adams et al., 2009). Ideally, the aim is to pick up early warning signs that can then be tracked and responded to appropriately – that is, to work in a precautionary way, acting 'before an identified threat reaches a point of irreversibility', to prevent an outcome (Ewald, 2002: 287, cited in Anderson, 2010).

Such a precautionary approach is hard to achieve in practice because it is difficult to identify signs and to predict what may unfold (Tazzioli, 2018). A pre-emptive approach recognizes that there are multiple potential futures that are not easily calculated, and, rather than try to identify and nullify defined threats, a broader strategy is required that aims to mitigate classes of issues, recognizing the partial unpredictability of emergent events (Anderson, 2010; Tazzioli, 2018). A pre-emptive approach does not seek to target specific events then, but rather to put in place a governance apparatus that responds adequately to all such events. For example, systems such as Eurosur and Jora, used by EU migration authorities to identify and trace illegal migrants, is less about targeting and policing the passage of specific groups, but, rather, running migration risk analyses that strengthen the governance assemblage to police the flow of all such migrants (Tazzioli, 2018). To a large degree, this involves recognizing the uncertainty of the future, widening the field of risk, and imagining and governing possible novel disruptions, rather than identifying the most probable eventualities and only targeting these (Amoore, 2013; O'Grady, 2018). Here, it is acknowledged that emergencies are inevitable and they cannot all be prevented. As such, there is a need, on the one hand, to try to circumscribe the horizon of possibilities by limiting the potential for a situation to arise (e.g. building flood defences, installing security apparatus, cutting fire breaks, installing avalanche netting), and, on the other, to be prepared for multiple possibilities to occur, regardless (Leszczynski, 2016).

Preparedness includes using data to model potential ways to tackle unfolding crises, identifying which approaches work best in different scenarios, codifying these into response plans, and making sure that required resources are already in place (e.g. having a stockpile of flu vaccines, or salt for gritting frozen roads, or trained personnel with suitable skillsets) and these are maintained over time to ensure ongoing resilience (Amin, 2013). These plans can then be quickly implemented if the situation occurs (Anderson, 2010). These contingency plans might be run as mock, simulated exercises (such as a field-based emergency response to a disaster) so that responsible individuals have some first-hand experience of having to handle unfolding events. Some of these exercises are purely virtual simulations, where software and models offer visions of the future and users are asked to tackle the emergency (O'Grady, 2018).

Precautionary and pre-emptive approaches have long been a feature of intelligence work and national security, using gathered data to identify people of interest and what actions they might be planning and, if possible, prevent their realization, and to be able to recognize and pre-empt a broad variety of risks and threats that could arise at any time, in any place. This work expanded enormously post 9/11, with a major step change in state-led surveillance (through the deployment of new state-run data-gathering technologies – such as a massive expansion of CCTV in public spaces, along with thermal cameras, high-definition aerial/satellite imagery, MAC (media access control) address tracking of smartphones, new indexical IDs for accessing services, automated screening of passengers at airports, and enhanced border controls – the mining of state databases, and accessing commercial data-driven systems), along with extensive predictive profiling, as exposed by the Snowden revelations (Amoore, 2006; Lyon, 2014). It has also become an aspect of welfare services and policing. For example, in the UK, a number of local authorities work with companies such as Xantura and CallCredit to undertake risk assessment to identify 'troubled families' and calculate the likelihood that a child is living at risk with respect to hunger or abuse and to direct services accordingly (Dencik et al., 2019; Redden et al., 2020). The Think Family database of Bristol's Integrated Analytical Hub combines 35 social, education, health and policing datasets to assess child welfare and to direct service provision; and Kent's Integrated Dataset draws together data from 250 health and social organizations and emergency services for predictive decision-making (Dencik et al., 2019).

Many police forces have turned to big data policing as a means to tackle crime (Brayne, 2017; Jefferson, 2018). New command-and-control centres are being built that employ enhanced and extensive multi-instrumented surveillance (e.g. high-definition CCTV, drone cameras, sensors, bodycams, community reporting, as well as scanning communications and social media) to identify and antic-ipate issues and direct on-the-ground policing in real-time (as well as act as a deterrent to criminal acts) (Brayne, 2017; Wiig, 2018). Data fusion initiatives link together data across criminal justice agencies (Shapiro, 2020), and digitally mediated crime scene tools are creating databanks of material evidence. New digital tools are enabling insights to be extracted from data sources, to predict and pre-empt crime, and to populate models to run scenarios and produce contingency plans (Shapiro, 2020).

Predictive policing uses a wide range of data, including longitu-dinal data relating to 'event-based concerns (frequency of arrests, emergency phone calls, incident reports and complaints), place-based concerns (known addresses of criminal suspects, locations of gang activity, places where crime is common), types of crime', personal information, gang activities, location information (street layout, traffic patterns, surveillance devices) and administrative data, to anticipate the location of future crimes and to direct police officers to increase patrols in those areas (Dencik et al., 2018; Shapiro, 2020). In the case of the PredPol system, used by several US police forces, the goal is to predict where crime will happen over the next 10–12 hours and to dispatch officers accordingly (Andrejevic et al., 2020). Importantly, this approach 'does not dismantle the patrol; it reformats the patrol along the axes of time and space to suit managerial impera-tives', and is a means of more closely directing police work (Shapiro, 2020: 150). Other systems focus on offender behaviour, seeking to track existing, and identify potential unidentified or future, criminals (Brayne, 2017; Jefferson, 2018), or to predict recidivism risk among defendants in the courts system (Shapiro, 2020).

Such anticipatory governance aims to be proactive rather than reactive, and to pre-empt and prevent crime before or as it happens (Aradau and Blanke, 2015). This can include acting as a deterrent through an increased police presence in an area or visiting individuals to let them know they are already under surveillance, or undertaking pre-emptive actions – for example, at public protests, detaining leaders, checking and searching attendees, nullifying potential trigger points, or 'kettling' (containing) the crowd (Dencik et al., 2018). These systems work in conjunction with, rather than overriding, the professional judgement and discretion of police officers, who interpret and implement responses informed by the predictive assess-ments, and work with them in relation to their own temporalities, which might include resistance and delay (Dencik et al., 2018; Andrejevic et al., 2020).

An activity such as emergency management involves a number of different forms of anticipation, including forms of preparedness, prediction, precaution, pre-emption, and response and recovery (Anderson et al., 2020). The aim is to prevent events from occurring if possible, to be prepared for any eventuality, and to tackle and mitigate quickly any crisis that develops. As Pollitt (2008) notes, major disasters such as Hurricane Katrina highlight the importance of preparation over the long term, the need for expertise based on accumulated experience and to learn from previous events, the necessity for very fast action from the crisis onset, the need for short- and long-term contingency plans, and the effects of institutional reorganization on timely coordination. Such emergencies affect groups differently, with distinct biopolitics at play. For example, Anderson et al. (2020) detail how emergencies are often racialized in terms of preparation, effects, response and recovery (as was evident with Katrina).

Emergencies rupture settled rhythms and patterns, creating a state of exception in which something of value is placed at risk, with 'a sense that there is a limited time within which to curtail irreparable harm or damage' and to halt an emergency from spreading or cascading (Anderson, 2016: 178). They also raise the question as to whether the pre-existing order can be restored after the event, though this is the promise of emergency response (Anderson, 2016). The work of emergency services is a mix of ordinary and extraordinary work. Much of the time involves waiting for an event to occur and routine preparation work. Most emergency events are relatively mundane (such as a domestic fire), an extraordinary and devastating event for those experiencing it but also relatively unexceptional and routine for responders (Anderson et al., 2020). Other events are uncommon, major instances that require an atypical response, often involving coordination across agencies.

When emergencies arise, they produce two other temporalities beyond exceptionality. First, 'a rushing future that severs the present from the past and compresses the time for decision and action', creating a sense that 'there is no time except the time of *now* that requires some form of urgent action' (Anderson, 2016: 180). Reflecting on the past, running future scenarios and deliberation all involve delay which heightens the risk of the emergency deepening further. The latter relates to the second temporality, that of the 'interval': 'the time during which action can still make a difference' and 'the emergency can be brought to an end without [additional] loss, harm or damage' (Anderson, 2016: 180). An emergency ends when an interval closes and there are no others in play. In this sense, emergencies are highly contingent and non-teleological, where the future unfolds relationally, given circumstances and response (O'Grady, 2018). Prepared plans for possible events are important because they provide a ready means for quick action, slowing the sense of a rushing future and shortening intervals (Anderson, 2015). They are designed to contain the emergency and (re)produce 'recognizable cyclical or linear sequences of, for example, order-growth-development, disruption-stabilization-recovery, or disruption-adaptation-transformation. The goal is to drain an event of its eventfulness, making it into a recognized, completed happening' (Anderson et al., 2020: 626).

Conclusion

The management and regulation of societies are shot through with temporalities. Governance is enacted in and structured by time, being time-ordered in its formulation, implementation and operation. Temporality is used as a strategic resource in the workings of governance, and the control and regulation of temporalities, such as time rules, are key mechanisms of power. Modes of governance shape in direct and indirect ways the nature and production of everyday temporalities, reconfiguring the organization and experience of activities. Our lives are temporally ordered in relation to the temporal logics of governance regimes, patterned into rhythms and cycles, and coordinated and synchronized. The growing ubiquity and pervasiveness of digital technologies is having a profound effect on the logics, practices and timescapes of governance.

Digital technologies are increasingly mediating how activities are organized and undertaken, services and infrastructures operate, and spaces are produced. They extend the scope, extent and mechanisms of governance, and produce forms of governance that are more technocratic, prescriptive, algorithmic and rule-based. In particular, they have enabled extensive real-time management of urban services and infrastructures, and facilitated the development of anticipatory forms of governance that predict, prepare for, prevent, pre-empt and respond to events. Additionally, digital technologies augment, mediate and supplement pre-digital forms of governance – such as the shift to e-government and e-governance of traditional forms of bureaucracy, the extension of workplace surveillance and forms of temporal arbitrage (see chapter 8), and the longitudinal monitoring of indicators to enact forms of performance management (see chapter

4). Importantly, temporality is embedded into the very code through which digital technologies enact modulation and regulation, with code constituting algorhythms (Miyazaki, 2012; see chapter 6) that enact various forms of machine time (Mackenzie, 2006; see chapter 1). Machine times and their produced temporalities are reconfiguring the nature of governmentality, enabling enhanced disciplinary regimes and new forms of social control wherein the exercise of regulation is baked into how an activity is performed.

— 6 —

MOBILITY AND LOGISTICS

Mobility and the movement of people, goods and services consist of passages through time and space. Temporality, then, is explicitly a component feature, not an artefact, of mobility, though mobility also produces associated temporalities, such as time-space compression and lived time. This chapter examines the diverse temporalities of mobility through three brief case studies. First, it considers the effects of mobile/smartphones and locative/spatial media on everyday individual mobility and scheduling. It then charts how intelligent transport systems are used to manage in real-time the flow and rhythms of traffic. Lastly, it examines how various forms of information management systems (such as enterprise resource planning and supply chain management systems) are used to coordinate and synchronize the time-spaces of global logistics. What the three cases reveal is that networked technologies are fundamentally logistical media, with their instrumentality designed to condition the organization and flow of urban sociality, activity and economy (Shapiro, 2020). Logistical media arrange, segment, coordinate and synchronize the pace, tempo and rhythms of everyday life, structuring movement and interactions around circuits of information and mediated action (Rossiter, 2016; Shapiro, 2020). As discussed in the previous chapter, logistical media embody and enact a blend of disciplinary and control forms of governmentality, mediating, interpellating and tracking the flow and exchange of people, ideas and goods in forms that their designers, managers and operators deem most productive and valuable (Shapiro, 2020). They produce 'logistical life' – that is, 'life lived under the duress of the command to be efficient, to communicate one's purposes transparently in relation to others, to be positioned where one is required, to use time economically, to be able to move when and where one is told to' (Reid, 2006: 13, cited in Shapiro, 2020: 13). In other words, logistical media do not simply facilitate interaction and exchange; they make them productive and governable – a means to exert biopolitics (Rossiter, 2016).

Everyday mobility and scheduling

Mobility, including the routines and scheduling of time geographies, is one of the key facets of everyday life in which the digital is having tangible effects. Each day, we travel between sites to undertake activities, often in conjunction with other people. Traditionally, many of these activities occupy familiar times and places, dictated by established timetables and cultural/social conventions, such as work hours, public transit schedules and family mealtimes. These are repeated daily and weekly with some performative flourishes and detours, but largely form a well-ordered and sequenced pattern of routine (Crang, 2005). Others are occasional, such as meeting up with friends or business meetings, or having to meet a deadline, which might be planned in advance or at short notice and slotted into schedules. Some encounters and activities are serendipitous and unplanned, and time might have to be made for them, or are considered 'time fillers' to be accommodated in the gaps between activities (Southerton, 2006). To manage the ordering and scheduling of activities and to coordinate and synchronize events in time and space, individuals have long used time management tools such as paper calendars and diaries. The information these contain might be shared with selected others, such as family members or work colleagues, to keep them informed of plans and to coordinate activities and events. Communication systems, such as the telephone and postal mail, enabled planning and organization from a distance.

These traditional analogue technologies are being complemented and replaced by networked digital technologies, such as smartphones, spatial and locative media, and time management apps, which have different temporal affordances. The wide-scale adoption of mobile phones and smartphones and the rollout of ubiquitous computing (access to networking and computation from anywhere) have had a notable effect on the temporal organization of everyday life and the practices and experiences of mobility. Rather than communication and information being available at fixed points, the perpetual connectivity of mobile/smartphones means that their owners are always–everywhere available (Green, 2002). This perpetual

101

connectivity enables scheduling to become flexible, decoupled from clock time and timetables, and organized with respect to network time (Katz and Aakhus, 2002; Hassan, 2009). Schedules built around specific times and places give way to shifting times and places (Hassan and Purser, 2007). Meetings can be synchronized on the fly, recalibrated in reaction to unfolding events and real-time information (Sharma, 2014). For example, if a person is running late, they can call or message the person they are due to meet to rearrange their plans. In the case of a family, the temporal exigencies of several members and their multiple schedules are subject to what Nansen et al. (2009: 198, their emphasis) term 'reticular orchestration *and* improvisation' – an ever-shifting flexible dynamic. In other cases, individuals might never have had any fixed plans or schedule, beyond they would update each other on their activities and whereabouts and work out where, when and whether to meet, based on prevailing circumstances (Reading, 2009). In such cases, flexibility and continual negotiation and recalibration replace a schedule and punctuality, de-routinizing mobility patterns (Southerton and Tomlinson, 2005; Sharma, 2017).

Flexibility and recalibration are facilitated by locative and spatial media that situate and mediate interactions in time and space (Kitchin et al., 2017). The development of Web 2.0 technologies (that shifted the Internet from a broadcast medium to social engagement), the release of the Google Maps API in 2005, and the centrality of location-awareness in iOS and Android smartphone apps from 2009 encouraged the production of a variety of apps that mediate movement and social interactions within time-space, and provided alternative ways to know and navigate locales (Gordon and de Souza e Silva, 2011). Journey planning and routing apps recommend the most time-efficient trip and enable the real-time recalculation of the timings and route of travel as situations change, such as reacting to congestion or delayed/cancelled transit. Location-based services facilitate finding goods and amenities in a locale, permitting choice- and decision-making based on current mood or context (Huang et al., 2018). Location-based social media provide social check-in services or chat with nearby people based on spatial proximity (Saker and Evans, 2016). Apps that track and find nearby friends enable serendipitous encounters with them (Sutko and de Souza e Silva, 2010). Importantly, these apps permit tasks to be undertaken *in situ*, on the move and in real-time, augmenting a whole series of activities such as shopping, wayfinding, sightseeing and protesting.

While locative and spatial media provide useful orientating information that augments time-space decisions and choices and

102

serendipitous encounters, they can also work to structure and nudge user perception and movement (Kitchin et al., 2017). Suggested routes and timetables in journey planning apps provide a reified path that displaces routine and ad hoc practices and seeks to persuade the driver or passenger to take certain paths and mobility options (Chesher, 2012). Likewise, the filtering and prioritization of information within a location-based services recommender system work to direct decisions towards selected content (Graham et al., 2013). Indeed, the designers of some locative media are quite explicit in their desire to generate nudges. For example, Foursquare declared that it is in the 'business of changing user behavior' (Crowley, 2010). Given the commercial nature of most locative and spatial media, these nudges often have a specific consumption agenda.

Moreover, locative and spatial media enable fine-grained, longitudinal surveillance of mobility patterns. Since a smartphone is portable it enables the tracking of movement through time and space via the GPS sensor in the device, or externally through cell-tower connections, the scanning of its MAC (Media Access Control) address, or connections to Wi-Fi. Other logistical media – such as high-definition CCTV cameras with facial recognition, smart devices such as GPS-enabled fitness trackers and smart watches, smart cards used to access public transit or buildings, ANPR cameras, transponders for automated road tolls and car parking, on-board GPS in vehicles, and shared calendars – enable movement and location to be monitored in pervasive, continuous and automated ways (Kitchin, 2014b). Such data can be used by the state for urban management (as with intelligent transport systems) or policing and security (see chapter 5). Most recently, they have been used during the Covid-19 crisis to facilitate contact tracing, quarantine enforcement, travel permissions and social distancing/movement monitoring (Kitchin, 2020). They can be used by companies to understand customers better, enhance decision-making, spatially target advertising, optimize the layout of stores, monitor employees, enhance logistics and enforce security measures.

Locative and spatial media, then, alter how we understand, move through, coordinate and communicate in, interact with and build attachments to time-spaces (Leszczynski, 2015; Kitchin et al., 2017). Smartphones, and other connected devices such as tablets and laptops, place people in a distributed net of governmentality while also enabling choices. They facilitate mobile time shifting, converting 'dead time' to productive time through multitasking (undertaking several activities simultaneously), interleaving (switching back and

103

forth between activities) and metatasking (planning and interlinking of goals across activities) (Wajcman, 2008). Tasks, and parts of tasks, can become parallel endeavours of movement, such as working while waiting on a platform or travelling on a train. The result is a ratcheting up of activities and an increased sense of busyness, not necessarily due to the speed at which life unfolds but the crowding of activities and incidents into everyday situations that demands energy and attention (Tomlinson, 2007). For Colville (2016), the sense that life is getting faster is because the volume and intensity of tasks and interactions compel individuals to increase the pace at which they perform activities, and to be more flexible in doing so. Mobility is colonized by other tasks, which, along with the journey itself, are undertaken in a hurried fashion. At the same time, perpetual connectivity creates opportunities for disruption and interruption, exposing the temporal fragility and elasticity of mobile time (Trentmann, 2009). Time on a journey that might have been a chance to relax or to work on a specific task can be ruptured and recast by incoming calls and messages and demands to switch attention (Southerton, 2020). The asynchronous nature of messaging and emails provides some degree of control and autonomy over responding to such interruptions, but they nonetheless induce an affective reaction by establishing a need to respond (Kitchin and Fraser, 2020).

As such, while mobile/smartphones create flexibility and efficiencies, their temporal affordances also produce what Rosa (2017) refers to as temporal rebound effects. Such rebound effects include temporal density and fragmentation, with plans, sequencing, prioritization and synchronization being open to instability, which generates temporal anxieties and stresses, such as feeling harried. Smartphones enable the management of time while simultaneously creating more demands on time (Rosa, 2017), producing a connectivity paradox and temporal ambivalences regarding coexisting contradictions in the management and experience of time (Ytre-Arne et al., 2020). A related paradox concerns coordination. Smartphones provide a greater degree of individual autonomy and 'greater discretion over timing and scheduling of activity', but, in so doing, they 'generate multiply idiosyncratic schedules which in turn increase the problem of coordination' (Shove, 2008: 8). Orchestrating flexible schedules across individuals becomes a more challenging task because other peoples' schedules are also less stable and ordered (Nansen et al., 2009). The effects of this instability vary as power pervades perpetual connectivity, with those more senior being able to structure the unfolding time-spacing of others around their own circumstances and agenda (Wajcman, 2019). Indeed, temporal autonomy over scheduling and mobility is highly differentiated across social groups (e.g., class, gender, race), work status (e.g. role and level of precarity) and family circumstances (e.g. extent of care duties) (Kwan, 2000; Datta, 2020). Somewhat ironically, as detailed in chapter 8, the solution to temporal anxieties and stresses is another set of apps focused on time management and productivity.

Keeping traffic moving

Given the growth in car use, which often far exceeds the projected carrying capacity of road infrastructure, every major city has become dependent on intelligent transport systems (ITS) and their associated infrastructure to keep traffic moving. ITS are an explicit intervention into managing the temporal rhythms of traffic flow and the temporalities of journeys and time-spaces (e.g. travel time, deferring or addressing delay and waiting). They also embody and produce their own temporalities, particularly through the algorhythms at the heart of their operation and the routines in traffic control centres. For Miyazaki (2012: 5; 2013), the concept of an 'algorhythm' blends together the notion of an algorithm's sequence of step-by-step instructions with rhythm's time-based order of movement to consider how computation 'manifests itself as an epistemic model of a machine that makes time itself logically controllable and, while operating, produces measurable time effects and rhythms'. Miyazaki (2013: 520) contends: '[a]lgorhythms are vibrational, pulsed and rhythmized signals constituted both by transductions of physical fluctuations of energy and their oscillations as well as by abstract and logical structures of mathematic calculations'. He shows how the micro-temporal workings of such algorhythms produce and mediate everyday life. In the case of ITS, algorhythms seek to utilize nowcasting to create a eurhythmic refrain through a form of automated management, in which computation monitors and manages the system in an automated, automatic and autonomous fashion (Kitchin and Dodge, 2011). Such automation enables massive volumes of data from thousands of devices scattered across a city to be tracked and controlled in real-time far exceeding the capacity of human attention. However, rather than being a human-off-the-loop system (Docherty, 2012; see chapter 5), wherein full control to regulate traffic is ceded to the algorhythms, ITS are human-on-the-loop in which the system works independently and autonomously, but is overseen by a human controller who can actively intervene (Coletta and Kitchin, 2017).

Employing a form of rhythmanalysis (Lefebvre, 2004), which unpacks the ways in which time, space and lived experience are folded into, conditioned by and produced through various rhythms, Coletta and Kitchin (2017) examined how an ITS is used to manage traffic flow and temporalities in Dublin, Ireland. The Dublin Traffic Management and Incident Centre (TMIC) provides a single, integrated, 24/7 control room to house the core traffic management systems for monitoring and controlling the road transportation network and traffic flow in the Greater Dublin Area, including dealing with major events and incidents. As well as ITS staff, there are desks for an AA Roadwatch operator (who communicates traffic news to radio stations), the Gardaí (police service), Dublin Bus, and their own radio staff (who broadcast live traffic news between 7 to 10 a.m. and 4 to 7 p.m., Monday to Friday). The TMIC is a busy, time-critical, polyrhythmic environment, with overlapping work, machinic and algorithmic rhythms operating on different temporal cycles: the peaks of morning and evening rush hour; people entering or leaving the room for breaks or as shifts change; the voice and music on the radio; the operators typing at keyboards and switching between cameras; and hurried conversations or jokes and the sharing of screens as a situation unfolds. At all times, real-time data is flowing into the centre from a fixed network of 380 CCTV cameras, 800 sensors (inductive loops embedded in the road surface), a small number of Traffic Cams (traffic-sensing radars), a mobile network of approximately 1,000 bus transponders, phone calls and messages by the public to radio stations and the operators, and social media posts, which contingently and relationally shape the core patterns of activity.

At the centre of this activity is the traffic management system, SCATS (Sydney Coordinated Adaptive Traffic System). SCATS is an automated and adaptive system for managing the flow of traffic through a city. It synchronizes traffic lights automatically, calculating the timing of signal cycles and phases at junctions depending on traffic conditions in order to ensure the optimal flow of vehicles, minimize congestion and manage incidents. In so doing, it dynamically manages the polyrhythms of road transportation and pedestrian crossings. A cycle is the wait time at a junction and is subdivided into phases for different directions and types (e.g. vehicles, cycles, pedestrians) of flow. It is adaptive in the sense that the system automatically adjusts the cycles and phases dependent on a set of programmed rules and the volume of traffic in previous cycles and phases. SCATS operates at three levels of control: at the level of the single inter-section, a subsystem, and a system (McCann, 2014). A subsystem is an amalgam of closely related junctions, including a 'critical' junction and adjacent minor junctions and pedestrian crossings: 'Within a subsystem, all junctions operate at the same cycle time and will have offset values designed to provide synchronisation between the junctions at all times of day' (McCann, 2014: 15). The system level seeks to provide coordination between subsystems by linking them together using external offsets. Across the subsystems and systems, the adjustment of time is based on the degree of saturation (DS), a traffic demand measure that calculates whether road usage is under-saturated (few vehicles) or over-saturated (congested). Operators can intervene and override the original SCATS settings, as well as its present conditions. Interventions are circumscribed by the system configuration by ITS staff, which in turn refer to the Traffic Signs Manual by the National Roads Authority, which sets rules on the minimum and maximum times for phases.

Calibrating processes and practices are at the core of the production of linear and cyclic rhythms: timings are not given, but are built through the interaction of multiple adjustments that shape the measurement and practices of rhythms. Calibration takes into account the inter-actions within the TMIC as performed by the controllers, whether it is a weekday or weekend, as well as seasonal/daily rhythms and when schools are closed, as well as the flows of traffic and pedestrians, who through their movements and actions at junctions contribute to, and are affected by, the system's algorhythms. For example, by pressing a pedestrian-crossing button, an individual produces a temporary break in the traffic rhythm, closing down the main phase in order to run the pedestrian phase. Similarly, the number of cars and the gaps between them, as detected by the inductive loops, indicates whether a phase was too short or long and the next phase time is re-calculated automatically by the SCAT system. Public buses benefit from prioritization, so as they approach a junction the phasing will alter to accommodate their passage, generating a further alteration of traffic rhythms that need to be managed by the software, and which sometimes produce congestion in the other phases. Much of the data utilized in the traffic control room is shared with the public via a number of channels, enabling citizens to see and interpret the data themselves, self-regulate their interactions with the traffic system and manage time-based decisions for journey planning. For example, real-time information about the expected arrival of buses is shared via smartphone apps, websites, on-street digital signs, radio bulletins and social media. In addition, many travellers can use GPS navigation systems that automatically re-route drivers in response to real-time updates, often taken from other real-time datasets (e.g. Google Maps traffic updates that track the movement of Android phones).

Similar management systems exist for managing public transit. For example, in Dublin there are separate control rooms to manage the bus, tram and rail networks. The emergency services have their own control centres to guide responses to unfolding situations, with the police having access to the traffic control's camera network. In the case of an emergency, the traffic control room can expand to accommodate personnel from other agencies to provide a coordinated response (see chapter 5). Likewise, every airport has an air traffic control room that guides movement on the ground between gates and hangars and runways, and guides flight paths in the air taking account of other planes, weather and airspace regulations. They often have other control rooms relating to security throughout the airport, as well as for particular tasks, such as the automated systems that guide tens of thousands of bags through the complex (Kitchin and Dodge, 2011). Ports also have control rooms for tracking and guiding shipping, and for the movement of containers on and off ships, into storage areas, and in and out of the facility via road or rail. Agencies such as Frontex and the European Maritime Security Agency operate a larger-scale monitoring of the movement of shipping around Europe, particularly in the Mediterranean, seeking to identify 'irregular' movements as means to detect illegal migrant border crossings (Tazzioli, 2018).

Logistics and chains of supply

The time-space compression of modernity facilitated the expansion of trade globally, lengthening the supply lines of materials and services, extending markets and enabling companies to develop into multinational enterprises with global production networks. New developments in transportation and communications transformed the organization, management, volume, reach, complexity and timeliness of logistics and chains of supply across the planet (Cowen, 2014; LeCavalier, 2016). Since the late 1960s, the development of the container and associated infrastructure, cold-storage and warehousing infrastructure, massive cargo ships and wide-scale air freight, new information management systems, and conceptual and practical innovations in business logistics, organizational theory and supply chain management (such as holistic approaches, just-in-time manufacturing, and stock control), have further extended the time-space convergence and distanciation of the logistics industry, with significant effects on the growth of multinational businesses and global trading interdependencies.

Networked technologies and infrastructures have been central to creating efficiencies in the temporal organization of logistics, enabling the coordination and synchronization of the scheduling of operations and movement of goods and services from the numerous sites of raw materials, components manufacture, product assembly and distribution to stores and purchasers; facilitating the control and flexibility to respond rapidly to unfolding situations, ever-changing market conditions, and disruptions to normal operations; and engendering a shift to network time for ordering, tracking, delivery and other tasks that previously had to occur at a specific time (LeCavalier, 2016; Lyster, 2016; Rossiter, 2016). Systems such as enterprise resource planning (ERP) and supply chain management (SCM) permit the coordination and control of processes and operations within a large, dispersed organization, and with other companies and customers, on a real-time basis. ERP, for example, standardizes and combines an organization's multiple databases and systems (relating to purchasing, warehousing, inventory, transport, marketing, accounting, personnel management and rostering, project management, customer relations) into one all-encompassing system that ensures that information and processes are automatically and seamlessly available from one part of a business to another (Dery et al., 2006). SCM is used to organize as efficiently as possible the procurement, movement, management and storage of materials from suppliers through a company and on to customers (Chopra and Meindl, 2012). SCM is facilitated by a range of networked technologies to scan and track items, sort and guide them through automated distribution centres, undertake stock audits, and monitor the movements and performance of workers. Similarly, inventory management is used to improve stock forecasting – and thus anticipate and pre-empt future operations – by monitoring sales histories, seasonal sales cycles and local conditions. Distribution and logistics optimization software is used to track the real-time location of goods and delivery vehicles, calculate the most time- and cost-efficient routes, and schedule maintenance (Manyika et al., 2011). Billions of pieces of information are generated, circulated, tracked, processed and analysed daily by such systems in order to maintain corporate and logistical operations.

ERP, SCM and other logistical media act as space-time machines (Kitchin, 2019a), simultaneously producing a number of coeval temporalities across sites and domains, stretched out from the local to global, ranging from time-space convergence and distanciation, to pre-empting futures, to the lived temporalities of employees whose work they mediate. While increasing the speed and timeliness of operations, and reducing the turnover time of profit, are a key ambition, as important are synchronization, coordination, streamlining processes, and minimizing disruption and delay. The organizing logic of just-in-time, adopted by many corporations, is important here. Just-in-time seeks components, products and services to arrive at the right time, in the right sequence and amount, at the right place all the way along supply and distribution chains (Cheng and Lai, 2009). Initially applied to manufacturing, just-in-time has been extended across business enterprises. It aims to enable efficient operations and labour, eliminate unproductive time and non-value-added activities (such as inspection, stock-taking and materials handling that cost time and labour but add little value to the company or customer), create flexibility in responsiveness, avoid bottlenecks and back-ups, reduce waste, minimize the need for costly storage, and limit the risk of damage and obsolescence (Cheng and Lai, 2009; LeCavalier, 2016). In an ideal logistics scenario, goods are always in motion, with minimal time in storage along the chain. This is illustrated by the shift from warehousing to cross-docking distribution centres, where goods from production sites are unpacked immediately on arrival, sorted and shifted through the centre, and placed onto transportation heading to stores (Nyckel, 2021). By reconfiguring the temporality of supply, just-in-time reduces costs while increasing return on investment and meeting customer expectations in relation to service and price. As detailed in chapter 8, the concept is also being applied to labour, with 'just-in-time workers' who are employed on an on-demand basis, with flexible schedules and paid per gig, as a means of reducing labour costs and overheads (de Stefano, 2015).

The space-time machinery of logistics is well illustrated by the operations of corporations such as FedEx, Walmart and Amazon (LeCavalier, 2016; Lyster, 2016). These companies rely on a complex network of sites, infrastructures, transportation assets and information systems to organize their operations and gain competitive advantage. They are strongly data-driven enterprises and have long been at the forefront of innovations in technical systems to refine the time-space relations of their operations, from the global circulation of inventory and delivery, to the lived time of their workers and customers.

As of 2016, FedEx operated 669 planes, 90,000 vehicles and a global network of pick-up points and distribution centres (Lyster, 2016). It has its own global operations control centre to coordinate the worldwide shipping of packages and to plan contingency measures, such as anticipating adverse weather conditions and re-scheduling/ routing flights (Lyster, 2016). Its distribution centres use automated sorting and tracking systems to direct packages efficiently across its delivery network. Its systems enable it to move quickly tens of thousands of items daily: for example, its sort centre in Memphis handles the cargo of 150 planes between midnight and 3 a.m., with no package being stationary for more than 30 minutes, and no domestic items being in the facility for more than 90 minutes (Lyster, 2016). The organization of operations is hierarchical and strategic, but the use of smart technologies enables flexibility and localized tactics to deal with issues arising and to maintain operational resilience. Time is the critical organizing logic, with operations centred on meeting scheduled delivery times.

Founded in 1952, as of 2014 Walmart had 4,835 stores located in the United States, along with 158 distribution centres, employing more than 1.3 million people, as well as 6,107 international stores, and global sales of $473 billion (LeCavalier, 2016). Its stores sell an enormous number of product lines from over 100,000 suppliers, and millions of shoppers pass through its stores daily. As a discount seller with thin profit margins generated from low prices and high turnover, efficiency and productivity in distribution have been essential components in Walmart's operations from its founding (LeCavalier, 2016). Its aim is to have a constant flow of inventory cycling through its distribution warehouses, arriving at stores, passing onto shelves, then leaving via shopping baskets as efficiently and cost-effectively as possible. For example, its distribution centre DC 6094 (Bentonville, Arkansas), a 1.2 million-square-feet facility, turns over more than 90 per cent of its contents every day (c. the size of a mid-sized Panamax container ship) (LeCavalier, 2016). Indeed, speed, synchronicity, coordination and efficiency underpin Walmart's operations. To that end, it was an early adopter of inventory management and customer relations management systems, data centres and analytics, and satellite communications to coordinate and synchronize operations across sites and suppliers, along with barcodes to track stock and increase check-out efficiency (LeCavalier, 2016). It continues to be a thoroughly data-driven organization using various technologies

111

to track worker, store and supplier performance, inform decision-making, and drive time-space efficiencies across all its activities.

Amazon is a company founded on a time-neutral online shopping experience (orders can be placed at any time) on a platform that hosts tens of thousands of other retailers, and rapid delivery to a customer's preferred address. Rather than having to visit thousands of stores, the time-space of shopping is re-organized and radically extended through network time. To facilitate this business model, Amazon is reliant on a suite of information management systems to coordinate and synchronize its operations, anchored on data centres and what it terms 'fulfilment centers' (distribution centres) (Lyster, 2016). The latter are massive spaces that are organized around 'velocity thresholds' (temporal demand), with the most popular items located in zones and shelving options where they can be quickly picked and distributed; every zone is designed to hold up to seven days' stock (Lyster, 2016). In low-turnover zones, both directed (a product is always placed in the same location) and random storage (placed where there is available space, with the location recorded in the inventory system) are used (Lyster, 2016). The work of receivers, stowers and pickers is temporally organized to handle a certain number of items in a given time, scanning items at each stage as a means to track inventory, tasks and worker performance, and to ensure temporal targets of the company and customer are met. Each centre is acutely time-centred and pressured, with workers operating in an environment that Lyster (2016) characterizes as 'Taylorization at its extreme' (every task being allocated the most efficient time possible; also see Delfanti, 2021). In 2013, Amazon filed a patent for 'anticipatory package shipping', in which data relating to 'wish list activities, shopping carts, product searches, and the duration of mouse hovers over items' is used to pre-empt an order, placing an item in transit on the prediction that it will be purchased, with fallback mechanisms in place to nudge the potential buyer or re-route or gift items if no order is made (Nyckel, 2021: 266). Here, speed is created by acting on a predicted near future, with the system acting to ensure that its prediction occurs.

As a consequence of the time-space distanciation, just-in-time operations, and temporal arbitrage of logistics (and many other activities), locales are finding themselves ever more bound within a stretched-out progressive sense of time – that is, locales co-produce multiple temporalities that are stretched out across the globe. In the same critique in which she formulated the notion of power-geometry to highlight the unevenness in time-space compression across people and places (see chapter 1), Massey (1993) forwarded the concept of a progressive sense of place. Places, she argued, are not bounded, singular entities; rather, the character of a place is shaped as much by the flows emanating from afar, and interconnected processes and interdependencies, as by internal characteristics. People, goods, services and information from a plethora of locations move in and out of places daily, directly contributing to its sense of place. Just as Sharma (2014) recast power-geometries to power-chronology, it is productive to recognize that the temporalities of places are not bounded, but are progressive – that is, heterogeneously scaled and interconnected. Such a progressive sense of time is particularly evident in the discussion of the temporalities of development, planning and labour in the following chapters.

Conclusion

A diverse range of logistical media is thoroughly embedded in the operations of mobility, and mediates its experience. These media are having a number of significant temporal effects, from the personal movement and schedules of individuals, to the coordination and synchronization of large city-scale transport infrastructures, to the global organization of complex logistical operations. In other words, they produce a distinctly logical timescape. Logistical media are producing what Rossiter (2016: xiii) refers to as the 'logistical city'. In the logistical city, everyday life is organized around logistics and the control and coordination of movement and distribution across space and scales in order to produce globalized 24/7 capitalism and neoliberal urban governance. He continues: 'The logistical city is elastic; its borders are flexible and determined by the ever-changing coordinates of supply chain capitalism' (Rossiter, 2016: xiii). It is a city produced through algorithmic, data-driven systems, platforms, infrastructures and devices, which coordinate, synchronize and rely on a material geography of data centres, control rooms, warehouses, transport and utility systems, and intermodal terminals: a city that operates in network time (Rossiter, 2016).

While logistical media seek to produce efficient, ordered flow and eurhythmic refrain, they are riddled with paradox. For example, technologies designed to manage and mitigate more effectively the temporal affordances of network time – such as temporal fragmentation, density and arbitrage – provide the means for further reproducing, embedding and deepening them. The solution to this paradox is further technical innovation, with a turn in recent years to machine learning and artificial intelligence to automate some processes and create system intelligence that can inform decisions and operations. 'Smart' solutions to time management are aimed at individuals through scheduling and productivity apps (see chapter 8), and at organizations, systems and infrastructures. As yet, however, there has been a relative paucity of research that has examined the temporalities – the algorhythms and time-spaces – of existing and emerging digital technologies, or how their temporal affordances are impacting on the time-space organization, operations, lived times and futures of mobility.

— 7 —

PLANNING AND DEVELOPMENT

Planning and development are time-dependent and ordered endeavours that are future-orientated, seeking to shape explicitly the present future of the form, structure, operations and sense of place of locales. This chapter examines the temporalities of planning and development, focusing on urbanization and how cities are designed, planned and built; slide into decline and obsolescence; and cycle into a new phase of regeneration and gentrification – and the role of digital technologies in these processes. Much of the analysis also relates to rural areas, though there are undoubtedly also differences, particularly with respect to the scales of investment in technical innovations and the imperatives of urbanization and capital in (re)development. The chapter is divided into three parts. In the first section, the timings and futuring work of the planning system are detailed, paying attention to the effects of GIS, expert systems, spatial decision support systems, 3D spatial media (e.g. virtual reality, BIM (Building Information Modelling) and CIM (City Information Modelling)), Web 2.0 technologies (e.g. social media) and consultation platforms on planning work. This is followed by a discussion of urban development and, in particular, fast urbanization, which seeks an accelerated development lifecycle, and speculative urbanization, wherein construction is driven by the anticipation of future returns, considering the role of planning technologies and digitally mediated financialization. The third section examines deceleration in growth and investment, dereliction and decay as places lose attraction, competitiveness and value, and transition into new socio-temporal relations, and the use of data-driven planning and investment tools to guide and track strategic planning decisions.

Planning

Planning is a technical, administrative and political set of processes and practices for envisioning and guiding the design and orderly development of land use, the built environment and infrastructure. It is an ideologically inflected method of claims-making 'to define the city of the present through strategic claims on its future' and to justify a future version of the city by determining development trajectories and environments to be created (Lauermann, 2016: 77). Planning is multi-scalar in its scope, relating to individual properties, large schemes, local and regional development plans, national spatial strategies and planning frameworks, and cross-border and supra-national plans. Moreover, it is multi-domain in orientation, relating to housing, commerce, infrastructure and environment, and involves a diverse set of stakeholders in the private, public, non-governmental and civic sectors. Given its focus on the production of space, planning is understood to be a spatial discipline, dominated by spatial thought (Laurian and Inch, 2019). Nonetheless, it is principally concerned with managing continual transformation of space through time, and the maintenance or creative destruction of land and property.

Framing the operations of planning are a series of nested planning and development legislation, ministerial guidelines, government policy, capital programmes and investment strategies, each of which has different timing patterns and process rhythms. The planning process is generally divided into three phases: the pre-assessment phase of plan making and consultation; the assessment of, and decision on, development proposals, and the appeals process; and the monitoring of development, enforcement of planning conditions, and legal redress. In other words, there is an explicit sequencing of planning actions, usually against a statutory set of timings (e.g., the timeframes within which processes and decisions have to be completed) (Raco et al., 2018). Synchronization and coordination of the planning system is essential for its smooth operation, though it is complex to achieve in practice, given the many stakeholders involved in development and the multiple temporalities that need coordinating, such as investment cycles and electoral terms (Laurian and Inch, 2019). Consequently, there is often temporal slippage in the planning and development process, with delays, alterations, abandonment and backtracking. Rather than operating in smooth, linear fashion, the sequencing of planning is punctuated, full of discontinuities, side loops, tangents and steps backward (Raco et al., 2018).

116

Given its focus on managing ongoing change, planning is inherently a future-orientated endeavour and its vocabulary is highly promissory in nature (Laurian and Inch, 2019). In part, strategic city plans are reacting to a sense that a place is 'out of sync' or 'ahead of or behind the curve' with respect to urban place-making, branding and economic competitiveness. As Abram and Weszkalnys (2011: 3) note, planning establishes a 'manifestation of what people think is possible and desirable, and what the future promises for the better'. Even when considering issues such as the preservation of built heritage and the conservation of ecosystems, the future is invoked since the objective is to ensure how these will be achieved for present and future generations. Conversely, decisions are also made as to what is obsolescent, where use value is insufficient to merit protection and a property can be demolished to make way for the new (Laurian and Inch, 2019).

In neoliberal and market critique, the planning process is characterized as being overly top-down, bureaucratic, cumbersome, inflexible, slow and out of sync with the pace of development, politics and finance (Raco et al., 2018; Brighenti and Karrholm, 2019). Planning controls, it is contended, add financial cost, restrict market flexibility, and prevent quick reaction to market opportunities, creating uncertainty and undermining competitiveness (Raco et al., 2018). Conversely, for communities, planning processes can seemingly move too quickly, running ahead of a community's ability to mobilize and produce counter-proposals. Streamlining and speeding up the planning process further 'privileges those who can operate within compressed time scales, narrows the range of participants in the policy process, and limits the scope for deliberation, consultation, and negotiation' (Jessop, 2015: 102). Being able to add delay and forestall the planning process can be used strategically by land owners and developers to value-engineer plans, allowing assets to appreciate in value, and negotiate more favourable outcomes over the longer term (Moore-Cherry and Bonnin, 2020). In other words, market actors desire a planning system that has flexibility in temporal control that they can dictate, able to move rapidly or slowly as required – not one wedded to fixed timescales (Raco et al., 2018).

Digital technologies have been promoted as a route to streamlining and speeding up all phases of planning, and to the planning system becoming more inclusive and participatory in its futuring and decision-making. The initial use of digital computing for planning was in the late 1950s for the computation of land-use and transportation models. By the late 1960s, a cybernetic approach was promoted in which models of urban systems were to be used to guide planning decisions in supposedly rational, instrumental ways, divorced from politics, clientelism and vested interests (Webber, 1965; Forrester, 1969). Initial applications performed poorly and were largely rejected by the planning community (Light, 2003). Planning, it was argued, was a complex human practice inflected by culture and politics that produced negotiated outcomes, rather than a rote, rule-based science (Lee, 1973). In the 1980s, there was wide-scale adoption of computer-aided design and GIS in architecture, engineering, construction and commercial planning enterprises, with GIS becoming a mainstream tool within public planning departments in the 1990s, along with administrative and database software for managing case files (Drummond and French, 2008). Expert systems and spatial decision support systems were introduced in the same era (Kim et al., 1990) – though their use has remained limited and specialized – and there were initial forays into the use of virtual reality for exploring potential new developments in 3D (Doyle et al., 1998).

By the late 1990s / early 2000s, PPGIS (public participation GIS) was promoted as a means to practise collaborative planning with local communities (Elwood and Ghose, 2001). From the mid-2000s, this participatory turn was extended to include Web 2.0 technologies such as social media, web-based surveys, wikis, blogs, spatial media and crowdsourcing (Shipley and Utz, 2012). In the same period, dashboard platforms, designed to monitor longitudinally the performance of the planning system and the implementation, progress and impact of developments by visualizing the time-series of key performance indicators, began to be adopted (Kitchin et al., 2015). In addition, BIM started to gain traction as a data infrastructure for managing the full build cycle of a development project. BIM combines a detailed 3D model of the physical and functional aspects of a planned environment with a database of components, scheduling data for construction and installation, and their overall cost, which can be updated dynamically and shared across multiple project partners enabling close collaboration through the alignment and tracking of complex workflows (Crotty, 2011).

In the 2010s, there was a turn towards 3D spatial media, such as 3D modelling packages, 3D GIS, virtual reality (VR), augmented reality (AR) and CIM as a means to display and model 3D information about present and planned environments (Kitchin et al., 2021). In their most sophisticated form, these 3D spatial media provide photo-realistic environments that can be viewed and navigated from multiple perspectives, providing a deeply immersive phenomenological experience (Gordon and Manosevitch, 2010). Rather than trying to assemble cognitively several 2D plans or artists' impressions, the entire spatial form of a development is rendered in a familiar perspective (Ball et al., 2007). Moreover, it is possible to run time-series analysis showing the environment over the course of a day and across seasons (e.g., to observe shadowing effects as the sun's position changes).

Some of these technologies promote a form of technocratic e-planning in which the formalism and elitism of professional planning are complemented with sophisticated, intelligent, technical tools and rich spatially and temporally referenced datasets (Brighenti and Karrholm, 2019). The technologies are used to manage and integrate a large volume of spatial and longitudinal data, and streamline a complex planning system that involves creating and assessing plans in relation to a wide variety of standards, regulations and policies, and cross-referencing to previous proposals and existing development – and to undertake this work in a timely fashion. The interactive nature of the technologies enables rapid, iterative and cost-effective prototyping, providing an efficient means for exploring multiple and competing scenarios and objectives and their merits (unachievable using physical architectural models that are slow and expensive to produce) (Portman et al., 2015). However, the software used requires specialist skills to operate and expert knowledge to interpret, and the models produced are typically created by private companies (property developers and their procured architects and planning consultants) to promote their agenda.

When networked in nature, these planning technologies foster collaboration between stakeholders, which can reduce operational costs and increase efficiency amongst distributed teams by enabling interaction and iterative workflows, minimizing potential errors or conflicts, building trust, reducing the time for review, and short-ening the project lifecycle (Gu et al., 2011; Portman et al., 2015). Consultation and feedback are invited through online forms or 'town hall' meetings, where the public are shown paper printouts, architec-tural models and well-produced promotional videos of how a place will look once developed. It is hoped that online 3D and CIM will enhance this consultation by enabling the public to view proposed developments in a form that facilitates understanding for those with relatively low levels of spatial literacy (Gordon and Manosevitch, 2010). Beyond feedback, the public play no active role in producing or assessing plans. Urban planning futures within a technocratic framing are then the visions of the capitalist interests of developers, the paternalistic views of trained civil servants, and the ambitions of politicians.

In contrast, some technologies are being used to challenge these technocratic practices and restricted futuring, seeking to make the planning process more open, inclusive and democratic (Brighenti and Karrholm, 2019). For example, PPGIS and planning-related Web 2.0 technologies are promoted as a means to utilize the 'wisdom of crowds' for the benefit of communities, to empower residents in designing their own neighbourhoods, and to involve the public in open debate, deliberation and decision-making regarding proposed plans (Brighenti and Karrholm, 2019). Planning agencies routinely make key information and materials available online concerning applications and decisions, and utilize specialized planning consultation apps to foster feedback on plans and dialogue between planners and members of the public (Trapenberg Frick, 2016). Routine planning agency meetings and public consultation meetings can be held as hybrid events, simultaneously taking place face-to-face and online, and the discussion can be recorded and placed online for viewing in perpetuity so that it is no longer a one-off event (Trapenberg Frick, 2016). Outside of official planning channels, every citizen with a smartphone or computer has the opportunity to become an active citizen – to create advocacy groups, to record events and share them online, to foment reaction on social media, and to organize gatherings that can sway public opinion on proposed plans and produce alternative ones (Mandarano et al., 2010). And to do so quickly, including live broadcasting a planning consultation meeting with a running commentary (Trapenberg Frick, 2016). The speed and time horizon of planning consultation, along with its spatial reach (anyone online can potentially respond), have, thus, been radically compressed.

Within the planning literature, there is a general sense that such tech-mediated openness, transparency, participation and attempts to create a citizen-centric planning system are a positive development. Democratic e-planning, as Brighenti and Karrholm (2019) term it, re-distributes power from capital and political/policy elites to citizens and serves a progressive agenda of fairness and equity in planning. However, citizens hold diverse political views, and planning platforms and social media have been utilized by conservatives and popularists to destabilize the planning field, reinforce property rights, delay and halt development, lock existing spatial relations in time, and promote exclusionary futures (Trapenberg Frick, 2013). Speed is often a tactic, with activists seeking efficiencies in communication and response – such as 'one-click actions' that simultaneously send a template protest email and sign a petition – and disrupting planning processes as they take place, performing 'repertoire switches' in which participants rapidly move from one approach to another to place professional staff on the back foot (Trapenberg Frick, 2016). Protests can be highly organized, including prepared counter-narratives, training materials on participation tactics, organized live streaming and crowd response, and sharing material after public meetings. While technology-supported planning processes might, in some cases, provide more meaningful citizen involvement in decisions that affect residents, it does not necessarily follow that their use fosters deliberation and inclusion or tackles social and structural divides (Trapenberg Frick, 2016).

Fast and speculative urbanization

Planning technologies and the planning system are vital aspects of fast and speculative urbanization, along with a range of financial technologies that perform the algorithmic calculations and practices that aid decision-making and the financing of modern development. Fast urbanization refers to the rapid growth of cities, with a marked acceleration and intensification of development, and to the processes that remove the barriers that hinder and limit development and speed up planning-to-construction progress (Datta, 2017). Across much of the Global South, new cities are being planned and built, and existing cities are expanding, at an unprecedented pace as millions of people make the transition from the countryside to urban living and population growth surges (United Nations, 2019). The pace of development is extraordinary, even when compared to the rapid urbanization of Europe and North America during modernity.

For example, in 1949, only 11% of China's population was urban based, growing to 23% by 1992. By 2005, 44% of people (572 million) were living in urban settings, and the rate is forecasted to reach 64% by 2025 (920 million), with 221 cities exceeding 1 million inhabitants (Boyle, 2015). In the decade 2000–10, the spatial footprint of China's cities grew by 50% (23,600 square kilometres) (Chien and Woodworth, 2018). Shenzhen, a city on the Pearl River Delta near to Hong Kong, grew from a population of 59,000 in 1980 to 11.9 million in 2018 (with several million additional illegal or temporary work migrants) (United Nations, 2019), an example of an 'instant city' (Murray, 2017). In Changsha (Hunan Province, population 10 million), a 57-storey skyscraper was completed in just 19 days (Chien and Woodworth, 2018). The drivers and forms of urbanization vary depending on local context and national political economies. In some cases, urbanization is informal, with large-scale unplanned developments accreting in and around existing cities. In other cases, the construction is planned but piecemeal, consisting of many small-to-medium sized developments, re-development of existing sites, in-filling, and expanding a city's spatial footprint, or is master-planned on a grand scale to create whole new districts or entirely new cities (Datta, 2017).

There is a clear emphasis by states and vested interests on speed – to increase the pace at which the development process unfolds. As Chien and Woodworth (2018) note, 'speed is neither a coincidental outcome nor the obvious by-product' of development, but is 'a contingent feature of … fast-city modes of expansion. Speed is by design.' In this sense, speed is both a description of the pace of urbanization and an active component – a deliberate achievement and driver through the setting of timing targets. Speed is of the essence to address a set of pressing societal issues, including population growth, migration, overcrowding, infrastructural overcapacity, social and environmental issues, and climate change (Cugurullo, 2017). Through a speedy response, cities can 'achieve their "potential" as sustainable cities of the future' (Datta, 2017: 3) and eliminate or bypass the inertia and inefficiencies of present 'congested, impoverished, chaotic, unpredictable and deteriorating' urban regimes (Kundu, 2017: 124). Fast urbanization is a means to fast-track, future-proof and leapfrog social and economic development (Datta, 2018).

While addressing pressing urban crises is used to justify extensive, new urban development, the primary aim of the corporations involved is the production of capital. Speed is a means of reducing the turnover time of profit, with development a means of speculating on future returns. Indeed, these city-making endeavours are ultimately massive, speculative real-estate initiatives involving billions of dollars of investment across a number of stakeholders (e.g. banks and financial institutions, private investors, property developers, construction companies, infrastructure providers, state agencies) (Goldman, 2011a, 2011b). Over the past thirty years, the financialization of property has become more complex and temporally compressed, facilitated by a global digital, financial system that enables instant calculations and transfers, and the creation of new forms of financial products and investments. Capital can be quickly cycled from one sector and scheme to another, 'strategically bouncing from housing to office space, from equity to debt, from shares in infrastructural goods to toxic debt', to the benefit of large investors who consolidate power and wealth, 'with the full support of state administrators, regulators and legislators' (Goldman and Narayan, 2021: 227). While the developments built are designed to be long-term, sustainable settlements, the time horizons of private equity firms, which are characterized by liquidity, mobility and arbitrage, are often short term, looking to flip and leverage investments swiftly (Goldman and Narayan, 2021).

Speculators can quickly switch finance capital, anticipating value and market consolidation, looking to buy up land and property assets (and, in so doing, inflating prices) and then sell them on, and seeking to offload liabilities and risks onto others (usually the state and small investors) (Goldman and Narayan, 2021). As Goldman (2011b: 231) notes, city-making projects 'are being designed so that large institutional investors can remain vested long enough to capture the initial speculative spike in value, and leave', requiring urban managers to create 'a string of deals along the life of a large-scale project so that different types of investors can gain differently'. The result can be turbulence in development progress and boom and bust cycles, clearly evident in the 2008 global financial crisis as property-backed investments failed, exposing and creating wide-scale liabilities across jurisdictions, while at the same time creating fresh investment opportunities on distressed assets (Goldman, 2011a). For initial investors, greenfield development is attractive because the entire project can be controlled without having to deal with legacy built environments, infrastructure, populations. The space produced is more likely to be privately owned and governed (Kundu, 2017), meaning new developments are more likely to 'operate under the umbrella of new regulatory regimes that either replace, manipulate, or completely silence conventional public administrative bodies', depending on political economic context (Murray, 2017: 32).

The state – drawing on a blend of neoliberalism and state authoritarianism, inflected with nationalism and postcolonial relations, depending on jurisdiction – plays a significant role in this entrepreneurial, speculative urbanism (Datta, 2017). States use their executive powers and resources to back initiatives, encouraging and supporting new city-making through their strategic plans, policies and investments (grants, loans, subventions, public–private partnerships, in-kind infrastructure, contributing publicly owned land); reforming public administration to increase efficiency by speeding up service delivery; removing red-tape, deregulating planning and building controls; devolving and marketizing some of the work that states traditionally perform, through service contracts and privatization; and creating exceptions and exemptions to rules or providing preferential treatments to privileged stakeholders (Brenner et al., 2010; Datta, 2017). Through policies and state work, they set favourable market and labour conditions, nurture appropriate human capital, subordinate social policies to economic policies, and quell local resistance to development (Shin, 2017). They accelerate these endeavours through fast and mobile policy (McCann and Ward, 2011) and worlding practices (Ong, 2011), importing ideas, policies and regulations, and mimicking the pathways to development and masterplans, employed elsewhere. Moreover, states are an active market player in seeding and nurturing innovation, co-investing in schemes, and creating place branding and competitiveness measures to entice private capital (Shin et al., 2020). In the latter case, it is no coincidence that a number of new city endeavours are framed as smart and/or eco-cities – utilizing high-tech, future-orientated, sustainability narratives to try to create urban growth machines and to market what are ultimately massive real-estate initiatives (Datta, 2015).

As noted, how fast urbanization is constituted varies by place. In authoritarian post-socialist states such as China, or constitutional monarchies such as Dubai and Qatar, power is highly centralized and mega-urbanization projects can progress relatively quickly. Indeed, in both China and the Middle East, massive urbanization through master-planned mega-developments has been under way for some time. In the Chinese case, Chien and Woodworth (2018: 723) refer to the development system as an 'urban speed machine' in which speed is 'an expression of political imperatives and city-based accumulation strategies'. They argue that the pace and scale of urban development are rooted in the expectations and targets placed on political and public-sector officials. These officials, vested with concentrated political power, are given specific economic goals to be achieved within a set timeframe (usually three to five years), with failure to reach and exceed targets foreclosing careers. Key actors have strong incentives to embrace entrepreneurial growth agendas, to drive spatial planning, and to 'accelerate urban expansion projects and select large-scale mega-projects with significant spatial and economic impact, rather than piecemeal incremental urbanization' (Chien and Woodworth, 2018: 730). Officials are supported by a sizeable commercial planning consultancy sector, which is primed to deliver full city-scale spatial plans, typically within fourteen weeks (Chien and Woodworth, 2018).

In the Middle East, fast urbanization is viewed as the route to a post-oil future and a means to attract inward investment and diversify the economy into services, tourism and consumption (Bagaeen, 2007). Dubai has grown rapidly over the past thirty years, with hundreds of billions worth of real estate being developed, much of it signature buildings and developments designed by well-known architects, accompanied by a sizeable growth in population (473,000 in 1990, 2.8 million in 2018; United Nations, 2019). In the neighbouring United Arab Emirates, Masdar, a supposedly eco-friendly smart city for 40,000, is under construction in the desert, with an initial projected cost of $18–22 billion. Initiated in 2006, government approval was granted in 2007, quickly followed by a design competition for a new sustainable city. A two-year deadline was set for completing the first part of the project, with a 2015 target for the whole complex (Cugurullo, 2017). Construction started in February 2008, with the first six buildings completed in October 2010. Development slowed given the global financial crash, and completion is now projected for 2030 (Goldenberg, 2016). Similar, autocratic-state-backed new eco/smart city initiatives include King Abdullah Economic City in Saudi Arabia, Qatar Knowledge City and Khabary Future City in Qatar, and Al-Irfan in Oman (Datta, 2017).

In contrast, the democratic political system and the legacy of colonial administration in India produces a somewhat different approach to fast urbanization, one in which residual inertia and barriers can slow state entrepreneurship and private investment (Datta, 2018). In India, fast urbanization is well illustrated by the government plan to create 100 smart cities (as extensions to, satellites of, or redevelopments of existing cities), selected through a national competitive process (Datta, 2018). These mega-developments are part of a nationalist development agenda to modernize Indian cities, with opposition to their construction cast as being anti-Indian (Datta, 2015). Fast urbanization is seen as the antidote to the 'corruption, bureaucracy, inertia, nepotism and general unaccountability of those in power' – a means to achieve 'development, modernity and progress' and a postcolonial urbanism that transcends its colonial legacy, which has been stymied by 'an illegible state and "anti-development" activists working outside the limits of law' (Shaban and Datta, 2017: 205). Development has not proceeded as intended, however, for a number of reasons, including the embeddedness of state bureaucracy, opposition to the proposals, contestation over land rights, and turbulence in speculator investment (Datta, 2018, 2019).

In her extensive analysis, Ayona Datta (2019, 2020) demonstrates that multiple temporalities are at play in these initiatives. These include a complex dialectic relationship between the past and present in imagining and realizing postcolonial futures in which postcolonial and precolonial mythical time (with astrological, religious and mythological registers) are used in conjunction with network time to promote a nationalist urban agenda (Datta, 2019). She notes that, despite claims to speed, efficiency and rationality, the postcolonial modernity of India's fast urbanism is marked by an ambiguity between rational and mythological time, between linear and cyclical notions of progress and development, and between technocratic and mythological nationhood. In a case study of Shimla, a Himalayan city which was the former summer capital for the British administration, she contrasts the timescape of an envisaged smart city with that of a working-class area (built on the waste from the development of the colonial city under British rule), the latter of which is the designated site for smart redevelopment (Datta, 2021; see table 7.1). With respect to the lived time of residents in Delhi, she finds a marked contrast between the ordered time of the supposedly safe, smart city and the gendered time experienced by young women trying to navigate urban space (Datta, 2020).

Table 7.1 The timescapes of a smart and subaltern city

Smart city	Subaltern city
Network time, real-time	Clock time, cyclical time
National, global time	Local time, natural time
Speed, linear time	Delay, wasted time, contoured time
Instantaneous	Generational
Connected, time-space distanciation	Embedded, grounded
Smartness	Broken, disconnected, absent
Modern, new	Informal, legacy
Fast urbanism	Slow urbanism, slow violence, slow justice
Future: projected, efficient	Future: demolition, regeneration
Past is a resource	Past is a hindrance
Upper class and emerging middle class	Poor; class, caste, race, gendered time
Ordered, technocratic, predictive, control	Unruly, bureaucratic, discipline
Legitimate	Illegitimate

Source: created by the author; based on Datta (2021).

While the promoters of fast urbanization contend that it is required to create sustainable urban futures, it is clear that there are a number of troubling issues with the notion itself and how it is practised. Fast urbanization is both a political, state developmental project designed to fulfil state desires regarding urban and economic growth, and a speculative, capitalist-driven enterprise designed to leverage the future to accumulate profit in the present and in the short-to-long term. Fast urbanization is thus ideologically predisposed to serve a state's development agenda and the interests of political parties, politicians and their stakeholders and constituents, and the capital interests of finance and property investors. Profits largely accrue to a narrow set of private interests, who seek to exploit their power across the development cycle, from short-changing or dispossessing the owners of land (usually family-owned farmland or commons) (Datta, 2015; Shaban and Datta, 2017) through to selling units at marked-up prices and binding the state into long-term leasing arrangements and providing associated infrastructure (Shin, 2017). At the same time, financial institutions seek to offload risks and liabilities onto those who build, manage and occupy new settlements (Goldman and Narayan, 2021). In so doing, speculative endeavours generate high levels of indebtedness, orientate the state mind-set and operations around servicing debt, make it reliant on capital markets for finance, and create vulnerabilities to financial shock (Goldman and Narayan, 2021). Moreover, urban governance is shifted to private control, and urban citizenship towards neoliberal notions of choice and cultural capital (Herbert and Murray, 2015; Kitchin et al., 2019).

The target market of the new settlements are usually middle-to-upper-class populations who have the purchasing power to invest, so that the settlement becomes an elite enclave, a gated community at scale. Poorer people are left in the existing 'failed urbanism' or building their own informal city on the edges – or, in the case of landowners, being evicted and displaced (Watson, 2014; Shin, 2017). In addition, the tax base and spending power of those moving to the new enclaves is lost from the existing city, while state spending on large-scale infrastructure is skewed to new developments and away from meeting existing basic service and housing needs (Watson, 2014). Speculation, then, comes with a price, in terms of reproducing and deepening social inequalities, fundamentally failing to deal with issues such as congestion, overcrowding and overburdened services for the majority (Shin et al., 2020). Moreover, speed adds to that price, with quick-fix urbanization underpinned by superficial and partial urban policies that fail to address the problems they purport to tackle

(Cugurullo, 2017). Mega-developments consume valuable farmland and wildlife habitats and massive amounts of natural resources in their construction, and promote unsustainable, consumption-driven lifestyles (Chien and Woodworth, 2018). The claims to sustainability are seemingly little more than a discursive move to satisfy economic and political ambitions, with the speed of the development process providing little opportunity for public debate or alternative visions to be forwarded (Shaban and Datta, 2017).

Deceleration and shrinking cities

In contrast to fast urbanization, there are places where the pace of urbanization and urban processes have slowed to the point where the economy and population are declining and the urban footprint is shrinking. Rather than being orientated around speed and affirmative futures, these cities are haunted by their past and have a different set of temporalities, often characterized by sedateness, breakdown, dereliction, decay, ruin, maintenance and repair, degrowth and regeneration (Edensor, 2005; Erickson and Mazmanian, 2017). This temporal-spatial shift in the pace, tempo and rhythms of urban processes, and the present fortunes and future prospects and imaginaries of cities, is not new or a rare phenomenon. As Murray (2021: 348) notes, 'the temporalities of urban development ... [are] not like an uninterrupted line moving inexorably along a linear pathway. Real-estate capitalism works through recurrent cycles of feverish building followed by momentary bouts of stagnation and stasis.' Cities have always lost or gained population because of economic conditions, immigration, natural disasters or war. In the present era, a slowing down of economic performance and depopulation are common in post-industrial and post-socialist cities.

In the United States, 'rust-belt' cities, such as Detroit, Cleveland and Buffalo, have all experienced significant economic decline, population loss, and dereliction and demolition of building stock, as well as increasing social and racial segregation and polarization as wealthier white populations moved to the suburbs and other cities (Dilworth and Gardner, 2019). For example, 161,000 buildings (containing hundreds of thousands of residential units) were demolished in Detroit between 1970 and 2000 (Byles, 2005), and in the first decade of the twenty-first century it lost over 25 per cent of its population (Hollander and Németh, 2011). In Europe, 54 per cent of all urban regions, with a concentration in eastern and southern

Europe, had declining populations in the same period (Pallagst and Wiechmann, 2012). Even before the global economic crisis of 2008, it was estimated that one quarter of all cities internationally with populations of over 100,000 were in decline (Oswalt et al., 2006).

Depopulation impacts every domain of urban and regional development, including municipal budgets, infrastructure and amenities, housing market and mobility, labour market and employment, residential composition, and social inclusion and cohesion. A contracting population results in a growing imbalance between the supply and demand for housing and infrastructure (particularly social infrastructure such as schools and policing), together with a reduced demand for commercial services. As a result, these services become underutilized and poorly maintained, and are often abandoned or withdrawn (Haase et al., 2012). Local living conditions and quality of life deteriorate and unemployment rises, resulting in the emergence of vacant land and derelict buildings. The changing demographic profile – particularly the out-migration of the middle-class and younger, well-educated people, and a rise in the proportion of elderly people – perpetuates a cycle of abandonment and decline. This in turn places greater pressure on local authority budgets, which are simultaneously burdened with low fiscal income and high social expenditure (Haase et al., 2012). In other words, the city decelerates. This does not mean that capital ceases to seek ways to extract profit – indeed, abandonment and neglect provide opportunities for predatory entrepreneurs 'to extract value from the dead and dying remains of the built environment' through 'extractive economies of plunder and pillage' (Murray, 2021: 348). Decisions concerning the operation and targets of predatory tactics by private enterprise, and where public administrations should strategically (dis)invest, are increasingly guided and made algorithmically (Safransky, 2020). Indeed, data-driven planning and investment tools are becoming an important means of guiding and tracking strategic-planning, and social and economic, policies adopted by municipalities.

For some, a gradual pathway back to a viable, growing economy is through the temporary use of space through pop-up companies, community enterprises and living labs, putting buildings and open spaces back to productive work (Madanipour, 2017). Others see a re-injection of speed and fresh waves of speculation through regeneration schemes as a way to reverse decline. Large-scale redevelopment either refits existing building stock for long-term residential and commercial use, or demolishes stock to replace it with new construction, including infrastructure upgrades. Commentators caution, however, that growth-orientated solutions do not always lead to success and often amplify the adverse consequences of decline, or the regeneration and gentrification of locales displaces those already living there (Pallagst et al., 2009). Instead, they advocate for 'smart shrinkage', a planned approach designed to enhance quality of life that is freer of time stresses (Pallagst and Wiechmann, 2012). The focus is on stabilization and consolidation, redeveloping and recycling derelict land and buildings (including reverting to farmland), cost-efficient stock management, and improving the quality of remaining buildings and infrastructure. One approach to smart shrinkage is to embrace the slow urbanist agenda, examined in chapter 10.

Conclusion

Futuring, speed and timing are vital components of planning and urban development. A range of networked, digital technologies are employed within the planning process by state and private actors to enhance the design of future environments, make the planning system more inclusive and participatory, and streamline and compress the practices of planning. The private sector utilizes planning and financial technologies to plan, speculate on and market the future. The diverse deployment of these technologies contributes to the performance of fast and speculative urbanization, which seeks to optimize and make more efficient public administration, planning, service delivery, policy formation and infrastructure provision, and to facilitate rapid urban transitions and quick turnover of capital through the timely development of large-scale settlements. They are also used to manage deceleration in an urban growth machine, the processes of decline and dereliction, and attempts to extract capital from distressed assets and to rejuvenate and regenerate places.

This chapter has examined these diverse temporalities, charting the timescapes of planning and development in a range of geographic contexts. It is clear that the political economies and institutional regimes of different jurisdictions have a marked effect on the nature of fast urbanism and shrinking cities and their temporalities, inflected by the workings of global capitalism, autocratic politics, colonial legacies, national and local governance and legal frameworks, and coalitions of public administration and private stakeholders. While a number of scholars have undertaken useful research concerning the relationship between time, planning and urban development, it is fair to say that the predominant approach to understanding the use of digital technologies in planning and urban development has prioritized attention on the production of space. There is, therefore, a need for further work to: examine the production of time in the creation and decline of cities; to unpack the relationship between time, space, and planning, construction and financial technologies; to investigate the temporalities of fast and shrinking urbanization on the ground, through detailed, empirical case studies; and to scope out alternative temporalities that are not necessarily organized around the values and interests of corporations and states.

— 8 —

WORK AND LABOUR

The organization of the economy, the structuring, interconnections and operations of businesses, and the practices and experiences of labour are thoroughly imbricated with a multiplicity of temporalities. As discussed in chapter 2, the rise of modernity, capitalism, colonialism and globalization were aided significantly by the adoption of chronotechnologies that structured and disciplined labour, new workplace technologies that increased efficiencies and productivity in the production and circulation of goods and services, and transportation and communication technologies that created radical time-space convergence and distanciation. This chapter examines how the development and adoption of digital devices, systems, platforms and infrastructures is producing new temporal relations that are restructuring the timescapes of work and labour. It starts with a discussion of the time-space organization of business globally and locally, and the effects of digitally mediated time-space distanciation, labour offshoring, and temporal arbitrage. Next, it considers the changing nature of labour and how the digital is being used to manage, reconfigure and replace labour through the gig economy and automation. The final two sections examine the use of digital time management tools and digitally mediated workplace surveillance.

The time-space configuration of global labour

The introduction of networked digital technologies has produced a new wave of time-space compression that has had a profound effect on the configuration of the economy and labour locally and globally. Instantaneous communication, the ability to transfer and process

132

large amounts of information easily, oversee work, and monitor and control systems and infrastructures in real-time from a distance have facilitated radical time-space distanciation and fuelled the growth of service and consumption economies. The rise of a global informational economy was evident in the 1980s, enabled by a significant expansion of telecommunications and the nascent Internet, leading to a reconfiguration of the time-space organization of businesses and city-region restructuring (Graham and Marvin, 1996). Companies started to take advantage of instant communication to disperse parts of their operations to cheaper locations in the suburbs, elsewhere in the region or overseas, to take advantage of cheaper site and labour costs, and to restructure their logistics operations to make them more efficient (see chapter 6). Concurrently, they also concentrated some work into sites of command-and-control, creating agglomeration of services where co-location continued to produce spill-over effects. These processes became more widespread in the 1990s as the digital systems began to pervade the workplace and the Internet grew exponentially (Castells, 1996; Graham and Marvin, 2001). Companies took advantage of enhanced telecommunications and new information systems to extend their businesses internationally, entering new markets, creating subsidiaries and taking over local enterprises (Dicken, 2007). Further digitization of economic systems, the rollout of the Internet of things and cloud computing, the creation of new platform economies, the automation of work practices, and the rise of born-digital products and labour have opened up more and more aspects of the economy to time-space convergence and distanciation (Moriset, 2019).

Key components of the time-space restructuring of business operations are the exploitation and reinforcement of spatial divisions of labour enabled by the temporalities of network time. The spatial division of labour refers to the distribution of different stages of economic activity across space, with places specializing in particular aspects of work (Massey, 1984). For example, command-and-control centres of transnational corporations cluster in global cities, research and development activities locate in regions of highly skilled labour, mid-level service operations operate as back-offices sited in the suburbs of global cities or in regional cities in the Global North where skilled labour is cheaper and more readily available, while low-skill services and manufacturing take place in low-wage regions in the Global South (Dicken, 2007). These spatial divisions of labour exploit instant communication, time-space distanciation, and temporal arbitrage produced by ICTs, along with neoliberal and structural reforms of

133

the global economy facilitated through International Monetary Fund and World Bank initiatives (Shapiro, 2020). This is especially evident in the international offshoring of labour.

For example, by relocating some of their service operations to India, companies in Europe and North America reduce their wage bill, but do not suffer a loss in efficiency or productivity despite staff being located in a different time zone. Instead, companies use three forms of temporal arbitrage to save costs and maximize profit (Nadeem, 2009). First, they can exploit time zone differences to create a 24-hour global business cycle, with work passing between offices at the end of a local business day. Second, labour can be organized at the local site to align temporally with the main business hours of Europe and North America, with workers labouring throughout the night. Third, weaker laws concerning working hours and conditions can be exploited to employ people for longer hours, at a higher tempo and pace (e.g., call centre workers in the US typically have 45–60 seconds between calls, whereas the expectation is 5–10 seconds in India) (Nadeem, 2009). In all three cases, the labour of workers is temporally subordinate, synchronized and structured for the benefit of bosses, colleagues and customers located elsewhere. Cities such as Bangalore have capitalized on this temporal arbitrage to drive local economic development, becoming a site of fast urbanism as it expands rapidly (see chapter 7), though often at the cost of the well-being of workers who labour at unsocial hours (Nadeem, 2009). The timescapes of work – its timing, tempo, temporal practices and time patterns – are reconfigured with respect to network time and global arbitrage arrangements (Ladner, 2009). As such, rather than instant communication leading to the 'death of distance' (spatial relations being annihilated by time), as some commentators had pronounced (Cairncross, 1997), time-space relations have continued to be important to the organization of work and labour. Instead of networked digital technologies producing an even playing field of economic opportunities, they have reinforced patterns of uneven development.

Platforms, gig work and precarity

In the latter part of the twentieth century, widespread changes in the global capitalist economy, accompanied by a shift in political economy towards neoliberalism, undermined secure labour contracts and welfare state policy in the Global North. The labour compact between companies, unions and states, backed up by Keynesian economic policies and welfare state programmes that operated in the Fordist era, slowly crumbled under the pressure of globalization, deindustrialization, financialization and structural adjustment and austerity policies (Kasmir, 2018). The nature of work moved from stable, full-time jobs undertaken during a standard work schedule (Monday–Friday, 9 a.m. – 5 p.m.) towards a more flexible labour regime, in which individuals no longer expect to work long-term for an employer or stay within a single sector over their career. Instead, labour has become increasingly hired on short-term and part-time contracts, directly or through agencies and independent contracting, introducing wide-scale labour precarity in the working-age population (Hassan, 2009). More and more work has extended outside of standard hours and into the weekend, and become more flexible and unpredictable in timing, reacting to circumstance (O'Carroll, 2015). For example, according to the European Working Conditions Survey, in 2015, 44% of workers did not work the same hours every day, 37% did not work the same hours every week, and 39% did not have fixed starting and finishing times (Eurofound, 2017). 27% of employees reported being asked to occasionally come into work at short notice, with a further 9% on-call several times a month, and 3% several times a week.

Digital technologies have been at the forefront of unpredictable and precarious employment by facilitating labour scheduling at short notice and the efficient management of a fluid, churning labour pool, and through the development of platforms that enable a gig economy characterized by flexible labour. A platform is a socio-technical arrangement in which a hosting architecture supports the work of many individuals and businesses, facilitating the buying, selling and sharing of goods and services, and supporting social activity (Kenney and Zysman, 2016; Codagnone et al., 2019). Platforms act as digital enclosures, drawing together many entities into a shared ecosystem that produces multiplier effects and scales of economy, improves productivity and reach, reduces costs, and creates new markets (Andrejevic, 2009). A wide variety of platforms now exists, supporting all kinds of commercial activities. For example, Airbnb connects those looking for accommodation with potential hosts; Amazon sells products through its own store, which also acts as a shopfront for thousands of other businesses; Apple, Google and Microsoft provide common technology frameworks for others to build their own products, and a platform to host the developed apps; Facebook provides a means to interact with friends, but also a channel through which businesses can interact with and target customers. In many cases, the platform does not own the means of production, but generates value by providing a conduit for connection and transactions (Moazed, 2016). A significant aspect of these connections and transactions is the contracting of labour on a gig basis – that is, hiring and paying per job or task. Platform enterprises such as Uber and Deliveroo do not directly employ drivers to taxi passengers or cyclists to deliver food, but rather hire contractors who choose to perform the gigs on the terms and conditions offered through the platforms, which include clauses concerning timeliness and standard of service (Shapiro, 2020). Platforms change how companies are formed and grow, and disrupt how labour is performed and organized.

The best-known platform companies have transitioned from start-ups with a handful of employees to multi-billion-dollar, global enterprises in very short timespans (less than a decade in many cases). They could do so because of their use of cloud technologies, outsourced labour, regulatory arbitrage and injections of vast amounts of venture capital (Shapiro, 2020). Companies have used technical and infrastructural solutions that can be scaled quickly and accessed by anyone with an internet connection. Since they were hosting existing businesses or outsourcing labour to independent contractors, they did not need to on-board new employees or cover associated costs (such as minimum wage, overtime, health insurance, social security payments, redundancy) or invest in property as they entered new markets, reducing overheads and creating agility (Shapiro, 2020). Similarly, by outsourcing infrastructure, they reduced sunk investments, labour overheads and risk, and retained the agility to downscale or move suppliers if needed. Venture capital investments and saved overheads meant they could undercut traditional rivals and carry losses for a number of years while they built market share. They could also steal trade from traditional businesses by shifting customer perceptions regarding the timeliness and convenience of services (i.e., orders at the click of the button, and products arriving speedily), and ensure quality and oversight by outsourcing performance controls to reviews and ratings by customers (Shapiro, 2020). At the same time, they worked to establish markets quickly ahead of regulation, and then staunchly sought to block the introduction of new rules and laws (Woodcock and Graham, 2019). Speed in scaling, following Facebook's slogan of 'Move fast and break things' (Benjamin, 2019), has thus been vital to the success of platforms.

Codagnone et al. (2019) identify two types of new labour relations created by platforms and the gig economy: online labour markets, and mobile labour markets. Rather than being tied to particular employers located in specific places, such as offices or factories, and undertaking work at set hours, online labour markets enable workers to perform digital labour at a place and time of their choosing since there is no need for proximity between employers, workers and clients. Work consists of undertaking specific tasks for a fee, with two main kinds of task: performing numerous micro-tasks requiring low-to-middle-level skills (e.g. Amazon's Mechanical Turk), or undertaking an entire project requiring middle-to-high-level skills (e.g. Upwork) (Codagnone et al., 2019). Mobile labour market workers also do not need a fixed site and times to work. They do, however, need to be locally present to perform the tasks mediated by digital platforms – for example, undertaking low-skilled manual work and errands such as delivering food or assembling furniture (e.g., Deliveroo and TaskRabbit), or enacting higher-level tasks such as in-person consulting services and personal tutoring (e.g., Expert360 and TakeLessons) (Codagnone et al., 2019). In both online and mobile labour markets, the conditions of work have changed, with workers treated as independent, self-employed contractors who rely on their own resources to fulfil jobs (such as providing the computer, bike, car and fuel required, as well as space such as a home or rented office), and compete with each other for gigs that might have a variable fee depending on conditions (rising when demand is high, and falling when low) (Woodcock and Graham, 2019; Shapiro, 2020). In so doing, platforms separate employment from employers, deregulate the job market, and jettison the notion of baseline income and benefits (Gregg, 2018).

The gig economy alters the time-spaces of work. It disconnects workers from specific sites and timetables. In the case of online labour markets, it creates significant time-space compression, enabling workers from across the globe to compete for gigs. Mobile labour markets allow workers to supplement their income by undertaking piecemeal gigs outside of their usual working hours (Graham and Anwar, 2019). Gig work is often promoted on the basis that it provides flexibility and autonomy to set one's schedule (Chen and Sun, 2020). However, because the work is piecemeal and often time-dependent, workers are usually under temporal pressure to accumulate and complete gigs to make a living wage. This pressure is heightened by platform expectations concerning the pace of work and meeting deadlines, enforced through time management surveillance, and workers being pitted against each other to secure gigs, particularly when there is an oversupply of labour (Woodcock and Graham, 2019). This competition produces irregular working hours with little pattern to them, frenetically performed labour, a fluctuating flow of income, downward pressure on labour costs, and a reduced ability for workers to bargain for better conditions (Correll et al., 2014; Graham and Anwar, 2019). The result is precarious labour that lacks fulfilment, has few additional benefits (e.g. no holiday or sick pay, no pension, no access to skill development), has poor regulatory protections and few employment rights (Woodcock and Graham, 2019; Shapiro, 2020). As Lorey (2015: 21) notes, precarity means constantly 'living with the unforeseeable, with contingency'. Rather than flexibility and autonomy, lost in the agreement to work gigs 'is any hope that workers *can* control time', given that the approach to work is 'improvised and ad hoc, forever arriving "just-in-time"' (Gregg, 2018: 129), and is structured and synchronized around the temporal expectations of those offering the gig (Sharma, 2017). As such, gig workers perform temporal arbitrage, their time subordinate and calibrated to the temporal and capital imperatives of others (Sharma, 2014; Chen and Sun, 2020).

Beyond the altered timings of labour, flexible and on-demand work has knock-on consequences for other temporal aspects of everyday life. It reduces the capacity to synchronize times of work with family and friends, and, in the case of online work, blurs the boundary between home and work (Southerton, 2020). Synchronization issues are a particular issue for single-parent households, where there is a need to source childcare, and dual-income households where aligning work shifts and home care can be a challenge. In the latter case, a number of arrangements can be adopted to try to cope with desynchronization, such as sandwich arrangements, in which one person starts later and finishes earlier than the other; overlapping shifts, in which one person starts later and finishes later than the other; and consecutive shifts, in which one person starts work after the other has finished (Fagan, 2001, cited in Southerton, 2020). The latter two tactics can be used strategically to lessen the need for childcare and share other domestic duties, but they also mean that partners have less time together. Temporal pressures of work and dual-income arrangements have also led to the commodification of what traditionally were unpaid domestic tasks, such as purchasing childcare, cleaning and home maintenance services from the market. Here, 'households exchange money for time in order to facilitate more rewarding activities for personal relationships' and to cope with labour demands (Southerton, 2020: 59).

It is clear that the pressures that arise around these issues dispro-portionately affect lower-status groups – who are more likely to be working unsociable shifts and have less autonomy than higher-status groups – and women. Working women are more likely to be balancing workplace demands with domestic and caring work; they do more combined paid and unpaid labour than men and non-working mothers (Wajcman, 2015). Single mothers in particular have little discretionary time, and what they do have often involves their children, and women in dual-income households are more likely than men to be juggling and synchronizing domestic and work roles. For example, while both men and women experience work–family spillover (dealing with work while at home), women are more likely to experience family–work spillover (dealing with family issues while at work) (Wajcman, 2015).

Automation, autonomous systems and smart work

Since the 1980s, the technologies used to undertake work have undergone profound changes. Equipment used in manufacturing up until this point was expensive and rigid in specialization. It was designed for long-term, limited use, and therefore had little adaptability to accommodate shifting consumer preferences or react to competition. The shift to digitally mediated equipment enabled flexibility and diversification in production because machines became programmable, their configuration and use malleable, rather than hard-cast into the design (Shapiro, 2020). Moreover, digital mediation enabled assembly line work to become: semi-automated or automated through the use of programmable robotic machines, thus saving labour costs; and 'informated' (Zuboff, 1988, cited in Shapiro, 2020), producing a rich flow of data that could be used to evaluate and optimize work management flow and administration, increasing efficiency and productivity. These technical advances enabled organizational change, making workflow leaner and more agile, and allowing offshoring and outsourcing across sites, driving companies to compete not just on the products themselves but also on the efficiencies of global production and distribution (Rossiter, 2016; Shapiro, 2020). These trends have continued, gathered pace and moved beyond manufacturing operations to encompass all aspects of business, with significant consequences for labour.

Current projections are for much more extensive automation of commercial activities in the future. Manyika et al. (2017), for example, report that about 50 per cent of current work activities can be automated using existing technologies, and predict that up to a third of jobs in some sectors could be displaced by 2030. The joining up of networked information systems with robotic and digitally mediated machines is enabling a reconfiguring of global value chains, and introducing what has been termed Industry 4.0 (Rojko, 2017) or cyber-manufacturing (Lee et al., 2016). Industry 4.0 integrates business and manufacturing processes across an organization, combining manufacturing execution systems with enterprise resource planning systems to produce products within an adaptive and self-organizing system that learns from its execution (Rojko, 2017). Cyber-manufacturing involves using big data and analytics to monitor and predict operations in order to achieve better performance and processes and create a 'smart factory' (Lee et al., 2016). In both cases, the workplace becomes more data-driven and controlled by technologies that have varying degrees of autonomy to make operational decisions about production, with many systems working as human-on- or human-off-the-loop enterprises (see chapter 5).

Automation is now also becoming more common in service sectors. In retail, some elements of the shopping have become semi-automated, such as the use of self-service checkouts, and the work of staff is guided by algorithmic systems that select pick and delivery routes (Evans and Kitchin, 2018). Online shopping makes extensive use of recommender systems that nudge browsers into buyers, using machine learning algorithms to profile and micro-target customers based on their past consumption and the purchasing patterns of others. In law, legal tech is increasingly automating tasks related to contract review, due diligence, discovery, case research, billing and intellectual property infringements (Hartung et al., 2018). The same pattern of automation is occurring in medicine, pharmacy, finance, marketing, administration, and other sectors that have high degrees of formalized knowledge and rote practices (Steiner, 2012). The impact varies across sector, but involves a mix of labour substitution (machines replacing people or significantly augmenting their work) and performance and productivity gains through increased efficiency (Manyika et al., 2017).

The automation of work has several temporal effects on the workplace and work. Working with machines means working in conjunction with their temporalities. The labour of operators and other staff becomes organized around the rhythms and timings of automated work. The move to machine time, where processes are performed at a significantly faster pace than human labour, and the removal of operators and human oversight, which can slow down production, increase efficiency and productivity. Patterns of work, such as the timing of work tasks and work timetables, become disrupted. So does the potential for lifelong work within a company or sector, with a percentage of the workforce needing to retrain and adopt lifelong learning to remain employable (Acemoglu and Restrepo, 2020). Automation and intelligent systems that are responsive to changing conditions anticipate and reduce risk and uncertainty by providing rule-based, modelled, standardized responses (Pfeiffer, 2017). Such standardization also enables global replication of production and service structures that are 'less dependent on local oriented and situation-specific knowledge' and 'free from local connections, regional expertise and labour market specific configurations'; reduce local technical labour requirements; and enable more interoperable collaboration with partners (Pfeiffer, 2017: 116). Identical facilities worldwide create efficiencies, and ideas for improvements can be implemented swiftly (in the case of Intel, enhancements proven effective in one plant have to be implemented in others within a week) (Pfeiffer, 2017). As noted in chapter 6, the use of ERP and SCM systems alter the temporalities of logistics, enabling just-in-time operations. The use of advanced robotics also shifts the turnover time for factory refitting, with machines quickly becoming obsolete as technologies evolve and improve, and to meet the need to stay ahead of the curve to remain competitive. For example, the multi-million-dollar chip-making machines in an Intel fabrication plant are replaced every 18–24 months to ensure rollout of the last-generation chips and maintain market share.

Time management

The ordering and control of working time was a key innovation in modernity and capitalism. Work was no longer defined by the length of sunlight or by how long a task took, but by working hours. Holiday entitlements, five-day weeks and the age of retirement became institutionalized (Parkes and Thrift, 1980). An array of chronotechnologies were introduced to monitor and enforce this new temporal regime, including bells and horns to denote the start and end of shifts, shift-timetables, attendance registers, clocking in-and-out machines, public clocks and personal watches, and diaries and calendars (West-Pavlov, 2013). Workers were expected to exercise time management inside and outside the workplace. Inside, workers were to labour at an appropriate pace to meet targets and deadlines, and to schedule their activities to ensure coordination with fellow employees. Outside, they were to coordinate the sequencing and synchronization of their non-work activities to facilitate the temporal expectations of work, organizing their lives around timetabled working hours and necessary overtime (Southerton, 2020). Such expectations and norms concerning working times, work rate and productivity generated a sense of temporal discipline which became a part of a worker's subjectivity (West-Pavlov, 2013). Such expectations are still well entrenched, with the use of digital technologies extending and complicating matters.

To aid individuals in managing the time pressures and stresses of today's workplaces and labour practices, a raft of digitally mediated time management solutions, including shared calendars, productivity apps (e.g. task managers, note takers/organizers, brainstorm and time manager apps) and digital assistants have been developed. Time management apps 'help individuals arrange schedules, workloads and activities'; they help to manage the 'turbulence of day-to-day administrivia', and to cope with precarity, improvisation, unstable and ever-shifting scheduling, and the frantic pace and fragmentation of everyday life, while maintaining – or, indeed, increasing – efficiency and productivity (Gregg, 2018: 54). In so doing, they 'cut through competing demands for attention to help workers focus, freeing up time and energy for the most demanding and rewarding work' (Gregg, 2018: 85). They achieve this by adding new functionality to diaries and calendars and devolving and distributing to individuals some aspects of temporal control that might previously have been centralized within households or workplaces.

Time management apps typically merge personal diaries with business enterprise calendars (Wajcman, 2018). They are interactive and dynamic, and automatically link together different applications, such as calendars and diaries with email clients, contact lists, activity, task and goal managers, and social scheduling and event sites. By utilizing cloud services, they can be synchronized across multiple devices and platforms and be shared with contacts, who can view and update schedules and tasks, import events into their own diaries, and invite others to events in a calendar, enabling group coordination and logistical control of labour (Gregg, 2018; Wajcman, 2018). Updating can occur at any time and need not involve formal communication or negotiation, which social/group scheduling used to require. These apps have become a means to calibrate and value time, and to mediate and navigate choices about the allocation of time and timing (Wajcman, 2018). More recently, AI is being used to create 'intelligent' time management apps that seek to create predictive scheduling and smart planning. Timeful, for example, is a project that uses machine learning to 'nudge' people into making better decisions concerning time management (e.g. automatically scheduling optimal times to achieve goals), employing ideas from behavioural science (Wajcman, 2018).

These time management apps typically reflect an economic-utilitarian philosophy of time that treats it as a quantitative resource to be managed and exploited, and obscures the temporal politics the apps promote (Wajcman, 2018, 2019). Through continually tracking, managing and nudging activities, they provide a means to train users with respect to their codifying practices, and to continually reinforce these through repetitive use (Gregg, 2018). These codifying practices ignore the invisible work of affective labour, housework, caring and voluntary activities, and also the temporal rhythms and patterns marked by gender, age, race, ethnicity and other social differences (Wajcman, 2018). Indeed, the apps 'fuel a lifestyle that does not differentiate among work, home, and leisure space' (Gregg, 2018: 86), valorizing busyness, productivity and overachievement and vilifying time-wasting, and further eroding 'quality time' (Wajcman, 2019). The underlying logic is that all time should be colonized, ordered, controlled and put to productive use (Wajcman, 2019). As such, in seeking to assist and nudge their users, algorithmic approaches to time materialize 'a moral enterprise of time optimization' that mirrors that of the app developers – largely white, Silicon Valley tech bros (Wajcman, 2018: 1276). Paradoxically, the apps can aggravate the temporal problem that they seek to mitigate. Rather than freeing up time, they fill and coordinate time, which can create time scarcity and a sense of being harried, and they provide the means for further accelerating, fragmenting, desynchronizing, and increasing temporal density (Rosa, 2017). Of course, the solution to this aggravation is further technical innovation, with the next step likely to be fully fledged virtual personal assistants driven by artificial intelligence (Wajcman, 2018), which will likely only exacerbate the problem.

Importantly, as Sharma (2014: 44) notes, these apps and other temporal devices structure and normalize a conception of time where: 'time management is the individual's responsibility; one must work harder to stay in time; and being tired is a slow person's excuse for being unproductive'. Actively managing temporality becomes a means of self-improvement and remaining a useful worker. In other words, these apps act as technologies of the self (Foucault, 1978), in which the regime of governmentality – busyness, timeliness, over-achievement, being a workaholic – becomes internalized and self-practised, with individuals adjusting behaviour to meet and exceed expectations, and projecting such expectations onto others (see chapter 5). Mobile media, in particular, actively facilitate the outsourcing of efficiency and productivity onto the self. 24/7 connectivity, the endless workday and perpetual productivity, regardless of where one is or the time of day, become normalized. Competition is often embedded in systems designed to increase performance and productivity, for example through rating and ranking of individuals, units or institutions, encouraging workers to up the ante continually and overwork for potential reward – in the process, internalizing the competitive ethos (Beer, 2016). This self-responsibility is part of a larger trend in which the pressure to manage productivity successfully, to meet company and market expectations, and to anticipate and adjust to new labour market demands is transferred more and more to employees (Beckert, 2016; Gregg, 2018).

Temporal surveillance and control

To reinforce personal responsibility for meeting temporal expectations, as well as to impose employer expectations, are new regimes of digitally mediated workplace surveillance. Even a decade ago, almost 75 per cent of US companies actively monitored their workers' communications and on-the-job activities using a range of technologies and techniques: CCTV cameras, counting keystrokes, email and internet monitoring, measuring key performance indicators and target quotas, biometric profiling and psychometric testing (Ball, 2010). In warehouse and transport industries, locative media such as GPS and RFID (radio frequency identification) scanning track worker location, movement and progress (Rossiter, 2016). This 'data gaze' (Beer, 2016) has increased subsequently and has shifted beyond the workplace to include domestic environments, especially since the Covid-19 pandemic and the rise of home working, with work/home monitored by keystrokes, emails sent, calls made, status updates, meeting targets and deadlines, and always working with video on (Blumenfeld et al., 2020). The use of big data systems for continual observation and assessment of performance greatly intensifies the extent and frequency of monitoring and shifts the governmental logic from surveillance and discipline to capture and control (Deleuze, 1992; Savat, 2012). Here, the means of undertaking a task is also the means by which it is supervised; worker behaviour is thus actively reshaped (see chapter 5).

Digital systems can track progress and provide nudges in real-time, such as warnings or penalties, to encourage compliance with expectations. They can automatically record and log the history of employee performance. They can calculate what is theoretically possible to achieve in a set time under ideal conditions and use this to set targets. In effect, work systems and processes become what Agre (1994) terms 'capture systems', in which all activities can be broken down into discrete units that can be measured, verified, compared and evaluated in terms of efficiency, and organized, optimized and normalized through 'grammars of action' (forms and sequences of tasks) (Chun, 2016). The aim is to incorporate all elements of work within a data gaze and governmental logic in order to maximize output, eliminating 'idle time' and increasing the pace of work so that 'nominal working hours remain the same but real working hours are lengthened' (Nadeem, 2009). The result is time-delineated tasks that are often nigh on impossible to achieve in normal conditions (e.g., deadlines for deliveries that assume no congestion and maximum road speed are possible; or stacking a set number of items on shelves per hour in a supermarket that assumes no interaction with customers), designed to ensure workers give every last effort and value for labour cost (Rosa, 2017; Evans and Kitchin, 2018).

Such time targets and pressures are common in gig work, with apps being a means to control and discipline workers remotely (Chen and Sun, 2020). Further pressure to meet temporal targets is generated by customers. For example, food delivery workers usually have a set time to deliver orders to customers that does not vary, regardless of the time of day or route conditions (e.g., rush hours in kitchens over lunch and dinner, rush hours on the roads, gaining entry to gated buildings, and busy times for elevators) (Shapiro, 2020). Many of the platform apps that orders are placed through allow the customer to watch the progress through time and the geographic distance of the deliverer to destination, and to rate worker performance, prompting complaints regarding lateness that directly affect the worker through penalties or losing their position (Chen and Sun, 2020). Customers' desire for instant gratification is used to discipline workers who are navigating systems that operate sub-optimally much of the time. This inevitably creates time pressures and encourages workers to take risks to remain on schedule, resulting in high numbers of crash incidents and injury in the case of delivery workers (Chen and Sun, 2020).

Conclusion

There is an enormous interdisciplinary literature concerning the temporalities of business, work and labour. This chapter, then, has inevitably been a somewhat circumscribed discussion of how networked digital technologies are modulating and shifting the temporal relations of economic life. The focus has been principally concentrated on the time-spaces of labour, with scant attention paid to temporalities related to credit, financialization, competition, consumption, obsolescence, commuting, innovation, investment, speculation, work futures and the experiential temporalities of workplaces. Nonetheless, the discussion has made it clear that a number of profound changes are taking place in relation to work and labour, across scales from the local to the global. Digital technologies are producing radical time-space compression and a reorganization of economic relations; they are creating new timescapes of work by fragmenting and replacing labour; they are altering the lived time of labour through flexibilization, precarity and forms of arbitrage; and they are providing a new means for individuals and employers to take control and manage time. As examined in the next chapter, employers increasingly expect their workers to be always–everywhere available (Green, 2002), contactable through mobile communication and ready to enact work regardless of the time or day of the week (Kitchin and Fraser, 2020). For many workers, synchronizing work and non-work activities is a constantly negotiated process that causes significant personal disruption. As work drifts into time outside of paid working hours and overwork is valorized (Pang, 2016), labour becomes increasingly accelerated and fragmented, and workers are subject to greater time pressures and stresses that undermine the possibility of achieving a work–life balance (Rosa, 2015; Wajcman, 2015).

Digital technologies are set to be ever more embedded into the practices and processes of work. Platforming and automation will further fragment labour, time-space compression will deepen its spatial and temporal divisions, time management tools will become increasingly sophisticated in their operations, workplace temporal governmentalities will deepen the internalization of temporal expectations and workers will be subject to control through capture systems. Companies and consultancies are actively seeking ways to utilize networked technologies to produce new work futures: to disrupt existing temporal doxas, reconfigure temporal relations to

146

improve efficiencies and productivity, extract value from labour, reduce the turnover time of capital, increase competitiveness and exploit temporal arbitrage. These ambitions will have significant consequences for labour and workers. It is therefore important to track proposed developments and attempts to implement and mainstream them, to unpack their potential effects, and to consider how they might be countered or replaced with alternative scenarios (see chapter 10). The latter requires a sustained programme of futuring that is not solely driven by the imperatives of capital.

— Part III —

REMAKING DIGITAL TIMESCAPES

—— 9 ——

TEMPORAL POWER AND ITS
CONSEQUENCES

So far, the analysis has mapped out the digital timescapes and the multiplicity of temporalities being produced across several aspects of everyday life. The emphasis has been on the impact of the digital on the nature and forms of temporality being produced, how these temporalities shape and are shaped by everyday practices, and how they produce new timescapes that make a difference to the structuring and operation of domains and sites. Throughout, it has been noted that the temporalities produced by the digital do not always have a positive impact on residents and workers, and that they often reproduce and strengthen temporal power and deepen temporal inequalities. This chapter examines the operations of temporal power and some of the more problematic and pernicious temporal processes wrought by the use of digital technologies. It starts by examining the temporal inequalities between social groups, temporal arbitrage and slow violence, the operations of temporal power and uneven access to temporal sovereignty, and the (re)production of a new temporal doxa. The chapter then details what Virilio (1997: 19) termed the 'tyranny of real time', and issues arising from always acting in the present moment with little time for reflection or deliberation. This is followed by a discussion of the effects of digital technologies on lived temporalities and the creation of time pressures and stresses. The fourth section considers memory and history, and issues relating to mass datafication, access, forgetting, silencing and revisionism. The chapter closes by asking 'Who is the future for?', exploring how futuring work is riven with temporal power designed to produce futures that favour particular interests. The next chapter considers how these temporal concerns might be tackled, and fairer and more equitable temporal regimes enacted.

Temporal inequalities

Temporalities are differentially produced and controlled, generating numerous temporal inequalities. As Sharma (2014) contends, '[t]he social fabric is composed of a chronography of power, where individuals' and social groups' senses of time and possibility are shaped by a differential economy, limited or expanded by the ways and means that they find themselves in and out of time'. Many studies have identified differences in the temporalities experienced by men and women in relation to the balance of paid and unpaid work and access to 'quality time' (Bittman and Wajcman, 2000; Milojevic, 2008; Ladner, 2009). Women's time-space patterns of mobility and activities are generally more constrained and routinized, particularly if the household has children (Nowotny, 1994; Kwan, 2000). Indeed, women's time is more likely to be shaped by others, with the time-space activities of young women, for example, limited by parental curfews and fear of violence when navigating streets (Pain, 2001; Datta, 2020). Within-category variances exist as well, with childless women, women in dual-income households, single working mothers, and women able to afford nannies and childcare services experiencing varying temporalities and degrees of autonomy to control temporal relations (Wajcman, 2015). Cultural and religious expectations, and other social markers such as class, race, disability and sexuality, also inflect gendered time (Milojevic, 2008). As Datta (2020: 1321) notes, 'control over gendered time means the power to manipulate subjective identities of childhood, youth, single life, motherhood, parenthood, worker, and community' and to fit them within the hegemonic, capitalist and patriarchal temporal expectations. This includes the performance of domestic violence, with digital technologies being used to exercise coercive control and entrapment through surveillance, harassment, and threats of exposing online intimate images and other secrets, extending control over time and space, including after the relationship has ended (Cuomo and Dolci, 2021).

There are significant differences across workers with respect to patterns and control of working time (see chapter 8). Lower social-status groups tend to be the ones working irregular hours, allocated at short notice, and performed with contracts that convey few rights. They are also more likely to be performing temporal arbitrage in which workers render their own working hours and conditions subservient to others, synchronizing and recalibrating the temporality of their labour to align with 'an external relation; be it another person, pace, technology, chronometer, institution, or ideology' (Sharma, 2017: 133). Workers are socialized and coerced into organizing their temporal relations around the demands of others (Sharma, 2014; Chen and Sun, 2020). Such arbitrage can be stretched out across space, taking advantage of time-space distanciation and time-zone and labour-cost differences. Fast urbanism serves capitalist interests and generally aims to cater for the wealthy and middle classes (see chapter 7). In many cases, urban speculation dispossesses poorer people of their land and homes, but locks them out of the new developments (Datta, 2015).

Temporal inequalities are often so entrenched that they constitute regimes of slow violence: a continual, gradual, persistent, genera-tional unfolding of discrimination and crises that reproduce uneven and unequal social relations and are responded to, if at all, by slow justice in terms of judicial response and social reform (Heise, 2016; Datta, 2020). For Anderson et al. (2020: 629), slow violence is an 'an endured time with no interval or break ... [A] "stalled present" of "arrested movement" (Scott, 2014: 6) [that] offers no promise of transformation, betterment or improvement'. These temporal inequalities do not just relate to the present. As discussed in chapter 3, archives do not capture and store information equally across populations. Those in positions of power are more likely to direct who and what should be archived. Moreover, futuring and attempts to influence and control how the future unfolds are disproportion-ately driven by vested interests.

These temporal inequalities have real material, affective and biopolitical consequences for individuals and communities, creating temporal inconveniences, pressures and stresses that directly influence quality of life. They infuse peoples' qualitative experience of time and the experience of activities performed in time (Sharma, 2014). They can affect individual mental and physical health and well-being, mediate life chances and the ability to make ends meet, shape the condition of social relationships and alter future life trajectories. They inflect household harmony, reproduce structural divides and institutional discrimination against social groups, and constrain the future prospects of groups and neighbourhoods. As Sharma (2014: 51) notes, the biopolitical economy of time is designed to make 'clear which bodies will be taken care of' and which are to be exploited through forms of temporal arbitrage.

Such uneven and unequal temporal relations arise because some institutions and individuals have greater control and autonomy over temporal relations, often seeking to exploit this temporal power for their own ends, while others have relatively little autonomy, needing to structure their temporalities with respect to time rules and expectations. Temporal sovereignty is a key element shaping this variation. Temporal sovereignty is the possession of some degree of temporal power – that is, an ability to exert personal control and to resist the temporal aspirations and expectations of others, and to impose temporal relations onto others, indirectly or directly (Nowotny, 1994; Wajcman, 2015). Institutions possess temporal sovereignty through the state's authority to mandate and police time rules (Madanipour, 2017). They can impose temporal conditions related to the timings, timeframes and deadlines of public services. Companies possess temporal sovereignty through the employment relationship, being able to dictate working hours and routines, pace and tempo within the constraints of regulations (though they might abuse those constraints), and to use surveillance and capture systems to enforce compliance (Shove et al., 2009; Gregg, 2018). They use their lobbying power to influence time-space relations, such as the regulation of labour and working hours, or the temporality of the night-time economy, or the time rules related to product shipping and shelf-life.

Individuals utilize their social status and positions to direct in explicit or subtle ways the temporal lives of others (Wajcman, 2018). Southerton (2020) draws on Reisch's (2001) account of time wealth to denote the advantages that temporal sovereignty conveys. Those with time wealth possess: chronometric control, having the right amount of time to perform the activities they deem of value to their life; chronologic control, having access to the right time of day, week or season to undertake activities; autonomy over the allocation of activities within time; and the ability to synchronize performing activities with others. Few people have full temporal sovereignty. People in positions of power are bound within social relations, and institutions operate within wider commercial and geopolitical relationships, where compromises have to be made over timings and temporalities. Nonetheless, they have much greater levels of autonomy and control than others. Everyone, though, possesses some degree of temporal autonomy, even if that might be quite constrained. For example, one might have a reasonable degree of control over scheduling, but still have to take into account the calendars of family, friends, bosses, colleagues and fixed events (such as sports matches) (Kitchin and Fraser, 2020); a prisoner generally has little control over the temporal pattern of a day, but can make some time-related choices and enact temporal practices that subvert and resist the imposed time regime

154

(Kaun and Stiernstedt, 2020). In the latter case, subjects have little temporal worth and minimal temporal investment/credit to draw upon to meet their temporal needs (Sharma, 2014). 'Instead, their temporality is expected to uphold the time of others while existing outside normative time', with them surviving using 'subarchitectures of time maintenance' of their own devising (Sharma, 2014: 74).

Temporal power is not necessarily wielded directly by people and entities, but can be more diffuse and invested in and enacted through ideologies, systems and structural relations. Temporal logics infuse the rationales and workings of capitalism, neoliberalism, colonialism, organized religion, patriarchy, institutionalized racism and other systems of power and oppression that shape how society is organized and operates (see chapters 1 and 2). Indeed, temporal power and sovereignty are baked into social relations, (re)producing temporal doxa. The institutionalization of temporal orders, time rules, and rhythms and cycles, their embedding within technical systems, and their habitual, daily reproduction, reinforce and reproduce a doxic sensibility in which their logic and practices are internalized and taken for granted. In other words, we are socialized and structured into accepting and reproducing dominant temporal relations. Moreover, it can be difficult to imagine a fundamentally different temporal regime.

To evoke Mark Fisher's (2009) characterization of capitalist realism, a temporal realism operates in which temporal orders and relations have produced a pervasive atmosphere so thoroughly interwoven into our lifeworlds that it is seen as the only viable system – the natural order: the way things are. It is accepted as inevitable and commonsensical, so institutionalized and normalized that it operates without having to resort to coercion. That is not to say that there is no resistance, transgression or subversion, but much of this is concerned with reordering and seeking fairness and equity within, or devising tactics to survive, an existing temporal regime, rather than fundamentally transforming the prevalent order (see chapter 10). In the context of the digital era, the temporal doxa enacted through digital technologies are reinforced in the same way as the data doxa detailed by Smith (2018): technologies and their temporalities are valorized as the solution to a myriad of social and work problems and are a key driver of economic growth (fetishization); they are so thoroughly interwoven into everyday lives and institutional systems that is difficult to imagine life without them (habituation); and they sufficiently enhance and enliven activities and their performance that users are prepared to tolerate any negative aspects (enchantment). These relations reinforce the orthodoxy and reproduce the status quo.

The tyranny of real-time

Digital technologies have enabled an enormous growth in the real-time flow of information and feedback, and control and management of infrastructures, systems and processes. Data are being generated, distributed, processed and acted upon by algorithmic systems in machine time, with very short latencies. Such real-time actions produce a number of impactful outcomes, including enhanced efficiency, productivity and an ability to respond in a timely fashion to unfolding emergencies. However, there are also downsides, and a temporal politics, to acting speedily and in the moment.

The demands of living and acting in real-time – of always being connected and cognitively engaged through email, mobile phones, social and spatial media – creates a temporal regime that compels never-ending engagement, and produces stress through increased demands on peoples' time and attention, with few opportunities to disengage and relax (Gleick, 1999). While real-time technologies are promoted as a means to manage temporal density, time scarcity and pressures, they often contribute to and exacerbate these issues (Crang, 2007; Hassan, 2009). Moreover, they orientate us to the present – to be fixated on checking and responding to email and social media, discovering and following the latest news/weather, and monitoring when the next deadline or bus/train is due. They encourage individuals to operate in the moment with little reflection on the past, its relevance to the present, or historical continuities, or on the future and long-term ambitions and planning, and diverts attention from asynchronous temporalities (Hassan, 2009). Indeed, for Purser (2002: 160), to 'think and act in real-time terms requires a certain kind of wilful blindness to the past and future'.

The emphasis on speed and instant reaction means there is no time for reflection, contemplation, slow rational deliberation, considered answers, creative imagination or affect and emotion in decision-making and response (Purser, 2002; de Lange, 2018). Instead, individuals need to practice 'abbreviated thinking' and to act quickly in a context where systems are highly instrumental and means–end orientated with limited options, seeking to achieve results quickly and with as little fuss as possible (Hassan, 2009: 98). 'Users are compelled by the momentum of the now. Control in this context is almost impossible: take your time and you lose the sale, suffer a drop in efficiency, or miss the "valuable" connection' (Hassan, 2007: 55). There is, in the words of Kaun (2015: 222), 'an annihilation of interpretation', with systems following rule-based responses. Compressed time for thought and action means that actors, such as infrastructure managers, have to fall back on either learned routines or established unconscious cognitive biases (Purser, 2002), or come to rely on forms of automated management enacted through algorithmic systems (Coletta and Kitchin, 2017). Family and friends become hustled into decisions and actions that they might not take if given time to reflect. Acting in real-time thus erodes choice, and reflexive and meaningful action, and limits alternative and creative intervention (Leccardi, 2007). In other words, kairos (the right time to act judiciously) is trumped by action in the immediate present.

The reliance on algorithmic systems to process and respond to real-time data creates forms of technocratic governance in which an intense instrumental rationality (that is reductionist and functionalist in approach) and technological solutionism (that presumes that complex situations can be solved or optimized through computation) are applied (Kitchin, 2014a). Such an approach prioritizes optimization, efficiency and rational decision-making as the key bases on which to manage and improve everyday living (Bleecker and Nova, 2009), and assumes that the same technological solutions can be easily transplanted between places to produce similar effects (Kitchin, 2014a). Managing systems in real-time, then, creates a disengaged, decontextualized, rote, rule-based approach that lacks reflection, deliberation, communal debate, learning trajectory, and framing to local socio-temporal conditions beyond instrumented metrics. It thus fails to take account of the wider effects of culture, politics, policy, governance and capital that shape everyday life and how it unfolds (Kitchin, 2014a; de Lange, 2018). Technocratic forms of governance run counter to democratic politics, with real-time management excluding meaningful public participation in governance, bypassing the creative, political and messy role of people in shaping their own environments (Bleecker and Nova, 2009; Sharma, 2014).

Moreover, 24-hour news broadcasting, viral social media commentary, and the demand for immediate response place politicians under pressure to act as events unfold. In such circumstances, 'insisting on a few hours or even an entire day to make a decision is regarded as a sign of indecision and weakness. ... [W]hat used to be called statecraft devolves into a constant struggle with crisis management [in which l]eaders cannot get on top of issues, much less ahead of them' (Rushkoff, 2013: 42). Similarly, viral rumours can quickly wipe millions off the valuation of companies, or undermine the viability of a new product, before mitigation measures can be put in place. As Rushkoff (2013: 168) notes, '[t]hanks to feedback and iteration, any single Tweet can mushroom in a cacophony' that demands a quelling response that has little time for formulation.

Lastly, the immediate actions of the present create a recursive, iterative path dependency for the future, with decisions taken shaping a system's imminent performance (Uprichard, 2012). Real-time systems work to prefigure, through pre-determined, programmed responses and feedback loops, the unfolding of everyday life. This is leading, Uprichard (2012: 133) contends, to the present being increasingly embedded into institutional structures, and vice versa, with the result that the 'present itself becomes more and more plastic, to be stretched, manipulated, moulded and ultimately "casted" by those who can access more of it in the supposed "now"'. In this sense, real-time systems 'often sustain and naturalize prevailing relations of power' (Hope, 2006: 285). From this perspective, urban control rooms cast the present by iteratively prefiguring it through ongoing responses. The consequence of always living in the now, Uprichard (2012: 134) argues, is that we will increasingly 'cut our coats according to our present cloths', becoming rooted in a constant series of 'plastic presents' that limit the possibilities of alternate emergent futures and largely ignore the past or the future present. In other words, we manage systems and organizations always in the moment (Hassan, 2009), taking little account of history and wider temporal and social, political or economic context and trajectories (Bleecker and Nova, 2009).

Time scarcity and temporal pressures

As the discussion of scheduling and mobility in chapter 6, and time management in chapter 8, highlighted, digital technologies have expanded, speeded up and fragmented activities, converted 'dead time' to productive time, and enabled multitasking and metatasking. Perpetual connectivity has led to more interruptions, disruptions and expectations regarding productivity, along with the use of capture and surveillance systems to enforce busyness. Work culture and rewards encourage employees to become workaholics, and temporal arbitrage forces some workers to structure their temporalities around the temporal lives and expectations of others (Sharma, 2014).

The changing nature of work through fragmentation, real-time systems, just-in-time operations, arbitrage arrangements and on-the-fly coordination has eroded the collective organization of calendars (e.g. set mealtimes, staff meetings, work times, opening hours) and made synchronization a challenge. Many devices and apps are designed to be psychologically compelling and habit forming; to entice us to continually check-in and keep up to date with what is happening; and to engender anxiety and a fear of missing out if disconnected (Eyal, 2014; Kitchin and Fraser, 2020). Rolling 24/7 news cycles are centred on and amplify negative events, which, along with doomscrolling through social media feeds, creates a sense of perpetual crisis (Rushkoff, 2013). Digital media are now the primary means of communication, and pressure is exerted by family, friends, employers, colleagues and clients to be connected and available at all times, to stay up to speed with developments, and to respond in a timely fashion. Simultaneously, time scarcity and pressures, particularly related to work, reduce time to spend in person with family and friends, and place strains on relationships (Southerton, 2020).

While the effect of digital technologies on the pace and tempo of activities is often highlighted as a significant factor in creating time pressures (the experience of being rushed or harried) (Tomlinson, 2007; Hassan, 2009), it is clear that temporal density (an expansion and crunch in tasks to perform, and intense, overlapping temporal rhythms) and fragmentation (the breaking up of activities into smaller units of time, and more rapid switching between many tasks), which cause time scarcity (a lack of time to perform activities as required), are just as – or more – important (Southerton and Tomlinson, 2005; Southerton, 2020). Time pressure due to scarcity arises due to a 'mismatch between the temporal resources allocated to a given task, or a given number of tasks, and the time needed to do them properly', with this issue exacerbated by 'the fact that the number of legitimate claims that can be made on ... time-budget[s] seems to rise incessantly' (Rosa, 2017: 26). In the digital era, individuals are faced with the task of seeking what Southerton (2020: 79) terms 'dynamic stabilization', 'in which the volume of activities and tasks continually increase per unit of time, but those units of time cannot be expanded'. The European Working Conditions Survey details that, in 2015, 23% of employees across Europe reported working at a very high speed almost all of the time, with a further 40% working at a high speed for between a quarter and three-quarters of their time (Eurofound, 2017). 27% were working to tight deadlines almost all of the time, and another 36% between a quarter and three-quarters of their time. 10% of employees reported they rarely had enough time to get their job done, with another 17% reporting that they sometimes experienced work-related time squeezes (Eurofound, 2017). 16% of employees reported experiencing frequent disruptive interruptions that further fragmented their working day (Eurofound, 2017). This is compounded by trying to manage work pressures alongside those generated outside of work. The result is feelings of anxiety generated by time crunches and a lack of temporal control (Hassan, 2007). These anxieties lead to frustration and disorientation – and, if unchecked, depression and ill health (Hassan, 2009).

It should also be noted, however, that the relationship between time density, scarcity and pressure is not a simple correlation (density and scarcity lead to harriedness and anxieties). It is quite possible for two workers with the same temporal pattern of work to experience divergent levels of harriedness, with one feeling under pressure and the other taking it in their stride. In other words, context and other factors influence the experience of temporalities, which are multiple and nuanced (Pentzold, 2018). Certainly, lived time is perceived differently by individuals, inflected by situations, perspectives and affect (Grant et al., 2015). Moreover, feelings of temporal anxiety are often 'momentary experiences as opposed to an ongoing or ever-present condition' (Southerton, 2020: 117). Busyness and temporal density can also be self-imposed, individuals choosing to take on more work to try and get ahead, or pack their leisure and home life with activities as a means to display status, to exercise 'quality time' or to appease a sense of a guilt towards family members and friends for the other demands on their time (Pentzold, 2018). In between feelings of being harried, one can feel bored and listless due to habitual and repetitious rhythms, or being free of temporal density and crunches (e.g. in the evening, or at weekends, or on holiday) (Wilk, 2009). In other words, busyness and boredom coexist, with digital technologies often seen as the answer to both.

Somewhat paradoxically then, technologies designed to produce efficiencies and aid the management of time often create temporal density, scarcity and pressures (Crang, 2007). Rather than producing more quality time, technologies fill days with ever-more-extended tasks to undertake. A smartphone helps a user to save and manage time, but it also increases the horizon of availability and claims on attention (Rosa, 2017). Indeed, as Wajcman (2015) notes, digital technologies produce a number of such paradoxes. They open up new freedoms and individual autonomy, but they also create digital leashes and bind us into systems that demand response, labour and temporal arbitrage. Networked infrastructures speed up communication, but they also lead to more sedentary and stationary lifestyles (e.g., sitting in front of a screen for hours). Social media transform the time for social relationships among a dispersed community, and collective political action, but interactions often take place at fever pitch and can be unpredictable and destructive (Keightley, 2012). Despite dozens of new domestic technologies designed to make home life more efficient, the time spent on domestic tasks has not lessened and, in many cases, has increased (in the main because they are performed more frequently, or the time saved on one task is invested in another) (Wajcman, 2015). Digital technologies perform more work-related tasks, but they have not lessened the load of workers, who increasingly experience working-time drift (that is, working beyond contracted hours). In the UK, it is estimated that workers undertake 5.1 additional hours a week, and in some cases significantly more – much of it unpaid (Eurofound, 2016). The more devices and apps that are used, the more rushed and harried users often feel.

Retention, loss, access and the revision of history and memories

As detailed in chapter 3, the use of digital technologies has led to a step-change in the volume and granularity of data being generated across domains and stored for future re-use. Vast quantities of personal and commercially sensitive information are being ceaselessly generated as data footprints and shadows, and many collections of analogue records and artefacts are being rendered in digital form, with the data held in data infrastructures and digital archives. These data, and associated metadata, provide detailed longitudinal records that can be linked together, shared and scrutinized using data analytics to produce further insights. While the generation and storage of these data undoubtedly have profound, positive implications for the mediation of personal memory and for historical analysis, they also raise some significant, troubling ethical and practical questions.

Prior to the big data age, only a fraction of activities was captured and stored within archiving systems, and memories were transitory, unreliable and forgotten (Huyssen, 2003). What was captured were usually core pieces of information, sampled at a particular place and time, or relating to specific events. Activities and memories were recorded on paper (as text or photographs), which was bulky and

161

expensive to store, or more recently on magnetic tapes, hard disks and CDs. Social interactions were, in the main, not recorded and were only remembered by those who participated. Devices and infrastructures did not record their own use. Surveillance was targeted, time consuming and expensive. Now, all activities that are digitally mediated can be logged, stored, shared and quickly analysed and acted upon (Kitchin, 2014b). In theory, the digital data generated can be held indefinitely, providing granular, indexical logs of activity, mostly held by entities outside of the control of those to whom the data refer. Google, for example, stores indefinitely every interaction with its various services: for the Google website, every search conducted and link clicked; for Gmail, all the email transactions; for Drive, all the files and edits; for YouTube, what was viewed and comments; for Play Store, what apps were downloaded; for Calendar, diary engagements; for Android phones, location and every app installed and its use (Curran, 2018). These data are not deleted by Google itself, and, even if the user seeks to control data flows or to delete their data, these are often retained in a different form (e.g. as metadata, or derived, aggregated or anonymized data). In other words, Google does not forget. And nor do Facebook, Walmart, Amazon, Apple and other companies generating big data. These accumulated data provide an important resource for knowing users and targeting them with advertising and services, and for generating efficiencies in workflows.

This mass datafication raises questions about what can be recalled now and in the future, and about forgetting. Companies and states generating big data are creating data infrastructures that provide micro-level detail of past activities and mobilities. Much of these data reside in commercial and state infrastructures, with some limits on access, though the billions of pages and resources that make up the Internet ensure that 'private lives [have] become increasingly visible in a vast public archive of everyday life', in which past activities are instantly retrievable (Hand, 2016: 270). While the data held in data infrastructures are often quite thin, in that the records are mostly factual rather than discursive, the temporal, spatial and attribute granularity across populations provides an unprecedented level of detail for future historians regarding social lives. In some cases, such as social media and news stories, data in the form of posts and comments are more akin to thick memories, expressing opinions, values, beliefs and emotions, revealing social networks and the context in which they were made (Dodge and Kitchin, 2007). Both thin and thick cases prompt questions about privacy and whether data that were generated as the by-product of a system, or for a specific reason, should be made available for other purposes, including historical analysis (Solove, 2011), and whether, like human memory, they should be open to being forgotten (Dodge and Kitchin, 2007; Connerton, 2009).

Privacy has become a core debate with respect to datafication. Privacy is the ability to control how one reveals, selectively, aspects of oneself to the world, and is a condition that many people value and expect (Solove, 2011). Privacy is a structural condition of selfhood and of managing boundaries and relationships with others (Cohen, 2019) and ensures that other civil liberties, related to how individuals are treated, based on what others know about them, are maintained (Kammourieh et al., 2017). Consequently, most people expect their past to remain private unless it is knowingly made public. However, in the big data age, such selectivity has been undermined by an erosion of key privacy and data protection tenets, including data minimization (the data are only used for the purpose for which it is generated), notice and consent, and practices of data transposition. Those living in the present era cannot, then, expect their pasts to be largely erased and forgotten (Hoskins, 2011). Consequently, concerns over the loss of privacy are a live issue, with multiple active campaigns seeking to ensure privacy rights, including the right to be forgotten (see chapter 10).

Somewhat paradoxically, just as some fear the recording and storing of everything, others fear that digitally stored information is open to irretrievable loss, that not everything that should be archived is being captured and stored, and that what is being recorded is sometimes less informative than analogue equivalents (e.g., written letters often contain a richer narrative than relatively terse emails and text messages). Digital media suffer from two fundamental issues with respect to long-term storage. First, the rate of obsolescence is high for storage media, file formats and the software and technologies used to access and manage them (Kitchin, 2014b). Digital memory requires substantial backwards compatibility. Second, the shelf life of digital storage solutions is relatively short, with hard disks subject to bit-rot and technical failures, meaning they deteriorate much faster than paper and other analogue media. Consequently, one has to transfer data continually to the latest media and platforms (while ensuring they can be accessed with present software) to ensure future access. Cloud storage and the sharing and copying of data provide one solution, though cloud storage still suffers from obsolescence. A related problem is that digital media are often composites and lack stability (Roberts, 2015). For example, many websites link to or incorporate other websites or databases. Capturing the local material without also netting the incorporated material will lead to partial records, or what Wilson (2009) terms 'digital ruins'. Moreover, websites are rarely static, with some being regularly updated or replaced, meaning that, unless there is a continuous capture of site versions, most of the material is lost on updating.

Whereas older media such as paper records could be passively preserved (e.g., left stored in an attic for later discovery), digital data require an active preservation strategy (Roberts, 2015). While professional digital archivists prepare and implement preservation strategies that seek to ensure that records are kept for posterity, many organizations simply have back-up strategies to ensure data can be recovered if there is a technical failure. Similarly, most individuals have an ad hoc approach to data management, with poor structuring of files that require personal knowledge to decipher, and haphazard methods of backing up and storing data. Data can be protected by passwords, rendering them inaccessible if the password is lost. In many cases, data are treated as ephemeral and transitory, generated for a particular purpose and then abandoned or deleted. In the absence of active preservation, date generated today will not last a generation, potentially creating an information vacuum for future historians (Arthur, 2009). Even when there is a preservation strategy, the issue of access to private resources remains. A large proportion of big data are being generated and collated by companies who closely control access to the resource, given its commercial value. This means resources that are potentially of enormous interest to future historians are private walled gardens. In some cases, access might be granted to selected parties (with those chosen itself a means of controlling narratives arising from analysis), though it might also involve signing intellectual property right and non-disclosure agreements, and agreeing to terms and conditions that set out how and for what purposes the data can be used (Ben-David, 2020).

Similarly, there is a fear of forgetting history and memories. In the first case, the worry is that too much emphasis is being placed on living in the present moment and futuring, rather than learning from the past. While data infrastructures and digital archives multiply, commentators opine that history in education curricula, and the use of the past in acting in the present, are declining (Connerton, 2009). With respect to memory, some are worried that forgetting, or a lacklustre attention to memory, may arise because there is no need to remember personally, since the storing of memories is outsourced to mnemotechnologies (Hoskins, 2011). In addition, there is a concern about what is being recorded and retained. Traditional archives seek to store trustworthy information that is deemed useful for future re-use. Much of the data being generated and stored within big data systems are dirty, gamed and fake, lacking in veracity and quality (Kitchin, 2014b). The Internet is awash with disinformation, propaganda, conspiracy theories and fake news and memories. People post anonymously using pseudonyms. Fact and fiction, truth and lies, permeate the archive.

Just as this cocktail of information shapes present views and attitudes, it has the potential to inflect individual memory, influence collective memory, and aid the revisionist versioning of history (Hoy, 2009). What information is retained and how it is presented shapes what is recollected and how it is interpreted. Digital media enable information to be easily remixed and manipulated, and to be presented in persuasive ways (Wilson, 2009). It enables presentist takes on history, back-tracing the present through contemporary lenses and analytical techniques; historical selectiveness regarding which particular pasts are cherry-picked and which are deliberately ignored; and historical legitimization and instrumentalization, in which versions of history are used to justify the present and preferred futures (Moss, 2021). These were prevalent in the pre-digital age, but digital media provide new tools of collation and presentation, and have greatly expanded the speed and reach of circulation.

Who is the future for?

The future does not unfold to a projected blueprint in a seamless, planned fashioned. Few, if any, individuals meticulously live their lives to detailed blueprints with defined milestones and targets, or indeed have mid- to long-term future visions and plans beyond sketchy generalizations, such as attend college, get a job, meet a partner, have a family. People know that such plans and hopes are easily dashed, vulnerable to changes in circumstance, and so become wary not to invest too much faith in them (Urry, 2016). Even in cases where blueprints and milestones are produced, such as an urban development plan, stakeholders are aware that these are preferred outcomes and ambitions and the plan will not fully transpire as hoped, and in many cases will deviate significantly from its intended path. The future emerges in contingent, relational, contextual and contested ways. It sometimes unfolds roughly as expected, but is 'unpredictable, uncertain and often unknowable', the outcome of diverse, often muddled and contradictory, processes and 'unknown unknowns' (Urry, 2016: 1). Moreover, futuring and future-making are uneven and unequal endeavours riddled with temporal power, with some interests possessing greater ability to influence discourses, plan-making and activities that help to bring futures into existence (Adam and Groves, 2007). In this sense, the future might be made for everybody, but not necessarily in their interest.

Nonetheless, everyone has some level of agency over shaping their own future, and can contribute to household and social circle activities and plans, community initiatives and social movements to envision and produce desired futures. This agency, though, is structurally constrained by resources, opportunities and barriers, and can be contested and actively opposed by those with alternative visions, ambitions and plans (Adam and Groves, 2007; Urry, 2016). For a relatively small number of people, agency might be very limited, such as those with dementia who require extensive care and support. Most individuals, however, have the ability to make choices and decisions that directly and indirectly shape their life paths and futures, usually in negotiation with others: parents, teachers, partners, friends, employers, bank managers, government officials and so on. Those who are wealthy or occupy positions of power within organizations have greater autonomy and are able to use their resources to influence public perceptions and dictate pathways taken to try to secure preferred futures (Zapata, 2021).

Beyond the individual level, community groups, corporations, institutions, political parties and other groupings act as collective enterprises, leveraging their shared resources and agency to project, plan, produce and colonize futures. These enterprises employ a range of tactics and strategies to realize desired futures, such as: investing in research and development; generating evidence for future need and demand; devising masterplans; forming alliances; promoting their vision and plans through marketing, advertising, public relations and media features; lobbying politicians and public administration; making submissions to foresight processes; influencing policies and decision-making; seeking to lessen regulatory overheads; entering into public–private partnerships; offering sweetening deals; and aggressively challenging and undermining opposing views (Adam and Groves, 2007; Urry, 2016). Much of this work proceeds by obtaining credit to be paid back in the future in order to fund investments; future finance is used to produce the future (Beckert, 2016). Digital technologies play a crucial enabling, coordinating and operating role in all

166

of these endeavours, providing 'secondary agency' (Mackenzie, 2006) to those that utilize their computational and networked capabilities. However, powerful individuals and collective endeavours are not always successful in realizing their anticipated outcome because they are competing with other powerful interests, and there is a large degree of contingency in how events unfold in practice.

While some future-making is designed to realize the aims of social justice, fairness, equity and democracy, much is designed to serve particular constituencies and widen social divisions. This is particularly evident in the future growth strategies and speculative practices of companies in pursuing future profit for the benefit of shareholders, and in government policies and plans relating to investments for the future, such as welfare, pensions, education, housing and infrastructure programmes that reduce the tax burden for the wealthy while disinvesting from poorer communities (Pollitt, 2008; Urry, 2016). It is also evident in geopolitics, contestation over resources, war and the work of inter- and non-governmental bodies. As discussed in chapter 7, fast urbanization is a speculative, capitalist endeavour that serves property developers, finance companies and those seeking investment opportunities at the expense of poor landowners and those seeking homes. Smart city initiatives produce plausible and preferable scenarios and dispositions, using forecasts, living labs, prototyping and trialling, to create pathways for their adoption, in turn generating value for their developers and those that benefit from their deployment (Evans et al., 2016). In such situations, it can be difficult for local communities to devise and make alternative counter-futures that serve communal, rather than capital and state, interests.

Similarly, as discussed in chapter 8, the changes to the nature of work and labour relations, and regulations being sought by companies, are designed to produce employment futures that are to the benefit of the employer. It is an ongoing battle for trade unions and employees to counter such moves and protect and expand the future rights of workers. The slow violence of institutionalized racism and domestic violence structurally reproduce such relations into the future (Anderson et al., 2020; Datta, 2020). The futuring work of big business is an active player in climate change debates, seeking to oppose science-backed evidence and narratives concerning climate futures and their impact, and to limit the introduction of measures that might curtail consumption in order to reduce energy production and carbon emissions (Urry, 2013). The rights and well-being of future generations are sacrificed for profit in the here and now and the immediate time horizon (Adam and Groves, 2007). The future, then, is largely envisaged and produced for those who are doing the envisioning, not people yet unborn, as is often purported in promotional rhetoric.

Conclusion

How the past, present and future are imagined and produced are shot through with temporal power that creates a number of troubling temporal relations. This chapter has detailed some of the ways in which digital technologies are facilitating temporal power and the operation of temporal regimes, and are creating uneven and unequal urban timescapes. There are widespread inequalities in the lived temporalities of people and the temporal power to control temporal relations, influenced by a range of factors such as gender, class, race and disability. Those with greater temporal sovereignty are able to control timings and their use of time, providing them with the latitude to reproduce their social position and condition. Real-time systems are not neutral, value-free technical solutions to managing urban services and infrastructures. They serve the purposes of those that operate them, facilitating technocratic, instrumental forms of governance that supposedly sit outside of politics, while locking citizens into systems that demand attention and a limited range of timely action. The extensive array of digital technologies that permeate everyday lives and inflect their temporalities is creating a number of time stresses and pressures that affect individuals and groups differently, depending on circumstances and temporal sovereignty. Data infrastructures and digital archives are raising questions concerning the extent to which data are being generated and stored, privacy, access and data use, their long-term resilience, as well as how memories and history are being mediated and produced and whose interests they serve. Temporal power extends to futuring and future-making, and how the future is produced to serve the interests of elites, corporations and states, often widening rather than reducing social inequalities and divisions. The next chapter explores how these issues of temporal inequalities and power might be addressed in order to democratize the past, present and future, redistribute temporal power and reconfigure temporal regimes, and produce fairer, more equitable urban timescapes.

— 10 —

TRANSFORMING TEMPORAL POWER

So far, the book has detailed how digital technologies are transforming everyday timescapes. In many cases, the temporalities enabled by the digital produce opportunities and efficiencies that can positively affect individual lives. For example, enabling home working and avoiding commuting time, or delivering real-time streaming services for on-demand entertainment, or providing a means to optimize time management and create more 'quality time'. The analysis has also highlighted the ways in which temporal work of digital technologies serves a variety of interests, maintains and deepens temporal power and temporal inequalities, reproduces temporal regimes, and consolidates and normalizes temporal doxa. This chapter considers ways to democratize temporal power and challenge temporal doxa by reframing how temporal relations are conceived and setting out political and practical ways to claim temporal sovereignty, both individually and collectively. The first part of the chapter focuses on temporal ethics and justice, making a rhetorical case for challenging and transforming hegemonic temporal relations. It considers rights and entitlements regarding how time is produced, and a set of related ethical arguments concerning an ethics of care, an ethics of forgetting, deceleration, disconnection and asynchronicity, and an ethics of the future. The second part of the chapter concentrates on strategies and tactics that can be used to transform temporal relations and regimes, including counter-archiving, slow computing, slow urbanism and urban time policies, fast activism and participatory futuring.

Temporal ethics and justice

Ethics 'involves systematizing, defending, and recommending concepts of right and wrong behavior' (Fieser, 2003). Normative ethics seeks to define moral standards and how things should be, and applied ethics aims to translate these into practice to try to resolve contested issues (Vaughan, 2014). Temporal ethics, then, is concerned with setting the parameters for acceptable and expected temporal relations from a moral perspective (Kitchin and Fraser, 2020). In previous work, I have made the case for a set of related temporal ethics – an ethics of temporal care (Kitchin and Fraser, 2020), an ethics of forgetting (Dodge and Kitchin, 2007), an ethics of deceleration, disconnection and asynchronicity (Kitchin, 2017; Kitchin and Fraser, 2020), and an ethics of the future (Kitchin, 2019b; Kitchin and Fraser, 2020) – drawing on the related ideas of others. This section discusses these, along with the notion of temporal justice.

An ethics of temporal care

An ethics of care promotes moral action at the personal and collective level to aid oneself and others (Tronto, 1993; Held, 2005). Drawing on feminist thought, it promotes a relational and reciprocal approach to ethics that recognizes that people are bound together in webs of relationships that have associated responsibilities, obligations and duties, and they care for each other in many different ways. Some care is reciprocal, with people acting towards others in ways that reflect how they expect to be treated in return, and some is non-reciprocal, driven by obligation (acting as a parent, friend, worker or employer) or altruism (such as volunteering). An ethics of care seeks to make this notion of care more extensive within society, with people treating each other in ways that promote well-being, cooperation and the accumulation of social capital. In contrast to generalizable standards, rules and principles that act as instructions to treat people fairly, and which might be translated into universal rights, entitlements and responsibilities, an ethics of care focuses on lived daily practice. It is primarily concerned with how best to respond to address an issue, and how best to reimagine and recon-figure social and economic arrangements so they protect and nurture personal and societal interests.

What kinds of care are needed and how it is best expressed varies between individuals and groups, and across contexts and situations; what might work well for some is not necessarily optimal for all, and what is appropriate in one setting may not be in another. For example, a structured workday might suit some people, whereas others thrive in more flexible work arrangements. Enabling workers to adopt a temporal pattern that suits them best would demonstrate an ethics of care. So would shortening work hours, rotating shifts, lessening targets, reducing work pace, increasing the frequency and duration of breaks, enabling the right to disconnect, and providing a greater degree of temporal autonomy (Nadeem, 2009). Here, work arrangements are not dictated by rights and compliance, which might promote a one-size-fits-all approach, but by a desire to look after the interests of employees, which usually has spill-over effects for employers as workers are more content, committed and productive and there is less workplace churn and days lost to ill health (Kitchin and Fraser, 2020). The slow movement (see below) is an example of an ethics of care that has been somewhat formalized into various related approaches and practices (e.g. slow food, slow cities, slow tourism, slow computing). Similarly, an ethics of forgetting, of deceleration, disconnection and asynchronicity, and of the future are expressions of an ethics of temporal care. Importantly, these ethics of care reject the narrow prioritization of neoliberal and capitalist values of time and their erasure of other cultural and social temporal formations. Instead, they seek to cultivate and value the multiple, overlapping temporalities of communities and places, and to celebrate and protect their histories and ongoing unfolding (Olmstead, 2021).

An ethics of forgetting

As discussed in chapters 3 and 9, mass datafication and the long-term retention of captured information raises a number of ethical questions concerning what data are stored, who has access to them, how they can be joined together to produce further insights, and for what purpose they can be used. Data infrastructures that retain a fine-grained, longitudinal store of information are attractive to those that produce them because of their potential commercial and governance value. Yet such data are potentially harmful because they keep on record in perpetuity past activities, including those that an individual might sooner forget. In the past, much of this information would not have been captured, and that which was would only be stored for a short while before being deleted. For example, a conversation was only experienced by those in earshot, and their memory of it was the only record, which each party might remember differently; whereas, on social media, an exchange can be captured exactly as it unfolds, be stored forever, and viewed by millions as it happens and years later. Such records can potentially haunt individuals for a lifetime, whereas previously it would fade from view, particularly if a person moved to a new location.

Unlike the data infrastructures of social media companies, human memory is fallible and people forget. Forgetting serves a number of useful purposes. Forgetting enables people to move past their mistakes and build new lives, to live with their conscience, to deal with their demons and to reconcile their own paradoxes and contradictions (Dodge and Kitchin, 2007). Forgetting enables omission and reinvention that allows negotiation, reconciliation and forgiveness, and to be a part of society. It enables the building of a different future, one that is not eternally colonized by the past (Esposito, 2017). Building forgetting into data infrastructures would be an act of care. Schacter (2001) details six forms of forgetting – three concerned with loss and three with error. Loss-based forgetting consists of transience (the loss of memory over time), absentmindedness (the loss of memory due to distractedness at the time the memory relates to) and blocking (the temporary inability to remember). Error-based forgetting consists of misattribution (assigning a memory to the wrong source), suggestibility (memories that are implanted either by accident or surreptitiously) and bias (the unknowing or unconscious editing or rewriting of experiences).

To enact an ethics of care, each of these forms of forgetting could be built into digital systems to ensure a degree of imperfection, loss and error, while maintaining utility. Records would be removed over time; absentmindedness added by distractedness being built into the mode of capture; blocking would occur during queries; misattribution would be achieved by the mis-recording of part, but not all, of an event; suggestibility would involve plausibly rescripting or inserting records; and bias would be achieved by rescripting records in line with a designated pattern. In other words, a range of algorithmic strategies could be used, such as erasing, blurring, aggregating, injecting noise, data perturbing, masking and so on, to add disturbance and doubt to the databases (Dodge and Kitchin, 2007). At present, the main way to deal with this issue is through data protection and privacy laws (see Solove, 2011), including – in the European Union – 'right to be forgotten' legislation, which refers to the deletion of data and restricting the return of results for specified names within search engines (Esposito, 2017). Data protection and privacy are principally concerned with access to and sharing data, and some forms of data use, rather than the purging of data. Certainly, then, additional ways of tackling excessive retention are required.

An ethics of deceleration, disconnection and asynchronicity

Digital technologies directly contribute to time scarcity and to time pressures and stresses. An ethics of care that promotes deceleration, disconnection and asynchronicity challenges the logics of speed, connection and real-time action, and offers an alternative way to view and respond to these issues and to arrange the temporal relations of society (Honoré, 2005; Bleecker and Nova, 2009; Kitchin and Fraser, 2020). Such an ethics is principally a call to slow down everyday life; to enable, for those who want it, a downshifting in the pace and tempo of everyday life, a de-densification in their scheduling of tasks, and a work–life balance. It would allow people to disengage from network time, not to be constantly on call and wrapped up in an eternal present, not to always be striving to stay synchronized to the temporal demands of others. It is an ethics that de-normalizes overwork, stress and burnout, promotes temporalities that create well-being and flourishing, and encourages the enjoyment of 'quality time' and not feeling guilty or being penalized for doing so (Pang, 2016). It approaches the temporal management and governance of everyday life from the perspective of fairness, equity and community, rather than efficiency, optimization and supporting the profit-making of vested interests (Shaban and Datta, 2017). For example, it strives to create workplaces that actively value employee satisfaction and well-being (Gregg, 2018), and facilitates counteraction in the moment or through pre-emption, reclaiming time for debate, negotiation and collective action over technocratic response (Andrejevic et al., 2020). It is an ethics that encourages the production of temporal dissonance and to actively resist, subvert and transgress temporal expectations and power in order to produce counter-temporalities.

Ethics for the future

An ethics of future care is concerned with operations in the present that are orientated to producing better futures – that improve

173

well-being and the lives of future generations. As discussed in the previous chapter, futuring and future-making are uneven and unequal endeavours and are dominated by vested interests that hold influence in political, planning and investment decision-making. These actors seek to project, prospect and colonize the future in ways that serve their purpose, creating pathways through plans and locked-in financial commitments that foreclose alternative possibilities (Laurian, 2021; Weber, 2021). An ethics of the future seeks to disrupt this enclosure of futuring and to democratize future-making (Urry, 2016). This requires wider participation in future-making beyond vested interests and professionals, to include the public in its full diversity. This includes adopting responsibility for decisions and actions taken in the present that have consequences for an open-ended chain of future generations who currently have no voice or votes, and no appointed advocates to speak for them. Instead, future generations are reliant on present citizens to act responsibly on their behalf, many of whom are muted in such an endeavour. Clearly, such advocacy is having limited effect as actions in the present continue to extract value and borrow credit from the future, in turn leaving environmental and social legacies for them to endure. An ethics of future care takes a longer view, seeking to imagine alternative futures and to draw them back into the present to transform perspectives and actions. Rather than imagining and enacting prefigured futures that are iterations of present relations, it embraces uncertainty and the possibilities of radical reconfigurations of social and economic relations, in which path dependencies are severed or bumped onto tracks heading in a different direction (Zapata, 2021).

Temporal justice

Performing an ethics of care can be a significant way of claiming and enabling degrees of temporal sovereignty, and for recalibrating how society views and responds to temporal pressures and stresses. However, given the pervasive, structural and institutionalized nature of temporal power and inequalities, and that an ethics of care is a largely voluntary approach rooted in personal values, it cannot replace claims for rights and entitlements enshrined in regulations and legislation that seek to protect people by limiting exploitative arrangements and practices and providing some level of temporal autonomy. Indeed, an ethics of slowness is not straightforward to enact for those experiencing temporal arbitrage who have little temporal autonomy and cannot easily offload work to others, and have bills to pay and need to earn income regardless of conditions (Honoré, 2005; Tomlinson, 2007). Women, people of colour, immigrants and insecure workers in general, have less control over their time and are less able to free themselves from temporal orders (Wajcman, 2015). Their schedules are built around the needs and demands of others. They are more likely to be on-call, to perform piecework where the pace of labour directly affects payment, to be trying to time shift other activities between work and care duties, and to be subject to workplace surveillance and penalties (for missing targets, lateness, etc.), and are less able to turn down extended shifts and overtime. For gig workers, taking a holiday means receiving no income. Practising a temporal ethics of care in such circumstances is more difficult than for somebody working in a permanent position with defined salary, hours, vacations and conditions.

Temporal justice extends ethical arguments concerning what is right or wrong, to make a case – and fight – for temporal relations that uphold a set of principles and values (Hassan, 2009; Henckel and Thomaier, 2013; Miciukiewicz and Vigar, 2013). The aim is to enshrine these principles and values in universal rights, entitlements and a new set of rules, and to use them to transform social structures and the operations of institutions. In other words, temporal sovereignty for all is cast as a requirement, not a choice or obligation; it is political commitment to transform the structural integrity of temporal regimes into more just arrangements. Temporal rights seek to ensure degrees of temporal sovereignty and autonomy in which temporal power is wrested from elites and democratized (recognizing that such sovereignty is still shaped by social relations and obligations, such as parental and pastoral care duties). Such rights includes the right to what is archived; the right to what heritage is preserved and celebrated; the right to be forgotten; the right to slowness, disconnection and asynchronicity; the right to a secure and sustainable future; and the right to participate in how temporal regimes are constructed and operate.

While seeking justice and associated rights is generally taken to mean opposing exploitation and oppression and creating a fairer, more equitable and democratic society, it is important to note that there are different theories of justice (Sabbagh and Schmitt, 2016). A libertarian notion of justice, for example, prioritizes individual autonomy over the state and society, and contends that the free market is inherently just: citizens are enmeshed in the temporal relations they deserve or can afford. In other words, capitalism is a form of 'natural' justice in which the fittest survive and prosper. Egalitarianism, in contrast, argues for equality in the distribution of wealth and power across all members of a society, regardless of ability and inheritance; and utilitarianism seeks the greater good for the greatest number (Harvey, 1972; Kitchin et al., 2019). To date, there has been no concerted attempt to map temporal justice with respect to different schools of thought regarding social justice. Instead, generalist notions of temporal justice centred on notions of distribution (fair share) and procedure (fair treatment) prevail, with some consideration of retributive (fair punishment for wrongs) and restorative (righting of wrongs) justice through regulation and legislation.

Transforming temporal power

For an ethic of temporal care and of temporal justice to be realized, they need to be enacted through practical and political action, at either the individual or collective level. There are a number of ways such action can be expressed.

Community archives and counter-archiving

The production of community archives and counter-archiving have become an important means of providing an alternative set of records to state and corporate archives, and to challenge the selective, elitist assemblage of memory and history and its claimed authority (Cifor et al., 2018; Burgum, 2020). Community archives 'recognize the need to record and allow voices that otherwise might be lost the opportunity to be heard' (Hetherington, 2013: 18). They are 'increasingly used to address silences and unsettle mainstream histories', remedying erasures and misrepresentations of the past, and to record localized memories for future generations (Burgum, 2020: 4). Through their collections and activities, community archives facilitate self-representation and self-expression, and foster the formation and maintenance of collective memory for marginalized people (Caswell et al., 2017). They provide a powerful resource for producing counter-narratives to official history (Burgum, 2020).

While local, community archives have a long history, datafication and access to data infrastructure technologies have made archiving easier to perform and have led to a surge in interest in producing archival resources. As such, there has been a democratization of archiving, with members of the public able to create a range of data collections, from simple web-hosted pages through to professional-standard archives with governance structures, digital and physical infrastructure, and dedicated staff. Community archives are generally run as voluntary or semi-professional endeavours, and involve communal practices of participation, inclusion and negotiation in their operation (Burgum, 2020). They can also be quite precarious, given their lack of core, non-cyclical funding. In some cases, the formation of archives is reactive, initiated during or in the aftermath of an event to preserve materials such as ephemera of protests, leaflets, magazines, oral history interviews, meeting minutes and so on. For example, in relation to the Occupy Movement, a number of archiving initiatives were started while the protests were ongoing. Some of these were initiated by participants in the protest, who later formed working relationships with established archives for expertise and long-term archiving, such as the Tamiment Library and Robert F. Wagner Labor Archives in New York; and some by institutional archives, such as the Smithsonian National Museum of American History and the New York Historical Society, who sent archivists to events to collect and document material (Erde, 2014). In contrast to most archives, the Occupy Movement had a very different organizational structure and approach to record creating and keeping, operating in a non-hierarchical fashion with no centralized control over records (Erde, 2014).

With respect to professional archives, there have been some moves to encourage participatory archiving – in which citizens are asked to take an active role in the curation of collections and the operations of the archive – and activist archiving – in which archivists themselves become activists, campaigning on issues such as access rights or using the archival resource 'to support activist groups and social justice aims' (Flinn and Alexander, 2015: 331). In both cases, archivists recognize the power vested in them in terms of deciding what is archived, managing the presentation of and access to archives, and contributing to history-making processes, and they seek to redefine their own role and the role of their archives (Cifor et al., 2018). In effect, it is envisaged that an archivist shifts from being a custodian and gatekeeper to a facilitator of participation (Erde, 2014). Groups such as the Activist Archivists in New York, and the Resistance Project in London, run courses to teach community members how to archive, and provide guidance documents (Erde, 2014; Burgum, 2020).

177

Counter-archiving seeks to provide an alternative archive of the same archival material. Ben-David (2020) provides a discussion of constructing a counter-archive to Facebook's data infrastructure after it had shut down API access for researchers. Many researchers have constructed their own archives of Twitter data using its API, being able to organize and query the data in new ways (Zook and Poorthuis, 2015). Others have used web scraping techniques to harvest data from online platforms (such as InsideAirbnb that scrapes Airbnb data to construct a longitudinal archive of properties and prices; http://insideairbnb.com) and government databases (such as the scraping of judgments in asylum seeker cases in Ireland; Brown, 2021). While some counter-archives are generated principally for use by their creators, many are made publicly available to enable others to analyse the data, and to use them in campaigns against their original producers. Counter-archiving, then, provides epistemic resistance to the hegemonic order and authority of official archives (Ben-David, 2020).

Slow computing

Slowness is an ethics of care for oneself and for others. It is not simply about changing the pace of life, but about transforming perspectives about what matters, and enacting a different set of values. Several books set out a critique of speed and time density in contemporary life and outline a general philosophy of slowness (Gleick, 1999; Honoré, 2005; Crary, 2013). In some cases, the call for a 'digital detox' and to seize temporal autonomy fall within the self-help genre, focusing on personal action (Pang, 2016; Shojai, 2017); others take a more societal view, recognizing that the structural conditions that produce time pressures and stresses require collective action. An ethics of slow care has been translated into practical and political action across a number of domains – slow living (Craig and Parkins, 2006), slow food (Miele and Murdoch, 2002), slow tourism (Clancy, 2016), slow work (Berg and Seeber, 2017; Mountz et al., 2015) and slow cities (see below). Slow computing concerns the use of tactics at the individual and collective level to transform how digital technologies mediate the pace, tempo and temporal density of everyday life (Kitchin and Fraser, 2020).

The term 'slow computing' was first coined by Nathan Schneider (2015) to describe a self-aware, responsible approach to computing that considers how digital technologies 'affect ourselves and others around us'. He continued, 'Much as the Slow Food movement emphasizes local economies, traditional knowledge and ecology, Slow Computing means not merely opting for the most competitive, profit-driven hardware and software, but instead building a commons. It means cultivating digital lives that reflect our analog values' (2015). In this vision, and that developed by Kitchin and Fraser (2020), slow computing is about not simply reclaiming temporal autonomy, but practising an ethic of care in relation to all aspects of computing. Nonetheless, temporality is central to the notion, embodying Ruha Benjamin's (2019: 17) call to 'move slower and empower people' as a counter-ethos to Facebook's 'move fast and break things'. From a temporal perspective, slow computing is about formulating and adhering to a set of principles designed to resist and reconfigure hegemonic temporal relations, enacted through a set of individual and collective tactics. It is not a Luddite withdrawal from using technologies or a blank call for society to slow down, but rather it is using technologies in a way that serves individual well-being and the common good. As Honoré notes, '[s]low is about relearning the lost art of shifting gears', about 'doing things at the right speed' and avoiding the 'trap of trying to do more and more things in less and less time' (Ash, n.d.).

At an individual level, slow computing aims to seize some level of temporal sovereignty over everyday pace, tempo, scheduling and timings. As Carlo Petrini, founder of the Slow Food movement, contends: 'Being Slow means that you control the rhythms of your own life. ... If today I want to go fast, I go fast; if tomorrow I want to go slow, I go slow. What we are fighting for is the right to determine our own tempos' (cited in Honoré, 2005: 16). Key here is identifying opportunities to step outside of network time – particularly being always–everywhere available – and taking control of temporal practices where possible. Personal slow computing tactics include:

- practising structured rest and work, actively protecting time for sleep, rest and vacations by disconnecting from work activities outside of work hours, and blocking tasks at work, strategically scheduling meetings and keeping them to the minimal viable duration, and avoiding multitasking;
- creating boundaries around technology use, such as only logging on after breakfast, turning to silent all devices in late evening, removing apps that are compulsive and consume a lot of time, and turning off notifications that prompt immediate responses;

- stepping away from activities undertaken for other peoples' benefit and discouraging on-the-fly scheduling;
- avoiding the filling of 'dead time' with tasks; and
- engaging in analogue practices, such as insisting on device-free activities, organizing meetings on clock time, and using paper, not shared online diaries (Kitchin and Fraser, 2020).

Undoubtedly, these tactics can produce inconveniences and irritations. In many cases, they might be difficult to implement due to familial responsibilities and structural conditions. Yet, if implemented where possible, they have the potential to create greater temporal control, lessen time pressures and stresses, and oppose localized temporal power.

On their own, however, individual tactics have two constraints. First, they are reliant on the ability of people to claim and assert temporal sovereignty. As already detailed, this ability varies across populations, with those in marginal and precarious positions least able to choose and practise slow computing. Second, they are highly dependent on others adopting or accommodating slow living in order to be effective (Southerton, 2020). As such, individual tactics need to be supplemented with universal slow computing rights and entitlements gained through collective action. By parties working and campaigning together, procedures and protections for the temporal effects and power enabled by digital technologies can be put in place for everyone. The organization of collective tactics can be led by a number of actors, such as community groups and workers/unions (campaigns for rights, entitlements and worker welfare), companies (market-led regulation and competitive advantage), non-governmental organizations and political parties (policy and regulatory proposals) and public bodies (setting agendas, scoping and drafting new regulation/laws, implementing initiatives and policies, setting up and monitoring of governance and oversight) (Kitchin and Fraser, 2020). Important temporal rights relating to work and labour, for example, have been won through collective action, such as shorter, fixed working hours, defined holiday entitlements, duration of maternity/paternity leave, overtime payments and part-time conditions.

A recent set of related initiatives have been the calls for the right to disconnect, intended to combat working-time drift and workers being contacted outside of working hours for additional labour. After campaigns by unions, new laws have come into effect in France and Italy, with several other countries on the path to implementing similar

180

laws, which specify employees have the right to stay offline and not answer their phone or email outside of designated work hours (von Bergen and Bressler, 2019). Several companies in other jurisdictions have voluntarily introduced such rules aimed at protecting workers from stress-related illnesses and increasing innovation and productivity from well-rested and motivated staff; for example, in Germany, Volkswagen blocks work email being sent to workers after office hours, and Daimler permits workers going on vacation to automatically delete all new emails while they are away (von Bergen and Bressler, 2019).

Slow cities and urban time policies

One means by which an ethics of slow care has been enacted collectively is through the development of the slow cities movement. The CittaSlow movement was founded in Italy in 1999 by four mayors (of Greve-in-Chianti, Orvieto, Bra and Positano) who met to discuss the possibility of managing their towns in a way that enhanced quality of life by making healthy environments and sustainable local economies their core values. The aim was to counter the pace and cultural consequences of globalization by promoting an alternative model of local governance that prioritized hospitality, community, conviviality, well-being, social equity, sense of place, traditional culture, heritage, authenticity, local products and markets, local environments, ecological concerns, public transit and cycling, and recycling and renewable energy (Knox, 2005; Pink, 2008). In temporal terms, the movement has sought a more relaxed pace of life that respects seasonality and traditional rhythms of community life (Knox, 2005).

In other words, CittaSlow has sought to step back from capitalism and its associated temporalities in order to prioritize local concerns and traditional ways of life, demonstrating an alternative approach to life and politics (rather than adopting a confrontational, anti-capitalist/globalization activism, which might alienate possible adoptees and advocates) (Pink, 2008). In this sense, it has sought to create the conditions in which residents can experience and imagine a different kind of society – one which is not dominated by a corporately driven, neoliberal urban political economy and which counters the alienation of a global consumerist culture (Knox, 2005; Mayer and Knox, 2006; Pink, 2008). The movement does not reject the use of digital technologies, but prioritizes their use for improving the quality of environment, safeguarding local economies, producing renewable energy, and meeting sustainable development goals (CittaSlow, 2021).

The initial meeting of the mayors led to a 54-point list of principles and pledges, and the building of local alliances of public administration, local businesses and civic groups who supported the slow city ideals (Knox, 2005). The partnership soon became formalized as a wider, institutionalized CittaSlow movement, with a formal governance structure and strict rules for membership: towns and cities only being admitted after confirming a population of less than 50,000, demonstrating a commitment to the movement's principles, and undergoing a detailed audit of present practices concerning environmental policies and planning, infrastructure, technology, local produce and ways of life, hospitality and the rhythm of life, and sense of place (Knox, 2005). As of September 2021, there were 278 member cities in 30 countries, all but 49 of which were in Europe (with only 3 in Africa and 1 in South America), with certification for membership based on 72 requirements (CittaSlow, 2021). While the movement does promote sustainable forms of living and quality of life, it has been critiqued for its nostalgia, aspirational values, rigid rules, scope of ambition (it concentrates on towns and small cities in an era of large cities) and the extent to which it has successfully pushed back against global, capitalist relations (Knox, 2005; Semmens and Freeman, 2012). The philosophy is not adopted by all residents and stakeholders or embedded in all institutions within a locale, is actively resisted in some cases, and is vulnerable to changes in political leadership (Semmens and Freeman, 2012). Nonetheless, its member cities demonstrate that alternative temporal regimes can be imagined and partially produced.

Complementing the CittaSlow movement, and likewise with roots in Italy, is the campaign for urban time policies. In the early 1990s, several policies and laws were introduced in Italy to regulate the timings and scheduling of urban services and workplaces (Bonfiglioli, 1997). Italian municipalities with more than 30,000 inhabitants had to produce a territorial time plan that harmonized the timetables of public services with the needs of citizens, other stakeholders and each other (Radoccia, 2013). In other words, rather than scheduling being dictated by trading activities and every service provider setting opening hours independently, there was an attempt to synchronize timings to maximize the use of services and facilitate quality of life (e.g., to coordinate transport and kindergarten childcare timetables with workplace hours) (Henckel and Thomaier, 2013). These time plans had an explicit gender component that facilitated equality in the coordination of daily life and work rhythms, and access to parental care and public services (Radoccia, 2013). To plan and coordinate time policies, many municipalities established 'city times bureaux' (Bonfiglioli, 1997). Other time policies include restricted access during certain periods (e.g., limiting which vehicles can access some areas or roads during rush hours or limiting truck deliveries to evenings or very early hours), or staggering opening hours to spread loads, lowering prices at specific hours to move demand, and staggering half-day closing across neighbourhoods (Bonfiglioli, 1997; Henckel and Thomaier, 2013).

The CittaSlow movement and the creation of urban time policies have been largely Global North endeavours. In the case of CittaSlow, its logics has been centred on relatively small, long-established places where urban and economic development and population growth are fairly small or stagnant, and the adoption of a slow approach is a lifestyle choice and economic strategy. Shaban and Datta (2017) likewise argue for the reassertion of slow urbanism, but their context is the fast urbanization of the Global South, where rural-to-urban migration and entrepreneurial urban development are leading to the rapid expansion of cities. They note that, in places such as India, the slowness of postcolonial bureaucracy – along with corruption, nepotism and unaccountability of those in power – is viewed by development interests as an unnecessary brake on modernity and progress that requires reform. Yet this slowness provides a necessary counter to speculative urban development that serves the interest of capital but not necessarily the wider public good. Slow provides space for participation, assessment, negotiation, deliberation and tailoring development to local specificities; the potential for more equitable distribution of power in city-making, social justice in decision-making, and protection for those whom mega-developments ride rough-shod over; and the creation of more sustainable and resilient future cities (Shaban and Datta, 2017; Raco et al., 2018). It also creates a political environment in which land dispossession and dislocation are less likely, as are protests, violent resistance and political agitation that can derail projects (Kundu, 2017). Slow urbanism in this sense is not about blocking all development – after all, existing residents need higher-quality abodes, and a growing population needs to be accommodated. Rather, it is about providing checks and balances to ensure that development is appropriate and serves all citizens (Raco et al., 2018).

183

Fast activism

There has long been activism in relation to temporal power. During the nineteenth and twentieth centuries, unions campaigned with respect to working hours, holiday entitlements and age of retirement (Blyton, 1985). Tactics to encourage change included slowness, delay, unpunctuality, stretching authorized breaks, working to rule and absence (Tomlinson, 2007). In some cases, protests turned violent. For example, after chronometers were installed in railway workers' toilet facilities in Cairo, with fines issued to workers who took longer than five minutes, the devices were smashed and rail lines cut; in other protests related to work hours, timetabling and productivity, telephone and telegraph poles were felled and train and tram lines cut (Barak, 2013). In present-day India, small-scale, land-owning populations have organized resistance to the land grabs of the agents of fast urbanization, seeking to block, stall and renegotiate urban development plans (Kundu, 2017). By using militant politics of refusal and symbolic contestation, the aim is to bring a planned development to the brink of crisis, ferment political debate and prompt a change in plans, or at the very least gain satisfactory compensation (Pieterse, 2008).

In recent years, and in contrast to approaches that seek to transform society by slowing things down, activists have sought to employ speed to counter the fast tactics and policies of states and companies. As noted in chapter 4, a number of analysts have noted a growing desynchronization of political practices (which follow time rules designed to enable deliberation and negotiation) and the economic system (which seeks to accelerate processes to improve efficiency and productivity) (Hassan, 2009; Rosa, 2017). Fast policy has been a response by states. Fast activism is the counter-move by civil society seeking to re-synchronize grassroots political practices with the pace and tactics of neoliberal capitalism. Fast activism involves reactive protest that responds quickly to unfolding events, matching or exceeding the pace of opposition actors to disrupt their plans (Lauermann and Vogelpohl, 2019).

'Fast activists plan temporary and strategically timed campaigns', and, like fast policy-makers, will draw on proven actions practised elsewhere and existing expertise in local social movements, quickly organizing diverse coalitions to mobilize opposition and counter-moves (Lauermann and Vogelpohl, 2019: 1231). The aim is to nip proposals in the bud before political and policy decisions are made and contracts signed. To be effective, it requires experienced leaders who can utilize their expertise and their pre-existing networks of allies, who can rapidly build and coordinate an effective alliance and campaign, who know how to react to media cycles and use media platforms to spread persuasive messages and garner support, and are versatile enough to assimilate, and pivot in relation to, the tactics of fast policy (Lauermann and Vogelpohl, 2019). To be successful, strategic actions have to be prepared to occupy the channels used by fast policy-makers and comply with expected behaviours, such as following the rules of communicative capitalism in their media tactics (Kaun, 2017).

The Arab Spring protests, the Occupy Movement, anti-Olympic Games campaigns and the Hong Kong democracy movement are examples of fast activism utilizing digital technologies and platforms. In the early 2010s, a series of anti-government protests and uprisings quickly spread across much of the Arab world, leading to rulers being deposed in four countries (Tunisia, Libya, Egypt and Yemen) and major social violence and civil war in several others. Dubbed the Arab Spring, protesters utilized social media and mobile phones to spread political messages and for rapid coordination of rallies and political action, with the shared, real-time dissent vital for gathering and maintaining momentum (Khondker, 2011; Wolfsfeld et al., 2013). In the case of the Occupy Movement, protesters mobilized to protest at growing wealth inequalities, the effects of the financial crisis on families, corruption in the financial sector, and the lack of consequences for the financial industry from the crisis (Erde, 2014; Kaun, 2015). The movement quickly spread from New York to other cities in the United States and internationally, swapping information and tactics to leverage impact. Hosting an Olympic Games is considered by some to be a prestigious honour and each event is competed for by a number of candidate cities. However, it is also expensive, has infrastructure and environmental-impact legacy effects, and there is little evidence that they produce long-term economic benefits. Between 2013 and 2018, thirteen cities cancelled Olympic bids in response to anti-bid campaigns, with opposition coalitions drawing on local expertise, and inspiration and support from other cities, to mobilize quickly to counter the boosterist agenda of political and corporate supporters (Lauermann and Vogelpohl, 2019). In Hong Kong, pro-democracy protesters have sought to react quickly to political and policy moves in order to try to block and slow attempts by government to limit freedoms (Lee and Chan, 2018). They do so using a sophisticated set of coordination tactics, such as using burner phones, reconfiguring existing phones, utilizing encrypted communications, disabling audio and location permissions of apps, turning off GPS, deleting logs and using false accounts, and at protests covering faces with masks, wearing gloves and black clothes with no labels, spray-painting cameras, and paying for public transport with cash rather than traceable currency (Aiken, 2019; Lee and Chan, 2018). They have also created handbooks so that protesters in other jurisdictions can swiftly learn from and implement their approach (Aiken, 2019).

While, undoubtedly, fast activism had an influential effect in each of these cases, long-term positive outcomes were not always as hoped. In the Arab Spring case, the power vacuums created led to violent counter-state actions and a number of civil wars. The financial sector is as strong as ever globally, and in the United States the right-wing, pro-capitalist Trump administration was elected. In Hong Kong, the Chinese authorities continue to assert their power, introduce anti-democratic legislation and quell protest. Perhaps only in the case of Olympic Games protests have several campaigns been successful, though cities continue to bid to host the event. Nonetheless, each of these cases demonstrates that fast activism can mobilize large, active social movements and can have significant impacts, changing the political terrain and the everyday lives of citizens. It is also important to note, as discussed in chapter 7, that fast activism is a tactic not only of progressives, but also of conservatives who use fast activist tactics to block change and reinforce existing social divisions (Trapenberg Frick, 2016).

Participatory futuring

As noted, futuring endeavours are often driven by vested interests seeking to produce their desired future. In response, there have been calls for futuring work to be citizen-centric, and preferably conducted with, not for, communities. Such an ethics of the future requires a more inclusive, participatory approach to futuring – one that explores possible, preferred and prospective futures desired by citizens, and addresses pressing societal challenges such as climate change. Consultative and participatory futuring is a means to realize a more inclusionary approach to visioning and planning how the future might unfold. Rather than predicting the future or determining probable futures, consultative and participatory futuring are normative exercises designed to determine a preferred future and to anticipate and prepare for futures, and prevent some from being realized, seeking to redirect present future paths onto new trajectories. The parameters for this preferred future can range from utopian wishful thinking through to visions limited by the perceived plausibility, probability and prospects of achieving them. For change to occur, the vision must form a prospective future – that is, society must be prepared to act in order to try to make it happen (Dixon and Tewdwr-Jones, 2021). While utopian imaginings have often been dismissed as constituting a futile, unrealizable pursuit, others hold that they are important for opening up previously unconsidered ideas, instantiating hope and alternative anticipatory logics, making clear the contingent rather than teleological nature of the future, and insisting that things could and must be better (Harvey, 2000; Zapata, 2021). Utopian thinking provides a testbed for exploring and debating what kind of society citizens wish to inhabit (Kitchin, 2019b; Dixon and Tewdwr-Jones, 2021). In other words, an ethics of the future must be aspirational, experimental, hopeful – utopian, to some degree, in its ambition.

Consultative futuring is a means by which several stakeholders – state, business, civil society organizations, academia – co-produce a vision of a preferred future through a facilitated process (Dixon and Tewdwr-Jones, 2021). The aim is to develop some level of consensus about the nature of society in the future and a route to realizing this future. The time horizon is usually medium to long term (20-plus years) rather than the short term, recognizing that transitional or transformative change requires a sufficient time period to occur (Dixon and Tewdwr-Jones, 2021). Rather than focusing on the views of a limited number of selected stakeholder groups, participatory futuring moves towards the inclusion of ordinary citizens and a process of co-creation. In so doing, it aims to capture the views and values of a wider constituency, many of whom will be still alive within any mid-to-long-term future produced. In co-creation, partici-pants are involved in setting the parameters of an initiative, including its aims, objectives, the approach adopted and outcomes, rather than just being involved in the central exercise (Dixon and Tewdwr-Jones, 2021). In this sense, it is more bottom-up in nature, co-managed by citizens, rather than a top-down process in which citizens have a voice but the programme and its outputs are controlled by a vested interest group.

Consultative and participatory futuring are generally foresight, rather than forecasting, initiatives (Dixon and Tewdwr-Jones, 2021). They can employ a number of methods to develop future visions and pathways. These include intelligence gathering about the possible futures – such as horizon scanning that seeks to monitor present trends, detect the drivers and pathways of present trajectories, and identify potential transitions or ruptures to social, economic and environmental systems; and interviews and surveys with stakeholders to gather their opinions about projected and ideal futures and strategic priorities (Dixon and Tewdwr-Jones, 2021). Other methods are used for imagining futures. Scenario-building consists of creating narratives or models about how a future phenomenon, such as a city or neighbourhood, might be constituted. It enables new ideas to be created, and existing assumptions about the future to be challenged. Producing scenarios can involve analysis and design to explore possibilities, constraints and opportunities, and testing activities to assess whether options are viable (Dixon and Tewdwr-Jones, 2021). Creating several scenarios enables discussion about the benefits and deficits of each, and re-fashioning iteratively or creating new scenarios. Projection consists of plotting the actions and milestones required to move from the present to achieve scenarios at a time in the future. Such plotting is sometimes termed roadmapping: charting the route and associated policies and resources required, and their sequencing, to progress towards a goal (Dixon and Tewdwr-Jones, 2021). Spatial strategies and city masterplans extensively use scenario building, projection and roadmapping to envisage how a place will evolve from the present over a specific period (usually the next 10 to 50 years).

In contrast, rather than projecting forwards, backcasting calculates back from a future vision to define the steps or pathways needed to realize its ambition (Adam, 2008). Backcasting frees its implementers from the forward momentum and path dependencies of the present future (the probable future), enabling the imagining of a more radical transformation. Levitas (2013) proposes 'utopia as a method', in which participants create an imaginary, speculative reconstitution of society that enables flourishing for everyone and not just a privileged few (see also Büscher, 2017). The method has three aspects: an archaeological mode (excavating and assembling the elements of what would constitute a utopian society), an ontological mode (defining the subjects, agents and roles interpellated in such a society) and an architectural mode (the institutional design and delineation of that society). Once the utopia is envisioned, then a process of backcasting can be undertaken to think through how the whole vision, or elements of it, might be realized. Consultative and participatory planning can be run in a number of ways, including

188

engagement workshops, town-hall meetings and citizen assemblies, and involve a range of techniques, such as focus group discussion, art and creative practice, and technically mediated experiences (e.g., PPGIS, social media, internet-supported forums and feedback surveys, and various forms of spatial media for experimenting with and exploring potential development scenarios) (Nesta, 2019; Boland et al., 2021).

Of course, foresight studies are aspirational. The visions and plans produced are desire lines – preferred pathways of development. The future, however, is highly contingent and relational, and its unfolding cannot be foretold. Nonetheless, foresight studies are more than thought experiments (Dixon and Tewdwr-Jones, 2021); aligning ambition, foresight, resources and actions can drive development in a certain direction. After all, new buildings start as vision and desire. In most cases, these are converted into blueprints, which then pass through a planning process, before being constructed. The initial vision was realized, though it might have been altered along the way and taken a more circuitous route to completion than anticipated. Foresight studies, and the plans and investments they generate, matter then, as does who is involved in their production.

Conclusion

This chapter has made a case for transforming temporal relations in order to address the imbalances and exploitations of temporal power enabled by the digital. It has argued for an ethics of temporal care and the need for temporal justice, and detailed a number of ways in which temporal power might be resisted and temporal sovereignty claimed. While these temporal tactics might provide some degree of care and justice, enabling temporal autonomy to be reclaimed and temporal relations reconfigured, they do so within the existing political economy and temporal regime, rather than radically reimagining and remaking the socio-economic and temporal-spatial organization of society. The counter-hegemonic actions outlined often lack an overarching strategic vision or a wider ideological framing, and enact politics with a small 'p'. In cases where an issue gains wider political currency, such as the right to disconnect campaign, they can either be subject to significant opposition or be co-opted into the neoliberal project, re-cast to serve capital's interest (hence the adoption of the right to disconnect by companies on their terms). The effect is to reshape some element of temporal arbitrage, while not diminishing

189

the overall temporal ambitions of efficiency, productivity and quick turnover of profit.

Where initiatives do have a wider political framing, such as with CittaSlow, their effects are usually quite localized, and similarly are co-opted by local companies as a business strategy to attract particular kinds of custom. The underlying temporal logics of governmentality remain the same. In this sense, the tactics adopted do not create a new liberatory relationship to time, but, rather, further normalize the temporal regime they seek to tweak (Sharma, 2017). Nonetheless, counter-temporal tactics are important in the sense that they enact what Macgilchrist and Bohmig (2012: 97) term 'minimal politics', creating 'tiny fissures' in the hegemonic temporal regime. The constant refrain of small actions 'ensures that democracy – understood as practices of conflict and disagreement – is enacted on a daily basis', and while individual actions might not usher in funda-mental shifts in the operation of a temporal regime, collectively they potentially widen a fissure sufficiently to enact institutional change (Macgilchrist and Bohmig, 2012: 97).

For a radical transformation of temporal power, however, minimal politics needs to be bundled up and framed within a more sustained, strategic, ideological movement to transform the hegemonic political economy. For some, this means a concerted political movement of radical incrementalism (Pieterse, 2008) to temper and recon-figure capitalism in order to reduce its structural asymmetries and divides, rather than revolution (Marcuse, 2012). Others argue that a 'genuinely humanizing' society (Harvey, 1972: 314) requires capitalism to be up-ended and replaced with a more equitable political economy and social system (Kitchin, 2019b). This is no easy task given that capitalism is so thoroughly hegemonic and robust; many global crises have made little impression on its acceptance as the 'common-sense' way of underpinning how society is organized and operates (Fisher, 2009). One solution to this resilience is to use speed to bring about its demise. Accelerationism is the notion that 'the only radical political response to capitalism is not to protest, disrupt, or critique, nor to await its demise at the hands of its own contradictions, but to accelerate its uprooting, alienating, decoding, abstractive tendencies' (Mackay and Avanessian, 2014: 4). Rather than trying to slow down capitalism, accelerationism embraces speed and the new technologies and practices that accelerate everyday life because, on the one hand, they rush capitalism towards its inherent internal contradictions and potential collapse, and, on the other, they can be used to forge more emancipatory relations (such as a genuine

190

sharing economy, rather than one underpinned by capital). As such, digital technologies and network time offer opportunities to rebuild society in a different form and cannot be left to capitalism and the Right, but must be co-opted by progressives (Williams and Srnicek, 2013; Mackay and Avanessian, 2014).

— 11 —

MAKING SENSE OF DIGITAL TIMESCAPES

Time, technology and everyday life are complexly interrelated. Their entanglement produces a varied set of timescapes that shape, and are shaped by, everyday activities and experiences. The principal objective of this book has been to examine how a diverse set of digital devices, systems, platforms and infrastructures is transforming the production of temporalities. The concept of timescapes has been the central analytical framing for the analysis. Explicit in its formulation is the entwining of places, activities and temporal relations – that everyday life consists of the production of multiple, intersecting temporalities that are inflected by space and matter, and are 'embodied in specific and unique geographical context' (Adam, 2004; Liu, 2021: 14). The various facets of everyday life do not possess a singular temporality, but consist of a plethora of unfolding rhythms, cycles, tempos, beats and other temporal relations, which operate within and reproduce temporal regimes, and are shaped by temporal power and its resistance. Charting the timescapes of sites and domains, then, provides a holistic understanding of how everyday life is produced within and through the temporal in ways that are contextual, contingent and relational. The exploration of timescapes has purposively been synoptic in order to consider critically a range of processes, practices, domains, technologies and temporalities. Such a synoptic approach has value because it reveals the varied ways in which timescapes are produced and what they mean for personal lives, communities, and how everyday life is planned, managed, governed, serviced and experienced.

The core argument developed throughout the book is that penetration of digital technologies into social, political and economic life has profoundly altered timescapes and time consciousness. The digital has become the key means of mediating temporal relations and organizing temporal power. Digital technologies have led to new time-space configurations, enabled new temporal practices, competencies and skills, and radically altered our sense, expectations and experiences of time, quickly forming a new temporal doxa. Just as temporal and spatial relations underwent profound changes in the late nineteenth and early twentieth centuries, driven by the introduction of new communication, media, transport and utility technologies, and new temporal policies and practices, a similar transition has occurred at the end of the twentieth century and in the first two decades of the twenty-first. These new temporalities have become thoroughly normalized by individuals and organizations, becoming routine and expected ways of understanding, orientating and acting temporally.

Mass datafication, the development of mnemotechnologies, new data infrastructures and the creation of digital archives have transformed: the scope and granularity of information being retained for future generations; access to past records, personal and collective memory; and the epistemology of historical research and how the past is understood. The time rules, timetables, tempos, cycles and rhythms of politics, as well as how temporality is used as a resource, have been reconfigured through instant communication, 24/7 media, social media, instant polling and performance analytics. Fast and mobile policy-making is dependent on the rapid circulation of knowledge through internet channels, as well as predictive analytics, simulation, modelling, and prototyping and testbedding to colonize the future. The systems and practices of government and governance have become thoroughly digitally mediated over the past thirty years; interactions with all levels of government and the state are increasingly undertaken through e-government portals, services and infrastructure are monitored and controlled in real-time, and algorithmic systems are used to predict, prevent, pre-empt and respond to emergencies, in turn shifting governmentality from discipline towards control.

The everyday scheduling and mobilities of individuals have been reshaped by mobile/smartphones and locative/spatial media, producing greater flexibility but also temporal density and fragmentation. The operation of transportation has been made more efficient through real-time intelligent systems, and the coordination and synchronization of local and global logistics have been reorganized and optimized through the use of enterprise resource planning and supply chain management systems. A range of planning/spatial technologies, such as GIS, BIM and planning support systems, along with digitally mediated financial systems, are driving development and fast urbanization, and how cities, towns and rural areas are designed, planned, and built, slide into decline and obsolescence, and cycle into a new phase of regeneration and gentrification. Much work and labour has become thoroughly digitally mediated, either practised with or monitored through an enormous number of specialist and generic digital devices and systems. In turn, labour has become more flexible, precarious, efficient and productive. Moreover, the time-space distanciation produced by networked technologies has enabled companies to expand further globally and reconfigure their operations, taking advantage of extended mechanisms of control, labour offshoring, temporal arbitrage and just-in-time logistics. Digital technologies are central to the configuring and operations of contemporary political economies, and the logics and functioning of capitalism, accelerating the turnover time of capital and colonizing the future.

While digital technologies are certainly transforming timescapes, the changes wrought are not always positive. Timescapes are saturated with temporal power and riven with temporal inequalities. Indeed, much of the social sciences literature examining how digital technologies are impacting society and economy identify problematic effects and trends that offset and counter gains made with respect to timeliness, efficiency and productivity. These include: mass datafication, issues of forgetting, and the control of mnemotechnologies and the production of history; the densification and fragmentation of temporalities, and the mismatch of time orders and horizons within and across domains which create arrhythmia and asynchronicity; the tyranny of real-time and acting in the present with little time for deliberation; time density and time pressures that impact on individual lives; the slow violence of structural inequalities on communities that fast policies ignore; and disparities in the ability to project, plan, produce and colonize the future that unequally serve vested interests.

While there are undoubtedly problematic and pernicious effects wrought by digital technologies with respect to temporalities, the temporal regimes and doxa being reproduced are open to resistance, subversion and transformation, including through the strategic use of the same technologies. Temporal power is always open to rupture and the claiming of temporal sovereignty and autonomy. There is a long history of individual and collective action to counter temporal power and reconfigure temporal relations. This has continued in the digital era, with a number of ideas and ideals being forwarded that are rooted in broader notions of an ethics of care and social justice. These include an ethics of forgetting; an ethics of deceleration, disconnection and asynchronicity; an ethics of the future; and temporal justice. These ideas and ideals have been translated into politics and praxes in a number of ways, including counter-archiving and building community archives, slow computing, slow urbanism and urban time policies, fast activism, and participatory futuring. While these actions can make a substantive difference to addressing temporal inequalities, lessening time pressures, ameliorating temporal arbitrage and providing greater degrees of temporal autonomy, they do not transform the underlying political economy that sustains and exploits temporal power. The question, then, as to how to produce genuinely fair and equitable timescapes remains open.

While the analysis of these digital timescapes, temporalities and their consequences has been reasonably broad in scope, it has also been selective. Everyday life is complex, multifaceted, interdependent and dynamic, with social and economic relations and operations stretched from the local to the global, and numerous interlinkages across domains of activity. As such, there are many other digital timescapes and temporal relations that the analysis has omitted or only dealt with in a cursory way. For example, the book could have included chapters in Part II concerning the timescapes of infrastructures and utilities, housing, education, health, welfare and the environment, amongst others, or focused on particular sites such as the home, the street, shopping malls, parks, the countryside or public transit. Moreover, each of the chapters in Part II could be expanded into a book-length treatment in their own right (indeed, many of the works cited have done so). The analysis predominantly related to the Global North and was rather universal in its argument, treating domains in a relatively generic way rather than drawing out the variations in temporalities across places due to culture, politics, governance, economy, environment and history. Likewise, time's persistent partner, space, has been ever present in the text, but has been somewhat backgrounded to concentrate attention on temporality. These shortcomings are not just limited to this book, which takes a much wider view in terms of domains, technologies and temporalities than most other related texts, and the remainder of the chapter discusses how they might be addressed, detailing an agenda for making sense of digital timescapes.

A research agenda

While there is a relatively extensive literature concerning the relationship between digital technologies, temporality and everyday life, there is significant work still to be done to make further sense of digital timescapes. The work can profitably follow a number of routes, all of which need to be interdisciplinary in practice, drawing together insights, concepts, approaches and methods from across science and technology studies, media studies, sociology, geography, urban studies, philosophy, political science, anthropology, history, memory studies, libraries and archives, and other disciplines.

As table 2.1 highlights, there is a vast array of digital technologies and infrastructures that augment and produce everyday life, and mediate the production of temporalities. The focus of attention, however, is somewhat uneven, with some technologies, such as mobile- and smartphones and the apps they host, and digital archives, receiving more interest. Undoubtedly, these technologies are important vectors for shifts in temporal relations, particularly with respect to individual experiences. Other technologies, however, are often just as consequential for activities within domains, mediating the temporalities of work, consumption, travel, leisure and so on, and require further empirical investigation to chart how they: shape the production of time; forge and maintain timescapes; affect the complex interrelation of past, present and future; and have diverse consequences for individuals, systems and domains. Detailed studies are needed to examine the temporal affordances of particular digital technologies, including how and in what ways variations within the same classes of technologies make a difference, how different classes of technologies vary in affordances, and how technologies contribute to the production of temporalities in conjunction with other technologies. The latter point is important; the temporalities of home, work or public space are not produced by single technologies working in isolation but through the entanglement of several co-eval technologies that might work to produce eurythmic arrangements or create arrhythmia and discord.

A key focus in unpacking the temporalities produced by digital technologies should be further consideration of how they variously affect individuals who are from the same social group, and examining differences across social groups. As noted, digital technologies help to produce temporal power, and maintain temporal inequalities and slow violence. Many studies have noted different temporalities experienced across gender, race, class, sexuality, age, disability, culture and religion, and other social markers such as household structure, employment status and job type. Intersectional work is less well developed and needs redress. Further studies are required concerning the workings of temporal power and patterns of inequalities across the full panoply of digital technologies across all domains, and these need to be linked into the wider literature around algorithmic violence and justice. An important component of such work is to chart how temporal power and inequalities are being resisted, and how they might be further challenged and reconfigured. Just as time is differentially experienced, it is variously understood across groups and cultures. Approaches to studying temporality, then, need to be mindful of diverse conceptions and orientations to time, and to account for these in their analysis, rather than trying to shoehorn them into the temporal framing of the analyst. This requires researchers to be sensitive to their positionality and situatedness in undertaking a study, and reflexive and nuanced in their interpretations.

Similarly, there is an unevenness of attention in the mapping of timescapes. Sites such as home and work, and domains such as production and mobility, have attracted more interest and empirical study to date than politics, policy, public space, health and education. Within these sites and domains, there is a need to examine not just how digitally mediated temporalities are affecting individual experiences, but also how they are reconfiguring the practices and operations of services, management, governance and labour, and are having system effects. This includes charting in detail the various temporalities that are being enacted within domains, the processes and temporal power driving them, the specific effects of temporal affordances and how these are being enhanced or tempered by other factors, and the extent to which temporalities are domain-specific affordances. It should also include work that charts the history of temporalities within a domain, and how temporal relations have evolved in contingent, relational and contextual ways, and a critical examination of futuring, future-making and potential future temporal relations. Such work needs to be sensitive to the interdependencies of time and space, being careful to avoid producing accounts in which time is rendered spaceless. To be sure, in making sense of some phenomena, the temporal is a core explanatory frame, such as time rules shaping the practice of politics; nonetheless, spatiality co-inflects action. Time rules are enacted within and produce time-spaces.

As well as examining the timescapes of specific sites and domains, research is required on the ways in which timescapes are variously

197

scaled from the household to the global, stretching out as a progressive sense of time in which temporalities elsewhere are connected and co-produced across scale. This is well illustrated with respect to fast urbanization, in which the network time of finance and the global circuits of master-planning expertise are grounded in, and drive, local temporalities of development. The scaling of temporalities equally applies to other domains, such as the home through the streaming of television from distant servers, or multiplayer games where contestants are distantly located but temporally co-present, or through the time-space distanciation and temporal arbitrage at work across multinational companies and logistic chains. In addition, there is a need to map out further the ways in which various timescapes intersect, working in concert or disharmony to produce urban chronotopias that collectively constitute a city's temporal landscape. Domains such as work, home and mobility are thoroughly inter-related and intertwined. Home and work are not divorced sites, with some work activities occurring at home, and home activities being organized from work. Moreover, mobility links the sites together, and work and home activities can be performed on the move. The tempo-ralities of households, business and public space co-produce the temporalities, sense of time and time-geographies of neighbourhoods.

Such work needs to be sensitive to the variances in timescapes across sites, neighbourhoods and cities. Just as there are differences across individuals and groups, there are variances within and across sites and places. In part, this is due to those who occupy those spaces, but it is also shaped by broader institutional and structural factors such as culture, governance, politics, political economy and history that contextualize the production of temporal orders and regimes. It is clear that the temporalities within cities vary across space – for example, the time-spaces of a city centre with its concentration of businesses and night-time economy being quite different to a wealthy, leafy suburb, which differs from a working-class estate or, in the context of the Global South, an informal settlement. Indeed, the temporalities of cities in the Global North and Global South might have some similarities and some marked differences, and there might be substantial variances within each. For example, within the Global North, the dynamism of a world city produces quite different devel-opment temporalities to the deceleration and decline of a shrinking city. In the Global South, fast urbanization varies in character between places, and not all places experience network time to the same extent, with lower levels of connectivity and less social and economic activity mediated by digital technologies. Care therefore needs to be taken to avoid universalist and deterministic accounts that treat all sites and places as if they are the same. While there has been some mention of temporalities in the Global South, it has been largely absent in the book, for good reason. Likewise, indigenous notions of time have been little examined. I am not an expert on the use of digital technologies and temporality in the Global South, or indigenous timescapes, and there is a distinct politics enacted by a Global North scholar writing about issues in which they are not well versed. I leave it to others, then, to produce a more informed, nuanced and situated analysis.

In all of these analyses, any research conducted needs to attend to the four issues detailed at the end of chapter 1. First, it will need to gauge the extent to which temporal relations are an outcome of other processes, or are the causal mechanisms driving how a process operates. Just because there are identifiable temporal effects, it does not automatically follow that it is time that is shaping the phenomena. Second, it should be careful to avoid a deterministic and teleological analysis of the effects of digital technologies on temporality, instead seeking a contingent, relational and nuanced analysis that places the role of digital technologies in wider context. Third, it will have to be sensitive to the multiplicity and (dis)continuities of temporalities that coexist. While digital technologies are transforming temporal relations, they are not fully replacing the temporalities of modernity – clock time and sacred and eschatological time remain important and will continue to do so. Fourth, there is a need for analysis to be situated in relation to the positionality of the analyst and the literature from which they are drawing theory and empirical examples.

This discussion of a future orientation and agenda for making sense of digital timescapes and addressing present shortcomings has its own limitations. There are undoubtedly many other issues and questions that need attention, and these will continue to grow as new technologies are developed and they are folded into everyday life. Moreover, the conceptual toolkit for making sense of timescapes will continue to evolve as new ideas and insights emerge and build on the valuable work to date. Hopefully, this chapter has constituted a useful piece of futuring to guide a research agenda and the book has contributed in a productive way to advancing how we understand time, temporality and everyday timescapes in the digital era, providing a coherent, grounded, synoptic analysis. Time might be produced, but there is no escaping it; we need therefore to understand its nature in order to produce more equitable and just digital timescapes.

REFERENCES

Abram, S. and Weszkalnys, G. (2011) Introduction: Anthropologies of planning – temporality, imagination, and ethnography. *Focaal – Journal of Global and Historical Anthropology*, 61(1): 3–18.

Acemoglu, D. and Restrepo, P. (2020) The wrong kind of AI? Artificial intelligence and the future of labour demand. *Cambridge Journal of Regions, Economy and Society*, 13(1): 25–35.

Adam, B. (1990) *Time and Social Theory*. Cambridge: Polity.

Adam, B. (1998) *Timescapes of Modernity: The Environment and Invisible Hazards*. London: Routledge.

Adam, B. (2004) *Time*. Cambridge: Polity.

Adam, B. (2007) Foreword. In R. Hassan and R. Purser, eds., *24/7: Time and Temporality in the Network Society*, ix–xii. Stanford University Press.

Adam, B. (2008) Of timespaces, futurescapes and timeprints. Presentation at Luneburg University, Luneburg, Germany. http://citeseerx.ist.psu.edu/viewdoc/summary?doi=10.1.1.594.1289.

Adam, B. and Groves, C. (2007) *Future Matters*. Leiden: Brill.

Adams, V., Murphy, M. and Clarke, A. E. (2009) Anticipation: Technoscience, life, affect, temporality. *Subjectivity*, 28(1): 246–65.

Agre, P. (1994) Surveillance and capture: Two models of privacy. *Information Society*, 10(2): 101–27.

Aiken, S. (2019) Inside digital resistance in Cypherpunk Harbour. Medium, 1 Oct. https://medium.com/crypto-punks/digital-resistance-security-privacy-tips-from-hong-kongprotesters-37ff9ef73129.

Amara, R. (1981) The futures field: Searching for definitions and boundaries. *The Futurist*, 15(1): 25–9.

Amin, A. (2013) Surviving the turbulent future. *Environment and Planning D: Society and Space*, 31(1): 140–56.

Amoore, L. (2006) Biometric borders: Governing mobilities in the war on terror, *Political Geography*, 25: 336–51.

Amoore, L. (2013) *The Politics of Possibility: Risk and Security beyond Probability*. Durham, NC: Duke University Press.

Anderson, B. (2010) Preemption, precaution, preparedness: Anticipatory action and future geographies. *Progress in Human Geography*, 34(6): 777–98.

Anderson, B. (2015) Governing emergencies: The politics of delay and the logic of response. *Transactions of the Institute of British Geographers*, 41: 14–26.

Anderson, B. (2016) Emergency/everyday. In J. Burges and A. L. Elias, eds., *Time: A Vocabulary of the Present*, 177–91. New York University Press.

Anderson, B., Grove, K., Rickards, L. and Kearnes, M. (2020) Slow emergencies: Temporality and the racialized biopolitics of emergency governance. *Progress in Human Geography*, 44(4): 621–39.

Andrejevic, M. (2009) Privacy, exploitation, and the digital enclosure. *Amsterdam Law Forum*, 1(4): 47–62.

Andrejevic, M., Dencik, L. and Treré, E. (2020) From pre-emption to slowness: Assessing the contrasting temporalities of data-driven predictive policing. *New Media & Society*, 22(9): 1528–44.

Appadurai, A. (2013) *The Future as Cultural Fact: Essays on the Global Condition*. New York: Verso.

Aradau, C. and Blanke, T. (2015) The (Big) Data-security assemblage: Knowledge and critique. *Big Data & Society*, 2(2): 1–12.

Arthur, P. L. (2009) Saving lives: Digital biography and life writing. In J. Garde-Hansen, A. Hoskins and A. Reading, eds., *Save As … Digital Memories*, 44–59. Basingstoke: Palgrave Macmillan.

Ash, A. (n.d.) The best books on Slow Living recommended by Carl Honoré. Five Books. https://fivebooks.com/best-books/slow-living-carl-honore.

Bagaeen, S. (2007) Brand Dubai: The instant city or the instantly recognizable city. *International Planning Studies*, 12(2): 173–97.

Ball, J., Capanni, N. and Watt, S. (2007) Virtual reality for mutual under-standing in landscape planning. *International Journal of Information and Communication Engineering*, 1(11): 661–71.

Ball, K. (2010) Workplace surveillance: An overview. *Labour History*, 51(1): 87–106.

Bańbura, M., Giannone, D. and Reichlin, L. (2010) Nowcasting. *European Central Bank Working Paper No. 1275*. www.econstor.eu/bitstream/10419/153709/1/ecbwp1275.pdf.

Barak, O. (2013) *On Time: Technology and Temporality in Modern Egypt*. Berkeley: University of California Press.

Barassi, V. (2020) Datafied times: Surveillance capitalism, data technologies and the social construction of time in family life. *New Media & Society*, 22(9): 1545–60.

Beagrie, N. A., Lavoie, B. and Wollard, M. (2010) *Keeping Research Data Safe 2*. London and Bristol: JISC. www.beagrie.com/jisc.php.

Beckert, J. (2016) *Imagined Futures: Fictional Expectations and Capitalist Dynamics*. Cambridge, MA: Harvard University Press.

Beer, D. (2016) *Metric Power*. London: Palgrave.

Beer, D. (2019) *The Data Gaze: Capitalism, Power and Perception*. London: Sage.

Ben-David, A. (2020) Counter-archiving Facebook. *European Journal of Communication*, 35(3): 249–64.

Benjamin, R. (2019) *Race After Technology*. Cambridge: Polity.

Berg, M. and Seeber, B. (2017) *The Slow Professor: Challenging the Culture of Speed in the Academy*. University of Toronto Press.

Berman, M. (1982) *All That Is Solid Melts into Air: The Experience of Modernity*. New York: Simon & Schuster.

Berry, D. (2017) The post-archival constellation: The archive under the technical conditions of computational media. In I. Blom, T. Lundemo and E. Røssaak, eds., *Memory in Motion: Archives, Technology and the Social*, 103–25. Amsterdam University Press.

Bittman, M. and Wajcman, J. (2000) The Rush Hour: The character of leisure time and gender equity. *Social Forces*, 79(1): 165–89.

Bleecker, J. and Nova, N. (2009) *Asynchronicity: Design Fictions for Asynchronous Urban Computing*. New York: Situated Technologies.

Blom, I. (2017) Introduction: Rethinking social memory – archives, technology, and the social. In I. Blom, T. Lundemo and E. Røssaak, eds., *Memory in Motion: Archives, Technology and the Social*, 11–38. Amsterdam University Press.

Blumenfeld, S., Anderson, G. and Hooper, V. (2020) Covid-19 and employee surveillance. *New Zealand Journal of Employment Relations*, 45(2): 42–56

Blyton, P. (1985) *Changes in Working Time: An International Review*. Sydney: Croom Helm.

Bode, L. (2016) Political news in the news feed: Learning politics from social media. *Mass Communication and Society*, 19(1): 24–48.

Boland, P., Durrant, A., McHenry, J., McKay, S. and Wilson, A. (2021, online first) A 'planning revolution' or an 'attack on planning' in England: Digitization, digitalization, and democratization. *International Planning Studies*. https://doi.org/ 10.1080/13563475.2021.1979942.

Bonfiglioli, S. (1997) Urban time policies in Italy: An overview of time-oriented research. *Transfer: European Review of Labour and Research*, 3(4): 700–22.

Bonilla, Y. and Rosa, J. (2015) #Ferguson: Digital protest, hashtag ethnography, and the racial politics of social media in the United States. *American Ethnologist*, 42(1): 4–17.

Borgman, C. L. (2007) *Scholarship in the Digital Age*. Cambridge, MA: MIT Press.

Bowker, G. (2005) *Memory Practices in the Sciences*. Cambridge, MA: MIT Press.

Boyle, M. (2015) *Human Geography: A Concise Introduction*. Chichester: Wiley Blackwell.

Brayne, S. (2017) Big data surveillance: The case of policing. *American Sociological Review*, 82(5): 977–1008.

Brenner, N., Peck, J. and Theodore, N. (2010) Variegated neoliberalizations: Geographies, modalities, pathways. *Global Networks*, 10(2): 182–222.

Brighenti, A. M. and Karrholm, M. (2019) Three presents: On the multi-temporality of territorial production and the gift from John Soane. *Time & Society*, 28(1): 375–98.

Brockmeier, J. (2002) Remembering and forgetting: Narrative as cultural memory. *Culture & Psychology*, 8(1): 15–43.

Brown, S. (2021) Evidence and absence in the archives: A study of the Irish Refugee Appeals Tribunal Archive to assess the state practice of determining asylum in Ireland. Ph.D. thesis, Maynooth University.

Bruzelius, C. (2017) Digital technologies and new evidence in Architectural History. *Journal of the Society of Architectural Historians*, 76(4): 436–9.

Burges, J. and Elias, A. J. (2016) Introduction: Time studies today. In J. Burges and A. L. Elias, eds., *Time: A Vocabulary of the Present*, 1–32. New York University Press.

202

Burgum, S. (2020, online first) This city is an archive: Squatting history and urban authority. *Journal of Urban History.* https://doi.org/10.1177/0096144220955165.

Büscher, M. (2017). The mobile utopia experiment. In J. Southern, E. Rose and L. O'Keeffe, eds., *Mobile Utopia: Art and Experiments*, 12–18. Exhibition catalogue. http://eprints.lancs.ac.uk/89847/1/AMCatalogue_inners_lok.pdf.

Buthe, T. (2002) Taking temporarity seriously: Modeling history and the use of narratives as evidence. *American Political Science Review*, 96(3): 481–93.

Byles, J. (2005) *Rubble: Unearthing the History of Demolition.* New York: Three Rivers Press.

Cairncross, F. (1997) *The Death of Distance: How the Communications Revolution Will Change Our Lives.* Boston, MA: Harvard Business School Press.

Calhoun, C. (1998). Explanation in historical sociology: Narrative, general theory, and historically specific theory. *American Journal of Sociology*, 104: 846–71.

Castells, M. (1996) *Rise of the Network Society.* Oxford: Blackwell.

Castells, M. (1998) *End of the Millennium.* Oxford: Blackwell.

Caswell, M., Migoni, A., Geraci, N. and Cifor, M. (2017) 'To be able to imagine otherwise': Community archives and the importance of representation. *Archives and Records*, 38(1): 5–26.

Chen, J. Y. and Sun, P. (2020) Temporal arbitrage, fragmented rush, and opportunistic behaviors: The labor politics of time in the platform economy. *New Media & Society*, 22(9): 1561–79.

Cheng, T. C. E. and Lai, K.-H. (2009) *Just-in-Time Logistics.* Farnham: Gower.

Chesher, C. (2012) Navigating sociotechnical spaces: comparing computer games and sat navs as digital spatial media. *Convergence: The International Journal of Research into New Media Technologies*, 18(3): 315–30.

Chien, S.-S. and Woodworth, M. D. (2018) China's urban speed machine: The politics of speed and time in a period of rapid urban growth. *International Journal of Urban and Regional Research*, 42(4): 723–37.

Chopra, S. and Meindl, P. (2012) *Supply Chain Management: Strategy, Planning and Operation*, 5th edition. Harlow: Pearson.

Chun, W. H. K. (2016) *Updating to Remain the Same: Habitual New Media.* Cambridge, MA: MIT Press.

Cifor, M., Caswell, M., Migoni, A. and Geraci, A. (2018) 'What we do crosses over to activism': The politics and practice of community archives. *Archives and Public History*, 40(2): 69–95.

CittaSlow (2021) CittaSlow website. www.cittaslow.org.

Clancy, M. (2016) *Slow Tourism, Food and Cities: Pace and the Search for the 'Good Life'.* London: Routledge.

Codagnone, C., Karatzogianni, A. and Matthews, J. (2019) *Platform Economics: Rhetoric and Reality in the 'Sharing Economy'.* Bingley: Emerald.

Cohen, J. E. (2019) Turning privacy inside out. *Theoretical Inquiries in Law*, 20(1): 1–32.

Coleman, R. (2018) Theorizing the present: Digital media, pre-emergence and infra-structures of feeling. *Cultural Studies*, 32(4): 600–22.

Coleman, R. (2020) Making, managing and experiencing 'the now': Digital media and the compression and pacing of 'real-time'. *New Media & Society*, 22(9): 1680–98.

Coletta, C. and Kitchin, R. (2017) Algorhythmic governance: Regulating the 'heartbeat' of a city using the Internet of Things. *Big Data & Society*, 4: 1–16.

Colville, R. (2016) *The Great Acceleration*. London: Bloomsbury.

Conlon, D. (2010) Fascinatin' rhythm(s): Polyrhythmia and the syncopated echoes of the everyday. In T. Edensor, ed., *Geographies of Rhythm: Nature, Place, Mobilities and Bodies*, 71–81. Farnham: Ashgate.

Connerton, P. (2009) *How Modernity Forgets*. Cambridge University Press.

Correll, S. J., Kelly, E. L., O'Connor, L. T. and Williams, J. C. (2014) Redesigning, redefining Work. *Work and Occupations*, 41(1): 3–17.

Costello, S. (2020) The sensors that make the iPhone so cool. Lifewire, 4 Feb. www.lifewire.com/sensors-that-make-iphone-so-cool-2000370.

Cowen, D. (2014) *The Deadly Life of Logistics: Mapping Violence in Global Trade*. Minneapolis: University of Minnesota Press.

Craig, G. and Parkins, W. (2006) *Slow Living*. Oxford: Berg.

Crang, M. (2001) Rhythms of the city: Temporalised space and motion. In J. May and N. Thrift, eds., *Timespace: Geographies of Temporality*, 187–207. London: Routledge.

Crang, M. (2005) Time: Space. In P. Cloke and R. Johnston, eds., *Spaces of Geographical Thought: Deconstructing Human Geography's Binaries*, 199–220. London: Sage.

Crang, M. (2007) Speed = distance/time: chronotopographies of action. In R. Hassan and R. Purser, eds., *24/7: Time and Temporality in the Network Society*, 62–88. Stanford University Press.

Crary, J. (2013) *24/7: Late Capitalism and the Ends of Sleep*. London: Verso.

Crotty, R. (2011) *The Impact of Building Information Modelling: Transforming Construction*. London: Routledge.

Crowley, D. (2010) *Adventures in Mobile Social 2.0: Twelve Months of Foursquare, at Where 2.0*. Santa Clara, CA: O'Reilly Media Inc.

Cugurullo, F. (2017) Speed kills: Fast urbanism and endangered sustainability in the Masdar City project. In A. Datta and A. Shaban, eds., *Mega-urbanization in the Global South: Fast Cities and New Urban Utopias of the Postcolonial State*, 66–80. London: Routledge.

Cuomo, D. and Dolci, N. (2021) New tools, old abuse: Technology-Enabled Coercive Control (TECC). *Geoforum*, 126: 224–32.

Curran, D. (2018) Are you ready? Here is all the data Facebook and Google have on you. *The Guardian*, 30 Mar. www.theguardian.com/commentisfree/2018 /mar/28/all-the-data-facebook-google-has-on-you-privacy.

Datta, A. (2015). New urban utopias of postcolonial India: 'Entrepreneurial urbanization' in Dholera smart city, Gujarat. *Dialogues in Human Geography*, 5(1): 3–22.

Datta, A. (2017) Introduction: Fast cities in an urban age. In A. Datta and A. Shaban, eds., *Mega-urbanization in the Global South: Fast Cities and New Urban Utopias of the Postcolonial State*, 1–27. London: Routledge.

Datta, A. (2018) The 'digital turn' in postcolonial urbanism: Smart citizenship in the making of India's 100 smart cities. *Transactions of the IBG*, 43(3): 405–19.

Datta, A. (2019) Postcolonial urban futures: Imagining and governing India's smart urban age. *Environment and Planning D: Society and Space*, 37(3): 393–410.

Datta, A. (2020) The 'Smart Safe City': Gendered time, speed, and violence in the margins of India's urban age. *Annals of the American Association of Geographers*, 110(5): 1318–34. https://doi.org/10.1080/24694452.2019.1687279.

Datta, A. (2021) Distant-times. Presentation at the 'Infrastructural Times' workshop, Network on Infrastructural Regionalism, Regional Studies Association, online event, 14–18 June.

de Lange, M. (2018) From real-time city to asynchronicity: Exploring temporalities of smart city dashboards. In S. Lammes, C. Perkins, A. Gekker, S. Hind, C. Wilmott and D. Evans, eds., *Time for Mapping: Cartographic Temporalities*, 238–55. Manchester University Press.

de Stefano, V. (2015) The rise of the just-in-time workforce: on-demand work, crowdwork, and labor protection in the gig-economy. *Comparative Labor Law & Policy Journal*, 37: 471–504.

Delaney, A. (2019) Humanising policy from 'Warriors to Guardians': An evaluation of coordinated management and emergency response assemblages in Ireland and the US. Ph.D. thesis, Maynooth University.

Delaney, A. and Kitchin, R. (2020, online first) Progress and prospects for data-driven coordinated management and emergency response: the case of Ireland. *Territory, Politics, Governance*. https://doi.org/10.1080/21622671.2020.1805355.

Deleuze, G. (1992) Postscript on the societies of control. *October*, 59: 3–7.

Delfanti, A. (2021) Machinic dispossession and augmented despotism: Digital work in an Amazon warehouse. *New Media & Society*, 23(1): 39–55.

Dencik, L., Hintz, A. and Carey, Z. (2018) Prediction, pre-emption and limits to dissent: Social media and big data uses for policing protests in the United Kingdom. *New Media & Society*, 20: 1433–50.

Dencik, L., Redden, J., Hintz, A. and Warne, H. (2019) The 'golden view': Data-driven governance in the scoring society. *Internet Policy Review*, 8(2): 1–24.

Dery, K., Hall, R. and Wailes, N. (2006) ERPs as technologies-in-practice: Social construction, materiality and the role of organisational factors. *New Technology, Work and Employment*, 21(3): 229–41.

Dicken, P. (2007) *Global Shift: Mapping the Changing Contours of the World Economy*, 5th edition. London: Sage.

Dilworth, R. and Gardner, T. (2019) White flight. In A. Orum, ed., *Wiley-Blackwell Encyclopedia of Urban and Regional Studies*, 1–6. Hoboken, NJ: Wiley Blackwell.

Dixon, T. J. and Tewdwr-Jones, M. (2021) *Urban Futures: Planning for City Foresight and City Visions*. Bristol: Policy Press.

Docherty, B. (2012) *Losing Humanity: The Case against Killer Robots*. New York: Human Rights Watch. www.hrw.org/sites/default/files/reports/arms1112_ForUpload.pdf.

Dodge, M. (2019) Rural. In J. Ash, R. Kitchin and A. Leszczynski, eds., *Digital Geographies*, 36–48. London: Sage.

Dodge, M. and Kitchin, R. (2007) 'Outlines of a world coming into existence': Pervasive computing and the ethics of forgetting. *Environment and Planning B*, 34(3): 431–45.

Dodge, M. and Kitchin, R. (2009) Software, objects and home spaces. *Environment and Planning A*, 41(6): 1344–65.

Dodgshon, R. A. (1999) Human geography at the end of time? Some thoughts on the notion of time-space compression. *Environment and Planning D: Society and Space*, 17(5): 607–20.

Dodgshon, R. A. (2008) Geography's place in time. *Geografiska Annaler B*, 90(1): 1–15.

Doyle, S., Dodge, M. and Smith, A. (1998) The potential of web-based mapping and virtual reality technologies for modeling urban environments. *Computers, Environment and Urban Systems*, 22(2): 137–55.

Drummond, W. J. and French, S. P. (2008) The future of GIS in planning: Converging technologies and diverging interests. *Journal of the American Planning Association*, 74(2): 161–74.

Dutilleul, B., Birrer, F. A. and Mensink, W. (2010) Unpacking European living labs: Analysing innovation's social dimensions. *Central European Journal of Public Policy*, 4(1): 60–85.

Dyson, K. (2009) The evolving timescapes of European economic governance: Contesting and using time. *Journal of European Public Policy*, 16(2): 286–306.

Edensor, T. (2005) *Industrial Ruins: Space, Aesthetics and Materiality*. Oxford: Berg.

Edensor, T. (2010) Introduction: Thinking about rhythm and space. In T. Edensor, ed., *Geographies of Rhythm: Nature, Place, Mobilities and Bodies*, 1–18. Farnham: Ashgate.

Edensor, T. and Holloway, J. (2008) Rhythmanalysing the coach tour: The ring of Kerry, Ireland. *Transactions of the Institute of British Geographers*, 33: 483–501.

Ekström, A. (2016) When is the now? Monitoring disaster in the expansion of time. *International Journal of Communication*, 10: 5342–61.

Elsner, I., Monstadt, J. and Raven, R. (2019) Decarbonizing Rotterdam? Energy transitions and the alignment of urban and infrastructural temporalities. *City*, 23(4–5): 646–57.

Elwood, S. and Ghose, R. (2001) PPGIS in community development planning: Framing the organizational context. *Cartographica*, 38(3–4): 19–33.

Erde, J. (2014) Constructing archives of the Occupy movement. *Archives & Records*, 35(2): 77–92.

Erickson, I. and Mazmanian, M. (2017) Bending time to a new end: Investigating the idea of temporal entrepreneurship. In N. Dodd and J. Wajcman, eds., *The Sociology of Speed: Digital, Organizational, and Social Temporalities*, 152–68. Oxford University Press.

Esposito, E. (2017) Algorithmic memory and the right to be forgotten. *Big Data & Society*, 4(1): 1–11.

Eurofound (2016) *Working Time Developments in the 21st Century: Work Duration and Its Regulation in the EU*. Luxembourg: Publications Office of the European Union. www.eurofound.europa.eu/sites/default/files/ef_publication/field_ef_document/ef1573en.pdf.

Eurofound (2017) *Sixth European Working Conditions Survey – Overview Report*. Luxembourg: Publications Office of the European Union. Interactive data visualizations at www.eurofound.europa.eu/data/european-working-conditions-survey.

Evans, J., Karvonen, A. and Raven, R. (2016) *The Experimental City*. London: Routledge.

Evans, L. and Kitchin, R. (2018) A smart place to work? Big data systems, labour, control, and modern retail stores. *New Technology, Work and Employment*, 33(1): 44–57.

Ewald, F. (2002) The return of Descartes' malicious demon: An outline of a philosophy of precaution. In T. Baker and J. Simon, eds., *Embracing Risk: The Changing Culture of Insurance and Responsibility*, 273–301. University of Chicago Press.

Eyal, N. (2014) *Hooked: How to Build Habit-Forming Products*. New York: Portfolio Books.

Fagan, C. (2001) Time, money and the gender order: Work orientations and working-time preferences. *Work and Organizations*, 8(3): 239–67.

Fawcett, P. (2018) Governance, acceleration and time – emerging issues for governance theory and practice. *Critical Policy Studies*, 12(3): 367–72.

Fieser, J. (2003) Ethics. International Encyclopedia of Philosophy. https://iep.utm.edu/ethics.

Fisher, M. (2009) *Capitalist Realism: Is There No Alternative?* Ropley: Zero Books.

Flinn, A. and Alexander, B. (2015) 'Humanizing an inevitability political craft': Introduction to the special issue on archiving activism and activist archiving. *Archival Science*, 15(4): 329–35.

Florida, R. (2002) *The Rise of the Creative Class*. New York: Basic Books.

Forrester, J. W. (1969) *Urban Dynamics*. Cambridge, MA: MIT Press.

Foucault, M. (1978) *The History of Sexuality*, Vol. I. Harmondsworth: Penguin.

Foucault, M. (1991) Governmentality. In G. Burchell, C. Gordon and P. Miller, eds., *The Foucault Effect: Studies in Governmentality*, 87–104. University of Chicago Press.

Franceschini, F., Galetto, M. and Maisano, D. (2007). *Management by Measurement: Designing Key Indicators and Performance Measurement Systems*. Berlin: Springer.

Fraser, A. (2019) Land grab / data grab: Precision agriculture and its new horizons. *The Journal of Peasant Studies* 46(5): 893–912.

Freeman, E. (2016) Synchronic/anachronic. In J. Burges and A. L. Elias, eds., *Time: A Vocabulary of the Present*, 129–43. New York University Press.

Garde-Hansen, J., Hoskins, A. and Reading, A. (2009) Introduction. In J. Garde-Hansen, A. Hoskins and A. Reading, eds., *Save As … Digital Memories*, 1–26. Basingstoke: Palgrave Macmillan.

Gardiner, E. and Musto, R. G. (2015) *The Digital Humanities: A Primer for Students and Scholars*. Cambridge University Press.

Giddens, A. (1984) *The Constitution of Society: Outline of the Theory of Structuration*. Berkeley: University of California Press.

Giddens, A. (1990) *The Consequences of Modernity*. Stanford University Press.

Gleick, J. (1999) *Faster: The Acceleration of Just About Everything*. New York: Pantheon Books.

Goetz, K. H. and Meyer-Sahling, J.-H. (2009) Political time in the EU: Dimensions, perspectives, theories. *Journal of European Public Policy*, 16(2): 180–201.

Goldenberg, S. (2016) Masdar's zero-carbon dream could become world's first green ghost town. *The Guardian*, 16 Feb. www.theguardian.com/environment/2016/feb/16/masdars-zero-carbon-dream-could-become-worlds-first-green-ghost-town.

Goldman, M. (2011a) Speculative urbanism and the making of the next world city. *International Journal of Urban and Regional Research*, 35(3): 555–81.

Goldman, M. (2011b) Speculating on the next world city. In A. Roy and A. Ong, eds., *Worlding Cities: Asian Experiments and the Art of Being Global*, 229–58. Chichester: Wiley-Blackwell.

Goldman, M. and Narayan, D. (2021) Through the optics of finance: Speculative urbanism and the transformation of markets. *International Journal of Urban and Regional Research*, 45(2): 209–31.

Goodin, R. (1998) Keeping political time: The rhythms of democracy. *International Political Science Review*, 19(1): 39–54.

Gordon, E. and de Souza e Silva, A. (2011) *Net Locality: Why Location Matters in a Networked World*. Malden, MA: Wiley-Blackwell.

Gordon, E. and Manosevitch, E. (2010) Augmented deliberation: Merging physical and virtual interaction to engage communities in urban planning. *New Media & Society*, 13(1): 75–95.

Graham, M. and Anwar, M. (2019) Labour. In J. Ash, R. Kitchin and A. Leszczynski, eds., *Digital Geographies*, 177–87. London: Sage.

Graham, M., Zook, M. and Boulton, A. (2013) Augmented reality in the urban environment. *Transactions of the Institute of British Geographers*, 38(3): 464–79.

Graham, S. and Marvin, S. (1996) *Telecommunications and the City: Electronic Spaces, Urban Places*. London: Routledge.

Graham, S. and Marvin, S. (2001) *Splintering Urbanism: Networked Infrastructures, Technological Mobilities and the Urban Condition*. London: Routledge.

Grant, S., McNeilly, J. and Veerapen, M. (2015) Introduction. In S. Grant, J. McNeilly and M. Veerapen, eds., *Performance and Temporalisation: Time Happens*, 1–23. Basingstoke: Palgrave Macmillan.

Green, N. (2002) On the move: Technology, mobility, and the mediation of social time and space. *The Information Society*, 18: 281–92.

Greener, I. (2002) Theorizing path-dependency: How does history come to matter in organizations? *Management Decision*, 40: 614–19.

Gregg, M. (2018) *Counterproductive: Time Management in the Knowledge Economy*. Durham, NC: Duke University Press.

Gregory, I. N. and Geddes, A., eds. (2014) *Towards Spatial Humanities: Historical GIS and Spatial History*. Bloomington: Indiana University Press.

Grzymala-Busse, A. (2011) Time will tell? Temporality and the analysis of causal mechanisms and processes. *Comparative Political Studies*, 44(9): 1267–97.

Gu, N., Kim, M. J. and Maher, M. L. (2011) Technological advancements in synchronous collaboration: The effect of 3D virtual worlds and tangible user interfaces on architectural design. *Automation in Construction*, 20(3): 270–8.

Gullino, S. (2009) Urban regeneration and democratization of information access: CitiStat experience in Baltimore. *Journal of Environmental Management*, 90: 2012–19.

Haase, D., Haase, A., Kabisch, N., Kabisch, S. and Rink, D. (2012) Actors and factors in land-use simulation: The challenge of urban shrinkage. *Environmental Modelling & Software*, 35: 92–103.

Hägerstrand, T. (1967) *Innovation Diffusion as a Spatial Process*. University of Chicago Press.

Halpern, O., LeCavalier, J., Calvillo, N. and Pietsch, W. (2013) Test-bed urbanism. *Public Culture*, 25(2): 272–306.

Halpern, O. and Gunel, G. (2017) Demoing unto death: Smart cities, environment, and preemptive hope. *Fibreculture*, 29: 1–23.

Hand, M. (2016). Persistent traces, potential memories: Smartphones and the negotiation of visual, locative, and textual data in personal life. *Convergence: The International Journal of Research into New Media Technologies*, 22(3): 269–86.

Happer, C., Hoskins, A. and Merrin, W., eds. (2019) *Trump's Media War*. Basingstoke: Palgrave Macmillan.

Hartung, M., Bues, M.-M. and Halbleib, G. (2018) *Legal Tech: A Practitioner's Guide*. Oxford: Beck/Hart.

Harvey, D. (1972) *Social Justice and the City*. Oxford: Blackwell.

Harvey, D. (1989) *The Condition of Postmodernity: An Enquiry into the Origins of Cultural Change*. Oxford: Blackwell.

Harvey, D. (2000) *Spaces of Hope*. Edinburgh University Press.

Haskins, E. (2007) Between archive and participation: Public memory in a digital age. *Rhetoric Society Quarterly*, 37(4): 401–22.

Hassan, R. (2003) Network time and the new knowledge epoch. *Time & Society*, 12 (2–3): 226–41.

Hassan, R. (2007) Network time. In R. Hassan and R. Purser, eds., *24/7: Time and Temporality in the Network Society*, 37–61. Stanford University Press.

Hassan, R. (2009) *Empires of Speed: Time and the Acceleration of Politics and Society*. Leiden: Brill.

Hassan, R. and Purser, R. (2007) Introduction. In R. Hassan and R. Purser, eds., *24/7: Time and Temporality in the Network Society*, 1–24. Stanford University Press.

Heersmink, R. and Carter, J. A. (2017). The philosophy of memory technologies: Metaphysics, knowledge, and values. *Memory Studies*, 13(4): 416–33.

Heim, M. (1993) *The Metaphysics of Virtual Reality*. Oxford University Press.

Heise, U. K. (2016) Extinction/adaptation. In J. Burges and A. L. Elias, eds., *Time: A Vocabulary of the Present*, 51–65. New York University Press.

Held, V. (2005) *The Ethics of Care*. Oxford University Press.

Henckel, D. and Thomaier, S. (2013) Efficiency, temporal justice, and the rhythm of cities. In D. Henckel, S. Thomaier, B. Konecke, R. Zedda and S. Stabilini, eds., *Space-Time Design of the Public City*, 99–118. Amsterdam: Springer.

Herbert, C. W. and Murray, M. J. (2015) Building from scratch: New cities, privatized urbanism and the spatial restructuring of Johannesburg after Apartheid. *International Journal of Urban and Regional Research*, 39(3): 471–94.

Hetherington, K. (2013) Rhythm and noise: The city, memory and the archive. *The Sociological Review*, 61(1): 17–33.

Highfield, T. (2017) *Social Media and Everyday Politics*. Cambridge: Polity.

Hirsch, M. (2008) The generation of postmemory. *Poetics Today*, 29(1): 103–28.

Hollander, J. B. and Németh, J. (2011) The bounds of smart decline: A foundational theory for planning shrinking cities. *Housing Policy Debate*, 21(3): 349–67.

Honoré, C. (2005) *In Praise of Slowness: Challenging the Cult of Speed*. New York: HarperCollins.

Hope, W. (2006) Global capitalism and the critique of real time. *Time & Society*, 15(2/3): 275–302.

Hoskins, A. (2009) The mediatisation of memory. In J. Garde-Hansen, A. Hoskins and A. Reading, eds., *Save As ... Digital Memories*, 27–43. Basingstoke: Palgrave Macmillan.

Hoskins, A. (2011) Media, memory, metaphor: Remembering and the connective turn. *Parallax*, 17(4): 19–31.

Hoskins, A. (2014) The right to be forgotten in post-scarcity culture. In A. Ghezzi, A. Guimarares Pereira and L. Vesnic-Alujevic, eds., *The Ethics of Memory in a Digital Age: Interrogating the Right to Be Forgotten*, 50–64. New York: Palgrave.

Hoskins, A. (2018a) The restless past: An introduction to digital memory and media. In A. Hoskins, ed., *Digital Memory Studies*, 1–24. New York: Routledge.

Hoskins, A. (2018b) Memory of the multitude: The end of collective memory. In A. Hoskins, ed., *Digital Memory Studies*, 85–109. New York: Routledge.

Houser, H. (2016) Human/planetary. In J. Burges and A. L. Elias, eds., *Time: A Vocabulary of the Present*, 144–60. New York University Press.

Hoy, D. C. (2009) *The Time of Our Lives: A Critical History of Temporality*. Cambridge, MA: MIT Press.

Huang, H., Gartner, G., Krisp, J. M., Raubal, M. and Van de Weghe, N. (2018) Location based services: Ongoing evolution and research agenda. *Journal of Location Based Services*, 12(2): 63–93.

Humphreys, L. (2020) Birthdays, anniversaries, and temporalities: Or how the past is represented as relevant through on-this-date media. *New Media & Society*, 22(9): 1663–79.

Huyssen, A. (2003) *Present Pasts: Urban Palimpsests and the Politics of Memory*. Stanford University Press.

Issenberg, S. (2012) *The Victory Lab: The Secret Science of Winning Campaigns*. New York: Crown.

Jacobsen, B. N. and Beer, D. (2021) *Social Media and the Automatic Production of Memory*. Bristol University Press.

Jefferson, B. J. (2018) Predictable policing: Predictive crime mapping and geographies of policing and race. *Annals of the American Association of Geographers*, 108(1): 1–16.

Jessop, B. (2008) *State Power: A Strategic-Relational Approach*. Cambridge: Polity.

Jessop, B. (2015) *The State: Past, Present and Future*. Cambridge: Polity.

Kammourieh, L., Baar, T., Berens, J., Letouzé, E., Manske, J., Palmer, J., Sangokoya, D. and Vinck, P. (2017) Group privacy in the age of big data. In L. Taylor, L. Floridi and B. van der Sloot, eds., *Group Privacy: New Challenges of Data Technologies*, 37–66. Cham: Springer.

Kansteiner, W. (2018) The Holocaust in the 21st century: Digital anxiety, transnational cosmopolitanism, and never again genocide without memory. In A. Hoskins, ed., *Digital Memory Studies*, 110–40. New York: Routledge.

Kasmir, S. (2018) Precarity. In *The Cambridge Encyclopedia of Anthropology*. http://doi.org/10.29164/18precarity.

Katz, J. and Aakhus, M., eds. (2002) *Perpetual Contact: Mobile Communication, Private Talk, Public Performance*. Cambridge University Press.

Kaun, A. (2015) Regimes of time: Media practices of the dispossessed. *Time & Society*, 24(2): 221–43.

Kaun, A. (2017) 'Our time to act has come': Desynchronization, social media time and protest movements. *Media, Culture & Society*, 39(4): 469–86.

Kaun, A. and Stiernstedt, F. (2020) Doing time, the smart way? Temporalities of the smart prison. *New Media & Society*, 22(9): 1580–99.

Keightley, E. (2012) Introduction: Time, media, modernity. In E. Keightley, ed., *Time, Media and Modernity*, 1–22. London: Palgrave Macmillan.

Keightley, E. and Pickering, M. (2014) Technologies of memory: Practices of remembering in analogue and digital photography. *New Media & Society*, 16(4): 576–93.

Kenney, M. and Zysman, J. (2016) The rise of the platform economy. *Issues in Science and Technology*, Spring: 61–9.

Kern, S. (1983) *The Culture of Time and Space, 1880–1918*. Cambridge, MA: Harvard University Press.

Khondker, H. H. (2011) Role of the new media in the Arab Spring. *Globalizations*, 8(5): 675–9.

Kim, T. J., Wiggins, L. L. and Wright, J. R. (1990) *Expert Systems: Applications to Urban Planning*. Amsterdam: Springer-Verlag.

Kinsley, S. (2015) Memory programmes: The industrial retention of collective life. *Cultural Geographies*, 22(1): 155–75.

Kitchin, R. (2014a) The real-time city? Big data and smart urbanism. *GeoJournal*, 79(1): 1–14.

Kitchin, R. (2014b) *The Data Revolution: Big Data, Open Data, Data Infrastructures and Their Consequences*. London: Sage.

Kitchin, R. (2015) The opportunities, challenges and risks of big data for official statistics. *Statistical Journal of the International Association of Official Statistics*, 31(3): 471–81.

Kitchin, R. (2017) The realtimeness of smart cities. *Technoscienza*, 8(2): 19–42.

Kitchin, R. (2019a) The timescape of smart cities. *Annals of the Association of American Geographers*, 109(3): 775–90.

Kitchin, R. (2019b) Towards a genuinely humanizing smart urbanism. In P. Cardullo, C. di Feliciantonio and R. Kitchin, eds., *The Right to the Smart City*, 193–204. Bingley: Emerald.

Kitchin, R. (2020) Civil liberties or public health, or civil liberties and public health? Using surveillance technologies to tackle the spread of COVID-19. *Space and Polity*, 24(3): 362–81.

Kitchin, R. and Dodge, M. (2011) *Code/Space: Software and Everyday Life*. Cambridge, MA: MIT Press.

Kitchin, R. and Fraser, A. (2020) *Slow Computing: Why We Need Balanced Digital Lives*. Bristol University Press.

Kitchin, R. and McArdle, G. (2016) What makes big data, big data? Exploring the ontological characteristics of 26 datasets. *Big Data & Society*, 3: 1–10.

Kitchin, R., Lauriault, T. P. and McArdle, G. (2015) Knowing and governing cities through urban indicators, city benchmarking and real-time dashboards. *Regional Studies, Regional Science*, 2: 1–28.

Kitchin, R., Lauriault, T. P., and Wilson, M. (2017) Introducing spatial media. In R. Kitchin, T. P. Lauriault and M. Wilson, eds., *Understanding Spatial Media*, 1–21. London: Sage.

Kitchin, R., Cardullo, P. and di Feliciantonio, C. (2019) Citizenship, social justice and the right to the smart city. In P. Cardullo, C. di Feliciantonio and R. Kitchin, eds., *The Right to the Smart City*, 1–24. Bingley: Emerald.

Kitchin, R., Young, G. and Dawkins, O. (2021, online first) Planning and 3D spatial media: Progress, prospects, and the knowledge and experiences of local government planners. *Planning Theory and Practice*. https://doi.org/10.1080 /14649357.2021.1921832.

Knox, P. L. (2005) Creating ordinary places: Slow cities in a fast world. *Journal of Urban Design*, 10(1): 1–11.

Koramaz, T. K. (2018) Digital representation of urban history and notes from an exhibition, Urban Intermedia: City, Archive, Narrative. *Disegnare.Con*, 11(21): 1–6.

Koselleck, R. (2004) *Futures Past: On the Semantics of Historical Time*. New York: Columbia University Press.

Kuhn, A. (2010) Memory texts and memory work: Performances of memory in and with visual media. *Memory Studies*, 3(4): 298–313.

Kundu, R. (2017) 'Their houses on our land': Perforations and blockades in the planning of New Town Rajarhat, Kolkata. In A. Datta and A. Shaban, eds., *Mega-urbanization in the Global South: Fast Cities and New Urban Utopias of the Postcolonial State*, 123–48. London: Routledge.

Kwan, M.-P. (2000) Gender differences in space-time constraints. *Area*, 32(2): 145–56.

Ladner, S. (2009) 'Agency time': A case study of the postindustrial timescape and its impact on the domestic sphere. *Time & Society*, 18(2–3): 284–305.

Lambert, A., Nansen, B. and Arnold, M. (2016) Algorithmic memorial videos: Contextualising automated curation. *Memory Studies*, 11(2): 156–71.

Lash, S. and Urry, J. (1994) *Economies of Signs and Space*. London: Sage.

Lauermann, J. (2016) The city as developmental justification: Claims-making on the urban through strategic planning. *Urban Geography*, 37(1): 77–95.

Lauermann, J. and Vogelpohl, A. (2019) Fast activism: Resisting mobile policies. *Antipode*, 51(4): 1231–50.

Laurian, L. (2021, online first) Planning: Reclaiming the dream of better futures. *Planning Theory and Practice*. https://doi.org/10.1080/14649357 .2021.1956815.

Laurian, L. and Inch, A. (2019) On time and planning: Opening futures by cultivating a 'sense of now'. *Journal of Planning Literature*, 34(3): 267–85.

Lauriault, T. P., Craig, B. L., Taylor, D. R. F. and Pulsifer, P. L. (2007) Today's data are part of tomorrow's research: Archival issues in the sciences. *Archivaria*, 64: 123–79.

LeCavalier, J. (2016) *The Rule of Logistics: Walmart and the Architecture of Fulfillment*. Minneapolis: University of Minnesota Press.

Leccardi, C. (2007) New temporal perspectives in the high-speed society. In R. Hassan and R. Purser, eds., *24/7: Time and Temporality in the Network Society*, 25–36. Stanford University Press.

Lee, D. B. (1973) Requiem for large-scale models. *Journal of the American Planning Association*, 39: 163–78.

Lee, J., Bagheri, B. and Jin, C. (2016) Introduction to cyber manufacturing. *Manufacturing Letters*, 8: 11–15.

Lee, L. F. L. and Chan, J. M. (2018) *Media and Protest Logics in the Digital Era: The Umbrella Movement in Hong Kong*. Oxford University Press.

Lefebvre, H. (1991) *The Production of Space*. Oxford: Blackwell.

Lefebvre, H. (2004) *Rhythmanalysis: Space, Time and Everyday Life*, trans. S. Elden and G. Moore. Paris: Éditions Syllepse.

Leong, S., Mitew, T., Celletti, M. and Pearson, E. (2009) The question concerning (internet) time. *New Media & Society*, 11(8): 1267–85.

Leszczynski, A. (2015) Spatial media/tion. *Progress in Human Geography*, 39(6): 729–51.

Leszczynski, A. (2016) Speculative futures: Cities, data, and governance beyond smart urbanism. *Environment and Planning A*, 48(9): 1691–708.

Levitas, R. (2013) *Utopia as Method: The Imaginary Reconstitution of Society*. London: Palgrave.

Leyshon, A. (1995) Annihilating space? The speed-up of communications. In J. Allen and C. Hamnett, eds., *A Shrinking World? Global Unevenness and Inequality*, 11–54. Oxford University Press.

Light, J. S. (2003) *From Warfare to Welfare: Defense Intellectuals and the Urban Problems in Cold War America*. Baltimore: Johns Hopkins University Press.

Linz, J. J. (1998) Democracy's time constraints. *International Political Science Review*, 19(1): 19–37.

Liu, C. (2021) Rethinking the timescape of home: Domestic practices in time and space. *Progress in Human Geography*, 45(2): 343–61.

Lorey, I. (2015) *State of Insecurity: Government of the Precarious*. London: Verso.

Lowenthal, D. (2012) The past made present. *Historically Speaking*, 13(4): 2–6.

Luke, T. (1998) Moving at the speed of life? A cultural kinematics of telematic times and corporate values. In S. Lash, A. Quick and R. Roberts, eds., *Time and Value*, 162–81. Oxford: Blackwell.

Lupton, D. (2016) *The Quantified Self*. Cambridge: Polity.

Luque-Ayala, A. and Marvin, S. (2016) The maintenance of urban circulation: An operational logic of infrastructural control. *Environment and Planning D: Society and Space*, 34(2): 191–208.

Luque-Ayala, A. and Marvin, S. (2020) *Urban Operating Systems: Producing the Computational City*. Cambridge, MA: MIT Press.

Lynch, K. (1972) *What Time Is This Place?* Cambridge, MA: MIT Press.

Lyon, D. (1994) *The Electronic Eye: The Rise of the Surveillance Society*. Cambridge: Polity.

Lyon, D. (2007) *Surveillance Studies: An Overview*. Cambridge: Polity.

Lyon, D. (2014) Surveillance, Snowden, and big data: Capacities, consequences, critique. *Big Data & Society*, 1(2): 1–13.

Lyster, C. (2016) *Learning from Logistics: How Networks Change Our Cities*. Basel: Birkhauser.

Macgilchrist, F. and Bohmig, I. (2012). Blogs, genes and immigration: Online media and minimal politics. *Media, Culture and Society*, 34(1): 83–100.

Mackay, R. and Avenessian, A. (2014) *#Accelerate: The Accelerationist Reader*. Falmouth and Berlin: Merve Verlag / Urbanomic.

Mackenzie, A. (1997) The mortality of the virtual real-time, archive and deadtime in information networks. *Convergence: The International Journal of Research into New Media Technologies*, 3(2): 59–71.

Mackenzie, A. (2006) *Cutting code: Software and sociality*. New York: Peter Lang.

Maclaren, V. W. (1996) Urban sustainability reporting. *Journal of the American Planning Association*, 62(2): 184–203.

Madanipour, A. (2017) *Cities in Time: Temporary Urbanism and the Future of the City*. London: Bloomsbury Publishing.

Malpas, J. (2015) Timing space – spacing time. In S. Grant, J. McNeilly and M. Veerapen, eds., *Performance and Temporalisation: Time Happens*, 25–36. Basingstoke: Palgrave Macmillan.

Mandarano, L., Meenar, M. and Steins, C. (2010) Building social capital in the digital age of civic engagement. *Journal of Planning Literature*, 25(2): 123–35.

Manovich, L. (2020) *Cultural Analytics*. Cambridge, MA: MIT Press.

Manyika, J., Chiu, M., Brown, B., Bughin, J., Dobbs, R., Roxburgh, C. and Hung Byers, A. (2011) *Big Data: The Next Frontier for Innovation, Competition, and Productivity*. McKinsey Global Institute.

Manyika, J., Lund, S., Chui, M., Bughin, J., Woetzel, J., Batra, P., Ko, R. and Sanghvi, S. (2017) *Jobs Lost, Jobs Gained: What the Future of Work Will Mean for Jobs, Skills, and Wages*. McKinsey Global Institute.

Marcuse, P. (2012). Whose right(s) to what city. In N. Brenner, P. Marcuse and M. Mayer, eds., *Cities for People, Not for Profit: Critical Urban Theory and the Right to the City*, 24–41. London: Routledge.

Markham, A. (2020, online first) The limits of the imaginary: Challenges to intervening in future speculations of memory, data, and algorithms. *New Media & Society*. https://doi.org/ 10.1177/1461444820929322.

Martinez, D. E. (2011) Beyond disciplinary enclosures: Management control in the society of control. *Critical Perspectives on Accounting*, 22(2): 200–11.

Massey, D. (1984) *Spatial Divisions of Labour: Social Structures and the Geography of Production*. London: Macmillan.

Massey, D. (1993) Power geometry and a progressive sense of place. In J. Bird et al., eds., *Mapping the Futures*, 60–70. London: Routledge.

Massey, D. (2005) *For Space*. London: Sage.

May, J. and Thrift, N. (2001) Introduction. In J. May and N. Thrift, eds., *Timespace: Geographies of Temporality*, 1–46. London: Routledge.

Mayer, H. and Knox, P. (2006) Slow cities: Sustainable places in a fast world. *Journal of Urban Affairs*, 28(4): 321–34.

McCann, B. (2014) A review of SCATS operation and deployment in Dublin. In *Proceedings of the 19th JCT Traffic Signal Symposium & Exhibition, University of Warwick, Warwick, 18–19 September 2014*. www.jctconsultancy.co.uk /Symposium/Symposium2014/PapersForDownload/A%20Review%20of%20 SCATS%20Operation%20and%20Deployment%20in%20Dublin.pdf.

McCann, E. (2003) Framing space and time in the city: Urban policy and the politics of spatial and temporal scale. *Journal of Urban Affairs*, 25(2): 159–78.

McCann, E. and Ward, K. (2011) *Mobile Urbanism: Cities and Policymaking in the Global Age*. Minneapolis: University of Minnesota Press.

Melendez, S. and Pasternack, A. (2019) Here are the data brokers quietly buying and selling your personal information. The Fast Company, 2 March. www.fastcompany.com/90310803/here-are-the-data-brokers-quietly-buying-and-selling-your-personalinformation.

Miciukiewicz, K. and Vigar, G. (2013) Encounters in motion: Considerations of time and social justice in urban mobility research. In D. Henckel, S. Thomaier, B. Konecke, R. Zedda and S. Stabilini, eds., *Space-Time Design of the Public City*, 171–86. Amsterdam: Springer.

Miele, M. and Murdoch, J. (2002) The practical aesthetics of traditional cuisines: Slow food in Tuscany. *Sociologica Ruralis*, 42(4): 312–28.

Milojevic, I. (2008) Timing feminism, feminising time. *Futures*, 40(4): 329–45.

Miyazaki, S. (2012) Algorhythmics: Understanding micro-temporality in

computational cultures. Computational Culture, 2. http://computationalculture
.net/article/algorhythmics-understanding-micro-temporality-in
-computationalcultures.

Miyazaki, S. (2013) Urban sounds unheard-of: A media archaeology of ubiquitous infospheres. *Continuum: Journal of Media & Cultural Studies*, 27(4): 514–22.

Moazed, A. (2016) *Modern Monopolies*. London: Macmillan.

Moore-Cherry, N. and Bonnin, C. (2020) Playing with time in Moore Street, Dublin: Urban redevelopment, temporal politics and the governance of space-time. *Urban Geography*, 41(9): 1198–217.

Moretti, F. (2005) *Graphs, Maps, Trees: Abstract Models for a Literary History*. London: Verso.

Moriset, B. (2019) Reshaping of traditional industries. In J. Ash, R. Kitchin and A. Leszczynski, eds., *Digital Geographies*, 210–22. London: Sage.

Moss, T. (2020) *Remaking Berlin: A History of the City through Infrastructure, 1920–2020*. Cambridge, MA: MIT Press.

Moss, T. (2021) Usable infrastructure pasts: Mobilizing history for urban technology futures. Presentation at the 'Infrastructural Times' workshop, Network on Infrastructural Regionalism, Regional Studies Association, online event, 14–18 June.

Mountz, A., Bonds, A., Mansfield, B., Loyd, J., Hyndman, J., Walton-Roberts, M., Basu, R., Whitson, R., Hawkins, R., Hamilton, T. and Curran, W. (2015) For slow scholarship: A feminist politics of resistance through collective action in the neoliberal university. *ACME: An International Journal for Critical Geographies*, 14(4): 1235–59.

Murray, M. (2017) Frictionless utopias for the contemporary urban age: Large-scale, master-planned redevelopment projects in urbanizing Africa. In A. Datta and A. Shaban, eds., *Mega-urbanization in the Global South: Fast Cities and New Urban Utopias of the Postcolonial State*, 31–53. London: Routledge.

Murray, M. (2021) Ruination and rejuvenation: Rethinking growth and decline through an inverted telescope. *International Journal of Urban and Regional Research*, 45(2): 348–62.

Nadeem, S. (2009) The uses and abuses of time: Globalization and time arbitrage in India's outsourcing industries. *Global Networks*, 9(1): 20–40.

Nansen, B., Arnold, M., Gibbs, M. R. and Davis, H. (2009) Domestic orchestration: Rhythms in the mediated home. *Time and Society*, 18(2–3): 181–207.

NESTA (2019) *Our Future: By the People for the People*. London: NESTA. www.nesta.org.uk/report/our-futures-people-people.

Newman, J. and Howlett, M. (2014) Regulation and time: Temporal patterns in regulatory development. *International Review of Administrative Sciences*, 80(3): 493–511.

Nowotny, H. (1994) *Time: The Modern and Postmodern Experience*. Cambridge: Polity.

Nyckel, E.-M. (2021) Ahead of time: The infrastructure of Amazon's anticipatory shipping method. In A. Vollmar and K. Stine, eds., *Media Infrastructures and the Politics of Digital Time: Essays on Hardwired Temporalities*, 264–78. Amsterdam University Press.

O'Carroll, A. (2015) *Working Time, Knowledge Work and Post-Industrial Society*. Basingstoke: Palgrave Macmillan.

O'Grady, N. (2018) *Governing Future Emergencies: Lived Relations to Risk in the UK Fire and Rescue Service*. Basingstoke: Palgrave.

Olmstead, N. A. (2021) Data and temporality in the spectral city. *Philosophy and Technology*, 34(2): 243–63.

Ong, A. (2011) Worlding cities, or the art of being global. In A. Roy and A. Ong, eds., *Worlding Cities: Asian Experiments and the Art of Being Global*, 1–26. Chichester: Wiley-Blackwell.

Osborne, P. (2013) *Anywhere or Not at All: Philosophy of Contemporary Art*. New York: Verso.

Oswalt, P., Beyer, E., Hagemann, A. and Rieniets, T. (2006) *Atlas of Shrinking Cities*. Ostfildern: Hatje Cantz Publishers.

Özkul, D. and Humphreys, L. (2015) Record and remember: Memory and meaning-making practices through mobile media. *Mobile Media & Communication*, 3(3): 351–65.

Pain, R. (2001) Gender, race, age and fear in the city. *Urban Studies*, 38(5–6): 899–913.

Pallagst, K. and Wiechmann, T. (2012) Urban shrinkage in Germany and the USA: A comparison of transformation patterns and local strategies. *International Journal of Urban and Regional Research*, 36(2): 261–80.

Pallagst, K., Schwarz, T., Popper, F. J. and Hollander, J. B. (2009) Planning shrinking cities. *Progress in Planning*, 72(4): 223–32.

Pang, A. S.-K. (2016) *Rest: Why You Get More Done When You Work Less*. New York: Basic Books.

Parikka, J. (2013) Archival media theory: An introduction to Wolfgang Ernst's Media Archaeology. In W. Ernst, *Digital Memory and the Archive*, 1–22. Minneapolis: University of Minnesota Press.

Parikka, J. (2018) The underpinning time: From digital memory to network microtemporality. In A. Hoskins, ed., *Digital Memory Studies*, 1156–72. New York: Routledge.

Parkes, D. and Thrift, N. (1975) Timing space and spacing time. *Environment and Planning A*, 7(6): 651–70.

Parkes, D. and Thrift, N. (1980) *Times, Spaces and Places: A Chronogeographic Perspective*. Chichester: Wiley.

Peck, J. (2002) Political economies of scale: Fast policy, interscalar relations, and neoliberal workfare. *Economic Geography*, 78(3): 331–60.

Peck, J. and Theodore, N. (2015) *Fast Policy: Experimental Statecraft at the Thresholds of Neoliberalism*. Minneapolis: University of Minnesota Press.

Pentzold, C. (2018) Between moments and millennia: Temporalising mediatisation. *Media, Culture & Society*, 40(6): 927–37.

Pfeiffer, S. (2017) The vision of Industrie 4.0 in the making – a case of future told, tamed, and traded. *Nanoethics*, 11(1): 107–21.

Pieterse, E. (2008) *City Futures: Confronting the Crisis of Urban Development*. London: Zed Books.

Pink, S. (2008) Sense and sustainability: The case of the Slow City movement. *Local Environment*, 13(2): 95–106.

Pogačar, M. (2018) Culture of the past: Digital connectivity and dispotentiated futures. In A. Hoskins, ed., *Digital Memory Studies*, 27–48. New York: Routledge.

Poli, R. (2015) Social foresight. *On the Horizon*, 23(2): 85–99.

Pollitt, C. (2008) *Time, Policy, Management: Governing with the Past*. Oxford University Press.

Portman, M. E., Natapov, A. and Fisher-Gewirtzman, D. (2015) To go where no man has gone before: Virtual reality in architecture, landscape architecture, and environmental planning. *Computers, Environment and Urban Systems*, 54: 376–84.

Poster, M. (1995) *The Second Media Age*. Oxford: Polity.

Prey, R. and Smit, R. (2019) From personal to personalized memory: Social media as mnemotechnology. In Z. Papacharissi, ed., *A Networked Self and Birth, Life, Death*, 209–24. London: Routledge.

Purser, R. (2002) Contested presents: Critical perspectives on 'real-time' management. In B. Adam, R. Whipp and I. Sabelis, eds., *Making Time: Time in Modern Organizations*, 155–67. Oxford University Press.

Raco, M., Durrant, D. and Livingstone, N. (2018) Slow cities, urban politics and the temporalities of planning: Lessons from London. *Environment and Planning C: Politics and Space*, 36(7): 1176–94.

Radoccia, R. (2013) Time policies in Italy: The case of the middle Adriatic regions. In D. Henckel, S. Thomaier, B. Konecke, R. Zedda and S. Stabilini, eds., *Space-Time Design of the Public City*, 245–54. Amsterdam: Springer.

Rast, J. (2012) Why history (still) matters: Time and temporality in urban political analysis. *Urban Affairs Review*, 48(1): 3–36.

Reading, A. (2009) Memobilia: The mobile phone and the emergence of wearable memories. In J. Garde-Hansen, A. Hoskins and A. Reading, eds., *Save As ... Digital Memories*, 81–95. Basingstoke: Palgrave Macmillan.

Reading, A. (2012) Globital time: Time in the digital globalised age. In E. Keightley, ed., *Time, Media and Modernity*, 143–62. London: Palgrave Macmillan.

Reading, A. and Notley, T. (2018) Globital memory capital: theorizing digital memory economies. In A. Hoskins, ed., *Digital Memory Studies*, 234–50. New York: Routledge.

Redden, J., Dencik, L. and Warne, H. (2020) Datafied child welfare services: Unpacking politics, economics and power. *Policy Studies*, 41(5): 507–26.

Reid, J. (2006) *The Biopolitics of the War on Terror: Life Struggles, Liberal Modernity, and the Defense of Logistical Societies*. Manchester University Press.

Reisch, L. (2001) Time and wealth: The role of time and temporalities for sustainable patterns of consumption. *Time & Society*, 10(2/3): 387–405.

Rieder, G. and Simon, J. (2016) Datatrust: Or, the political quest for numerical evidence and the epistemologies of Big Data. *Big Data & Society*, 3(1): 1–6.

Roberts, L. (2015) Navigating the 'archive city': Digital spatial humanities and archival film practice. *Convergence: The International Journal of Research into New Media Technologies*, 21(1): 100–15.

Rojko, A. (2017) Industry 4.0 concept: Background and overview. *International Journal of Interactive Mobile Technologies*, 11(5): 77–90.

Rosa, H. (2003) Social acceleration: Ethical and political consequences of a desynchronized high-speed society. *Constellations*, 10(1): 3–33.

Rosa, H. (2015) *Social Acceleration: A New Theory of Modernity*. New York: University of Columbia Press.

Rosa, H. (2017) De-synchronization, dynamic stabilization, dispositional squeeze: The problem of temporal mismatch. In N. Dodd and J. Wajcman, eds., *The Sociology of Speed: Digital, Organizational, and Social Temporalities*, 25–41. Oxford University Press.

Rose, N. (1996) *Inventing Our Selves: Psychology, Power and Personhood.* Cambridge University Press.

Rose, R. (1990) Inheritance before choice in public policy. *Journal of Theoretical Politics*, 3: 263–91.

Rossiter, N. (2016) *Software, Infrastructure, Labor: A Media Theory of Logistical Nightmares.* London: Routledge.

Rushkoff, D. (2013) *Present Shock: When Everything Happens Now.* New York: Penguin Putnam Press.

Sabbagh, C., and Schmitt, M., eds. (2016) *Handbook of Social Justice Theory and Research.* New York: Springer.

Sadowski, J. (2019) When data is capital: Datafication, accumulation, and extraction. *Big Data & Society*, 5(1): 1–12.

Safransky, S. (2020) Geographies of algorithmic violence: Redlining the smart city. *International Journal of Urban and Regional Research*, 44: 200–18.

Saker, M. and Evans, L. (2016). Locative mobile media and time: Foursquare and technological memory. *First Monday*, 21(2). https://doi.org/10.5210/fm.v21i2 .6006.

Savat, D. (2012) *Uncoding the Digital: Technology, Subjectivity and Action in the Control Society.* New York: Springer.

Schacter, D. L. (2001) *The Seven Sins of Memory: How the Mind Forgets and Remembers.* Boston, MA: Houghton Mifflin.

Schatzki, T. (2009) Timespace and the organization of social life. In E. Shove, F. Trentmann, and R. Wilk, eds., *Time, Consumption and Everyday Life: Practice, Materiality and Culture*, 35–48. Oxford: Berg.

Schedler, A. and Santiso, J. (1998) Democracy and time: An invitation. *International Political Science Review*, 19(1): 5–18.

Scheuerman, W. (2004) *Liberal Democracy and the Social Acceleration of Time.* Baltimore: Johns Hopkins University Press.

Schmitter, P. C. and Santiso, J. (1998) The three temporal dimensions to the consolidation of democracy. *International Political Science Review*, 19(1): 69–92.

Schneider, N. (2015) Slow computing. *America*, 21 May. www.americamagazine .org/content/all-things/slowcomputing.

Schull, N. D. (2016) Data for life: Wearable technology and the design of selfcare. *BioSocieties*, 11(3): 317–33.

Schumpeter, J. (1942) *Capitalism, Socialism and Democracy.* London: Taylor and Francis.

Schwanen, T. (2007) Matter(s) of interest: Artefacts, spacing and timing. *Geografiska Annaler B*, 89(1): 9–22.

Scott, D. (2014) *Omens of Adversity: Tragedy, Time, Memory, Justice.* Durham: Duke University Press.

Semmens, J. and C. Freeman (2012) The value of Cittaslow as an approach to local sustainable development: A New Zealand perspective. *International Planning Studies*, 17(4): 353–75.

Sewell, W. H. (2005) *Logics of History: Social Theory and Social Transformation.* University of Chicago Press.

Shaban, A. and Datta, A. (2017) Slow: Towards a decelerated urbanism. In A. Datta and A. Shaban, eds., *Mega-urbanization in the Global South: Fast Cities and New Urban Utopias of the Postcolonial State*, 205–20. London: Routledge.

Shapiro, A. (2020) *Design, Control, Predict: Logistical Governance in the Smart City*. Minneapolis: University of Minnesota Press.

Sharma, S. (2014) *In the Meantime: Temporality and Cultural Politics*. Durham, NC: Duke University Press.

Sharma, S. (2017) Speed traps and the temporal: Of taxis, truck stops, and TaskRabbits. In N. Dodd and J. Wajcman, eds., *The Sociology of Speed: Digital, Organizational, and Social Temporalities*, 131–51. Oxford University Press.

Shin, H. B. (2017) Envisioned by the state: Entrepreneurial urbanism and the making of Songdo City, South Korea. In A. Datta and A. Shaban, eds., *Mega-urbanization in the Global South: Fast Cities and New Urban Utopias of the Postcolonial State*, 83–100. London: Routledge.

Shin, H. B., Zhao, Y. and Koh, S. Y. (2020, online first) Whither progressive urban futures? *City*. https://doi.org/10.1080/13604813.2020.1739925.

Shipley, R. and Utz, S. (2012) Making it count: A review of the value and techniques for public consultation. *Journal of Planning Literature*, 27(1): 22–42.

Shojai, P. (2017) *The Art of Stopping Time*. New York: Rodale Books.

Shove, E. (2008) *Rushing Around: Coordination, Mobility and Inequality*. Lancaster University.

Shove, E., Trentmann, F. and Wilk, R. (2009) Introduction. In E. Shove, F. Trentmann and R. Wilk, eds., *Time, Consumption and Everyday Life: Practice, Materiality and Culture*, 1–13. Oxford: Berg.

Smith, G. J. D. (2018) Data doxa: The affective consequences of data practices. *Big Data & Society*, 5(1): 1–15.

Smith, S. (2006) New York unveils new emergency management headquarters. *EHS Today*, 6 Dec. www.ehstoday.com/training-and-engagement/article/21908242/new-york-unveils-new-emergency-management-headquarters.

Snellen, I. Th. M. and van de Donk, W. B. H. J., eds. (1998) *Public Administration in an Information Age*. Amsterdam: IOS Press.

Solove, D. J. (2011) *Nothing to Hide: The False Tradeoff between Privacy and Security*. New Haven, CT: Yale University Press.

Southerton, D. (2006) Analysing the temporal organization of daily life. *Sociology*, 40(3): 435–54.

Southerton, D. (2020) *Time, Consumption and the Coordination of Everyday Life*. London: Palgrave Macmillan.

Southerton, D. and Tomlinson, M. (2005) Pressed for time – The differential impacts of a time squeeze. *The Sociological Review*, 53(2): 215–40.

Speed, C. (2012) Walking through time: Use of locative media to explore historical maps. In L. Roberts, ed., *Mapping Cultures: Place, Practice, Performance*, 160–80. Basingstoke: Palgrave.

Starosielski, N. (2021) Grounded speed and the soft temporality of network infrastructure. In A. Vollmar and K. Stine, eds., *Media Infrastructures and the Politics of Digital Time: Essays on Hardwired Temporalities*, 177–89. Amsterdam University Press.

Stehle, S. and Kitchin, R. (2020) Real-time and archival data visualisation techniques in city dashboards. *International Journal of Geographic Information Science*, 34(2): 344–66.

Steiner, C. (2012) *Automate This: How Algorithms Took Over Our Markets, Our Jobs, and the World*. New York: Portfolio.

Stiegler, B. (2009) *Technics and Time*, Vol. II: *Disorientation*, trans. S. Barker. Stanford University Press.

Stiegler, B. (2011) *Technics and time*, Vol. III: *Cinematic time and the question of malaise*, trans. S. Barker. Stanford University Press.

Stine, K. and Vollmar, A. (2021) Infrastructures of time: An introduction to hardwired temporalities. In A. Vollmar and K. Stine, eds., *Media Infrastructures and the Politics of Digital Time: Essays on Hardwired Temporalities*, 9–38. University of Amsterdam Press.

Stockdale, L. P. D. (2015) *Taming an Uncertain Future: Temporality, Sovereignty, and the Politics of Anticipatory Governance*. London: Rowan and Littlefield.

Strassheim, H. (2016) Knowing the future: Theories of time in policy analysis. *European Policy Analysis*, 2(1): 150–67.

Sui, D. (2012) Looking through Hägerstrand's dual vistas: Towards a unifying framework for time geography. *Journal of Transport Geography*, 23(1): 5–16.

Sutko, D. and de Souza e Silva, A. (2010) Location-aware mobile media and urban sociability. *New Media & Society*, 13(5): 807–23.

Tazzioli, M. (2018) Spy, track and archive: The temporality of visibility in Eurosur and Jora. *Security Dialogue*, 49(4): 272–88.

Terranova, T. (2017) FileLife: Constant, Kurenniemi, and the question of living archives. In I. Blom, T. Lundemo and E. Røssaak, eds., *Memory in Motion: Archives, Technology and the Social*, 287–305. Amsterdam University Press.

Thatcher, J. (2013) Avoiding the ghetto through hope and fear: An analysis of immanent technology using ideal types. *GeoJournal*, 78(6): 967–80.

Thatcher, J., O'Sullivan, D. and Mahmoudi, D. (2016) Data colonialism through accumulation by dispossession: New metaphors for daily data. *Environment and Planning D*, 34(6): 990–1006.

Thompson, E. M., Greenhalgh, P., Muldoon-Smith, K., Charlton, J. and Dolník, M. (2016) Planners in the future city: Using city information modelling to support planners as market actors. *Urban Planning*, 1(1): 79–94.

Thompson, E. P. (1967) Time, work, discipline and industrial capitalism. *Past and Present*, 36: 609–24.

Thrift, N. (1988) 'Vivos voco': Ringing the changings in the historical geography of time consciousness. In M. Young, ed., *The Rhythms of Society*, 53–94. London: Routledge.

Thrift, N. (1990) The making of a capitalist time consciousness. In J. Hassard, ed., *The Sociology of Time*, 105–29. London: Palgrave Macmillan.

Thu Nguyen, D. and Alexander, J. (1996) The coming of cyberspace time and the end of polity. In R. Shields, ed., *Cultures of Internet: Virtual Spaces, Real Histories and Living Bodies*, 99–124. London: Sage.

Tomlinson, J. (2007) *The Culture of Speed: The Coming of Immediacy*. London: Sage.

Townsend, A. (2013) *Smart Cities: Big Data, Civic Hackers, and the Quest for a New Utopia*. New York: W. W. Norton & Co.

Trapenberg Frick, K. (2013) Actions of discontent: Tea party and property rights activists pushing back against regional planning. *Journal of the American Planning Association*, 79(3): 190–200.

Trapenberg Frick, K. (2016) Citizen activism, conservative views and mega planning in a digital era. *Planning Theory & Practice*, 17(1): 93–118.

Trentmann, F. (2009) Disruption is normal: Blackouts, breakdowns and the elasticity of everyday life. In E. Shove, F. Trentmann and R. Wilk, eds., *Time, Consumption and Everyday Life: Practice, Materiality and Culture*, 67–84. Oxford: Berg.

Tronto, J. C. (1993) *Moral Boundaries: A Political Argument for an Ethic of Care*. New York: Routledge.

Tutton, R. (2017) Wicked futures: Meaning, matter and the sociology of the future. *Sociological Review*, 65(3): 478–92.

United Nations (2019) *World Urbanization Prospects: The 2018 Revision*. New York: United Nations Department of Economic and Social Affairs.

Uprichard, E. (2012) Being stuck in (live) time: The sticky sociological imagination. *The Sociological Review*, 60(Suppl. 1): 124–38.

Urry, J. (2000) Mobile sociology. *Sociology*, 51(1): 185–203.

Urry, J. (2013) *Societies beyond Oil: Oil Dregs and Social Futures*. London: Zed Books.

Urry, J. (2016) *What Is the Future?* London: John Wiley & Sons.

van Dijck, J. (2009) Mediated memories as amalgamations of mind, matter and culture. In R. P. Zwijnenberg and R. Vall, eds., *The Body Within: Art, Medicine and Visualisation*, 157–72. Leiden: Brill.

Vanolo, A., 2013. Smartmentality: The smart city as disciplinary strategy. *Urban Studies*, 51(5): 883–98.

Vaughan, L. (2014) *Beginning Ethics: An Introduction to Moral Philosophy*. New York: W. W.. Norton & Co.

Virilio, P. (1997) *Open Sky*. London: Verso.

von Bergen, C. W. and Bressler, M. S. (2019) Work, non-work boundaries and the right to disconnect. *Journal of Applied Business and Economics*, 21(2): 51–69.

Wajcman, J. (2008) Life in the fast lane? Towards a sociology of technology and time. *The British Journal of Sociology*, 59(1): 59–77.

Wajcman, J. (2015) *Pressed for Time: The Acceleration of Life in Digital Capitalism*. University of Chicago Press.

Wajcman, J. (2018) How Silicon Valley sets time. *New Media & Society*, 21(6): 1272–89.

Wajcman, J. (2019) The digital architecture of time management. *Science, Technology, & Human Values*, 44: 315–37.

Walter, M. and Andersen, C. (2013) *Indigenous Statistics: A Quantitative Research Methodology*. Walnut Creek, CA: Left Coast Press.

Watson, V. (2014) African urban fantasies: Dreams or nightmares? *Environment and Urbanization*, 26: 215–31.

Webber, M. (1965) The roles of intelligence systems in urban-systems planning. *Journal of the American Institute of Planners*, 31(4): 289–96.

Weber, R. (2021, online first) Foreclosing the future: How finance got there first. *Planning Theory and Practice*. https://doi.org/10.1080/14649357.2021.1956815.

Weltevrede, E., Helmond, A. A. and Gerlitz, C. (2014) The politics of real-time: A device perspective on social media and search engines. *Theory, Culture and Society*, 31(6): 125–50.

West-Pavlov, R. (2013) *Temporalities*. New York: Routledge.

White, J. (2016) Anticipatory logics of the smart city's global imaginary. *Urban Geography*, 37(4): 572–89.

Wiig, A. (2018) Secure the city, revitalize the zone: Smart urbanization in

Camden, New Jersey. *Environment and Planning C: Politics and Space*, 36(3): 403–22.

Wilk, R. (2009) The edge of agency: Routines, habits and volition. In E. Shove, F. Trentmann and R. Wilk, eds., *Time, Consumption and Everyday Life: Practice, Materiality and Culture*, 143–54. Oxford: Berg.

Williams, A. and Srnicek, N. (2013) #*Accelerate: Manifesto for an Accelerationist Politics*. http://syntheticedifice.files.wordpress.com/2013/06/accelerate.pdf.

Willis, K. S. (2016) *Netspaces: Space and Place in a Networked World*. Farnham: Ashgate.

Wilson, S. (2009) Remixing memory in digital media. In J. Garde-Hansen, A. Hoskins and A. Reading, eds., *Save As ... Digital Memories*, 184–97. Basingstoke: Palgrave Macmillan.

Wolfsfeld, G., Segev, E. and Sheafer, T. (2013) Social media and the Arab Spring: Politics comes first. *The International Journal of Press/Politics*, 18(2): 115–37.

Woodcock, J. and Graham, M. (2019) *The Gig Economy: A Critical Introduction*. Cambridge: Polity.

Ytre-Arne, B., Syvertsen, T., Moe, H. and Karlsen, F. (2020) Temporal ambivalences in smartphone use: Conflicting flows, conflicting responsibilities. *New Media & Society*, 22(9): 1715–32.

Zapata, M. A. (2021, online first) Planning just futures: An introduction. *Planning Theory and Practice*. https://doi.org/10.1080/14649357.2021.1956 815.

Zikopoulos, P. C., Eaton, C., deRoos, D., Deutsch, T. and Lapis, G. (2012) *Understanding Big Data*. New York: McGraw-Hill.

Zook, M. and Poorthuis, A. (2015) Small stories in big data: Gaining insights from large spatial point pattern datasets. *Cityscape: A Journal of Policy Development and Research*, 17(1): 151–60.

Zuboff, S. (1988) *In the Age of the Smart Machine: The Future of Work and Power*. New York: Basic Books.

Zuboff, S. (2019) *The Age of Surveillance Capitalism: The Fight for the Future at the New Frontier of Power*. New York: Profile Books.

INDEX